5/98

This is an unforgettable book. Its personal testament is a powerful reflection of the resistance, courage, and suffering of the people of East Timor. Anyone wanting to know how imperial power works, and how ordinary people stand up to it, must read Constâncio Pinto's remarkable story.

—John Pilger, journalist and filmmaker

Constâncio is a hero. Tortured, hunted, and forced into exile, he continues to struggle for East Timor's freedom. This book is a searing indictment not only of the Indonesian dictatorship, but the United States government, which arms and funds it....It is not enough to read this book. Ultimately, it is up to us to stop the reign of terror against the people of East Timor.

—Amy Goodman, WBAI/Pacifica Radio

The struggle of the Timorese for freedom and justice is one of the most inspiring of the modern era, vividly depicted here through participant eyes, with an authoritative review of the background and current situation. Their resistance is a tribute to what the human spirit can achieve, even in the face of awesome resources of violence and unimaginable horror. It teaches many lessons, and should serve as a call to action on many fronts, not least to help the people of Timor achieve the right of self-determination that they so richly deserve.

—Noam Chomsky, Institute Professor of Linguistics,
Massachusetts Institute of Technology

Constâncio Pinto's personal history, with Matthew Jardine's placing it in the context of Western realpolitik, will move and motivate anyone with a conscience. Constâncio has kept his spirit, commitment, and hope alive while surviving torture, brutality, and mass killings. We need only to read about these horrors to know that they must stop.

—Charles Scheiner, National Coordinator,
East Timor Action Network/U.S.

I0619940

To the People of East Timor:
Past, Present, and Future . . .

"There is a latent threat in each of the victims of [a] system which struggles against the consequences of its own acts. Even while celebrating the annihilation of its enemies, the system cannot fail to suspect that it is condemned to beget them."

— Eduardo Galeano

"Oppression helps to forge in the oppressed the very qualities that eventually bring about the downfall of the oppressor."

— Richard Wright

East Timor's Unfinished Struggle

Inside the Timorese Resistance

Constâncio Pinto and Matthew Jardine

South End Press
Boston, MA

Cover design by Beth Fortune
Cover photographs by Steve Cox
Maps by Matthew Jardine
Text design and production by the South End Press collective
Printed in the U.S.A.

Library of Congress Cataloging-in-Publication Data
Pinto, Constâncio.
East Timor's unfinished struggle: inside the Timorese resistance / Constâncio Pinto and Matthew Jardine.
    p.   cm.
Includes bibliographical references and index.
ISBN 0-89608-542-2. — ISBN 0-89608-541-4 (pbk.)
1. Timor Timur (Indonesia)—History—Autonomy and independence movements. 2. Pinto, Constâncio. I. Jardine, Matthew. II. Title

DS646.59.T55P55 1996
959.8—dc21   96-40951
                                                                                    CIP

South End Press, 116 Saint Botolph Street, Boston, MA 02115-4818
04 03 02 01 00 99 98 97 96   1 2 3 4 5 6 7 8 9

Contents

Preface

by José António Ramos Horta
co-winner of the 1996 Nobel Peace Prize

Special Representative of
the National Council of Maubere Resistance (CNRM)
of East Timor

The Nobel Committee hopes that this award will spur efforts to find a diplomatic solution to the conflict in East Timor based on the people's right to self-determination.

— October 11, 1996

Constâncio Pinto and Matthew Jardine have written a unique testimony of the struggle for freedom in East Timor. *East Timor's Unfinished Struggle* is necessary reading for anyone who wants to understand East Timor and who hopes to see self-determination for its people.

This book is especially important for readers in the United States, who have a special role to play in bringing international pressure on Indonesia to end its suppression of legitimate East Timorese aspirations for respect of their human rights, including the right of self-determination.

Such pressure is especially urgent now, in light of the recent awarding of the Nobel Peace Prize. Bishop Carlos Filipe Ximenes Belo and I share the hope that we can take advantage of the new international awareness of the occupation of East Timor to contribute decisively to a diplomatic solution.

The Nobel Peace Prize truly belongs to the people of East Timor and to Xanana Gusmão, who merits the award more than any other individual for his work on behalf of freedom for East Timor.

We are confident that, following the Nobel award, the peace plan of the National Council of Maubere Resistance (CNRM)—which Constâncio Pinto and Matthew Jardine have printed at the conclusion of *East Timor's Unfinished Struggle*—will become the basis of a diplomatic, peaceful resolution of our conflict.

East Timor's Unfinished Struggle makes an important contribution to that end.

—October 15, 1996
Sydney, Australia

Acknowledgments

We would like to thank all the members of the South End Press collective for their help and support on this project. A special thanks to Sonia Shah and Dionne Brooks who saw us through much of the early stages of the book and to Anthony Arnove, our editor for the critical final stages of the process. We are most appreciative of Anthony's excellent suggestions for improving the book, and his cooperative spirit and strong commitment, political and professional, to the project.

A special thanks to Jee Sun Lee, who laboriously (and accurately!) typed almost all of the more than 40 hours of taped interviews between the two of us, and to Mizue Aizeki, our first transcriber, who encouraged Jee Sun to take over the task.

There are a great many people who have contributed to this project: Elaine Brière, Steve Cox, Robert Domm, Jenny Groves, Jean Inglis, Allan Nairn, Charlie Scheiner, and Dave Targan. We thank them, and the many who we have surely forgotten to mention, for all their help.

From Constâncio Pinto

> Whether it is in Tibet or in Poland, the Baltics or the South Pacific, Africa or the Caribbean, it has been shown that force and repression can never totally suffocate the reasons underlying the existence of a people: pride in its own identity, capacity to preserve, without restriction, everything that identifies it as such, freedom to pass all this on to future generations, in brief, the right to encourage its own destiny.
>
> —Xanana Gusmão,
> October 5, 1989

To all my friends and *companheiros* of the struggle, from the old to the young, in the towns, cities, and villages within East Timor occupied by the Indonesian army and in the diaspora, to the courageous FALINTIL in the remote mountains of Matebian, Kablake, and Ramelau, my deepest gratitude and acknowledgment to all of you who risk your lives, continuing to uphold the sacred rights to self-determination and independence, the right of every people and every nation state regardless of the size of the population, the country, and the economic resources.

With great gratitude I would like to acknowledge and thank Xanana Gusmão, the undisputed leader of the people of East Timor, for his moral and political support, his talent, and his courageous leadership of the struggle.

I thank all my friends in the underground movement within East Timor and those abroad for their invaluable support during my persecution until I successfully escaped. I would like to acknowledge all members of the Executive Committee of the Clandestine Front for their moral, spiritual, and material support, even behind the bars of injustice. I would like especially to thank Kiak, Leo Lima, Maubere, Alla, Agus, Salarkosi, Domingos Sarmento, and others unnamed for the friendship and support that made my escape abroad possible. My special thanks to Pak Harto and his family, whose support can never be repaid.

Special appreciation goes to Allan Nairn, Amy Goodman, Sister Monica Nakamura, Dean David Targan, John Takahashi, Nelson Vieira, Charles Scheiner, Carolina Matos, and all others whose invaluable support made it possible for me to come to the United States to study at Brown University. I would like especially to express my gratitude to Dr. Rui Machette and the Luso American Foundation, in Portugal, and Brown University for providing me with a wonderful scholarship to further my education.

A special thank-you to my co-author, Matthew Jardine, who has turned my personal story into this book. Without his initiative and encouragement this book could not have been written.

Finally, I am grateful to my parents, brothers and sisters, my wife, Gabriela, and other relatives with whom, together or apart, I have shed many tears in sorrow and in happiness.

From Matthew Jardine

I would like to thank Constâncio, Gabriela, Tilson, and Tima for their kind and generous hospitality on numerous occasions when Constân-cio and I were working intensely on the book at his family's home in Rhode Island. One of the greatest aspects of working on this project was getting to know all of them better.

I am very grateful to Chase Langford and Ken Schwartz of the UCLA Department of Geography for sharing their cartographic expertise with me.

I also want to express my gratitude to Karen Nevins for her generous help in printing various drafts of the manuscript. In the same vein, I want to recognize "Special K" and "Dodgeball" for their assistance, support, and good humor.

A special thanks to Gerry Hale, Carol Bernstein Ferry, and all the members of my family.

Finally, I want to thank Mizue for her love and support, which made it possible for her to put up with me over the sometimes seemingly endless months of work that this book required. Most of all, I want to thank her for sharing her life with me.

Foreword

by Allan Nairn

When I first met Constâncio Pinto in August 1990, outside a cemetery in East Timor, he had already spent a decade and a half trying to cope with the consequences of a decision made routinely, almost casually, by officials in Washington.

When General Suharto, the Indonesian dictator, was contemplating invading East Timor in the latter months of 1975, he, in effect, asked permission from the U.S. government. Washington was his main political and military patron and the chief guarantor of his regime. Washington had welcomed Suharto's 1965 coup against the nationalist Sukarno, and had helped him stage the internal bloodbath that consolidated army rule. The U.S. government was steering financing to Indonesia through the World Bank and other sources and was providing military training, intelligence, and roughly 90 percent of its arms. Suharto wanted to make sure that he did not step on Washington's toes.

An August 20 Central Intelligence Agency (CIA) cable noted that "a major consideration on [Suharto's] part is that an invasion of Timor, if it comes, must be justified as an act of defense of Indonesian Security. He is acutely aware that conditions of U.S. military assistance to Indonesia specifically limit the use of this equipment to defensive purposes." It was therefore necessary to get Washington to overlook its own treaty conditions.

As to the future of East Timor, Washington did not appear to have strong feelings. A 1972 CIA report had called it of "little strategic significance." But Suharto deeply wanted to take East Timor. He and his army seemed to worry that if the old Portuguese colony won independence, the example of freedom next door might prove subversive in Indonesia.

When President Ford and Secretary of State Henry Kissinger met Suharto in Jakarta from December 5 to 6, 1975, they gave the green light for the invasion he was seeking. Years later, in 1991, I asked President Ford whether he had authorized the Indonesian invasion of East Timor at those meetings. He first replied, "Very honestly, I cannot recall precisely that detail." He argued—I think plausibly—that Timor was a minor matter on the U.S.-Suharto agenda, "a lower echelon priority." More central were matters such as the fact that "The Indonesians were anxious for greater military help and assistance," Ford said. "As I recall," he added, "we were very sympathetic to their request."

William Colby, the CIA director in 1975, later told me that Timor and the question of the Indonesian invasion "didn't loom very large" in the overall scheme of U.S. global operations at the time. Indeed, Indonesia itself was not seen as a major worry in Washington: "[A]fter the coup in '65 [Indonesia] really wasn't a matter of great moment to us because the threat that had previously existed with the largest communist party outside the communist region— [which] was a considerable concern at one point. . . [had] self-destructed," Colby said, referring to Suharto's 1965-67 slaughter of more than 400,000 communists, ethnic Chinese, and assorted dissidents. "[W]e didn't have that much concern about what was happening there."

Suharto, in Washington's view, had Indonesia well in hand, and if he wanted to take East Timor, then the government decided that it could indulge a friend. When I asked Colby what would have happened if the United States had vetoed the invasion, he said, "[we] certainly would have had a little diplomatic strain there" but the relationship would have continued. After all, Colby noted, "where would [Suharto] have gone?"

Avoiding "a little diplomatic strain," the U.S. government gave the green light. Sixteen hours after Ford and Kissinger left Jakarta, the invasion was underway.

I first arrived in Timor 15 years into the genocide. After years spent working as a journalist in countries ruled by some of the world's most repressive governments, I was struck immediately by an air of fear like I'd never seen elsewhere.

The secret police of the Indonesian Intel watched the churches, schools, and markets. People would come up beside you on the street. Whispering tensely in banned Portuguese, they would speak urgently of loved ones killed and ask you to tell the outside world. They would slip you petitions and lists of the dead and ask that they be delivered to the Secretary General of the United Nations, the President of the United States, the Prime Minister of Australia, or the parliament of Portugal. One nervous young man said,

> We have ideas but it is difficult to express them. In public we cannot be seen with any foreigner. When the secret [police] see us, they take pictures, and when the foreigners leave they persecute us. In the school the teacher cannot speak about the situation [in East Timor]. If they speak, they will be arrested.

The first words out of Bishop Carlos Ximenes Belo's mouth when I called on him at his residence were: "There is intelligence everywhere, so people feel afraid to speak. I don't know if I can talk to you. This is not like the United States." At the time, Belo's mail and phone were cut off, and two doors down from his home, the army had held a meeting debating whether to assassinate him. The meeting, chaired by Colonel Prabowo, General Suharto's son-in-law, decided against killing Bishop Belo and warned him to be quiet instead. Belo had smuggled out a letter to the Secretary General of the United Nations stating that the East Timorese were "dying as a people and as a nation." The letter called on the Secretary General to organize a free referendum on Timor's future.

Visiting Mário Carrascalão, the Indonesian-appointed Governor of

East Timor, I was surprised to hear him confirm that the army maintained a string of torture houses. Inside these buildings, the Intel would torture people with razors, electric shock, and iron bars. One could be called in for discussing "politics," meeting in an unauthorized public assembly, "expressing enmity against the state," listening to foreign shortwave radio, or because an informer suspected you of thinking prohibited thoughts. Carrascalão explained that the torture facilities were completely beyond his authority. "That's the army's job," he said.

I did not meet any East Timorese who hadn't lost family and friends. As Colonel Gatot Purwanto, the occupation intelligence chief, confirmed to me, the Indonesian armed forces have killed roughly one-third of the East Timorese population.

Many farmers had been moved from their mountain fields so the army could maintain surveillance. The harm to food production left children stunted and mentally slowed. At a rural eastern schoolhouse that had been occupied as an army barracks a few years before, the teacher explained that a basic schooling problem was "lack of nutrition for the children—children growing up not to their intellectual capacity." There had also been the problem of finding teachers since "the intelligentsia" had largely been killed. Amnesty International had reported in the early years of the Indonesian occupation that the army had a strategy of targeting "the whole stratum of educated Timorese."

School teaching was Constâncio's public trade in 1990 and 1991. And though he secretly worked, in his second life, as the leader of the civilian underground, he was still able to maintain a conscientious classroom presence. One day, leaving the funeral of a young man who had been shot by the army, I met a girl from his class who explained that "Mr. Constâncio" was a tough grader, but that the students liked him because "he is so nice."

The ability to keep some semblance of normal life amid the executions, hunger, and strain was one of the many impressive things about the civic culture of the East Timorese. By that time, virtually all Timorese institutions, save the Catholic Church, had been crushed. Peasant leagues, student groups, and political parties had been banned. Countless leaders had been executed. The occupation army's aspiration was, as their "Established Procedures" manual put it, to maintain "control over all aspects of the life of the community."

Yet the Timorese, on their own, had rebuilt a society underground. Meeting in small groups with blinds drawn and lookouts posted outside, they created a complex underground that sustained rites of public gathering, political education, and speech, while at the same time serving the function of organizing against the Indonesian occupation.

One quickly noticed in Timor that the occupation was, on the one hand, totalitarian, and, on the other, unsuccessful. Timorese society was still alive. The spirit was evident in the excitement with which many people greeted the news that a delegation from the United Nations and the Portuguese parliament would soon visit East Timor. (The United Nations technically recognizes Portugal as the administering power of East Timor.) In 1975 and in 1976, the UN Security Council had passed resolutions calling on Indonesia to "withdraw... without delay" from East Timor. But the United States had blocked enforcement of those resolutions, as U.S. Ambassador Daniel Patrick Moynihan later noted in his memoir. Now, though, the Timorese hoped that the Portuguese and UN delegation's visit would finally lead to concrete UN action on Timorese self-determination.

The army convened meetings in towns and neighborhoods nationwide and warned the Timorese that they would kill anyone who demonstrated or tried to speak to the delegation. They said that they would kill any protesters after the delegation left and then kill their families "to the seventh generation." Some officers added that they had already dug mass graves to bury Timorese protesters.

Many East Timorese organized despite the threats. When the army went hunting for activists, some two dozen young people took sanctuary inside the Motael Church in Dili.

At the last moment, under pressure from the governments of Australia and the United States, the Portuguese and UN delegation visit was called off. The army raided the Motael at 1:30 a.m., after the news was announced. Indonesian soldiers and police dragged the young people out and, according to eyewitnesses I spoke to, executed one, Sebastião Gomes, with a point-blank pistol shot to the gut. Gomes bled to death on the steps of the church. The Timorese were stunned. The army had violated their final sanctuary. The message was clear: there is no place to hide.

Arriving back in Timor hours after the Motael raid, I found a packed church with people weeping and praying on their knees. A plan emerged that the two-week commemoration of Sebastião's death would be a procession across town to the Santa Cruz Cemetery, where people would lay flowers on Sebastião's grave.

By sunrise that morning, November 12, 1991, Dili was on full alert. Occupation troops and police were lined up all along the route of the march. Army vehicles were going to and fro with officers speaking into walkie-talkies. It was a full-scale mobilization involving units of every sort. As the Timorese came out of the mass—about a thousand people were there—the young people reached under their shirts and pulled out home-made bed sheet banners. As they unfurled the banners on the seaside road, an electric current ran through the crowd. The banners called on Indonesia to withdraw from East Timor, referred to the 200,000 Timorese dead, defended the Catholic Church, and even attacked Colonel Gatot Purwanto by name. People were waving the flags of banned political parties and holding embroidered portraits of Xanana Gusmão, the leader of the Timorese resistance.

As the procession wound toward the cemetery, people joined from homes, schools, and offices on the way. Nuns were at the front singing hymns. The crowd multiplied many times. Some of the bolder young people ran up to soldiers, gave the "V" sign for victory and peace, and shouted *"Viva East Timor!" "Viva Sebastião!"* and *"Viva Xanana!"*

It was an unheard-of display of defiance. Occupied Dili had never seen such an event. Many people in the crowd did not know if they would reach the cemetery alive. But then we turned the corner and saw that there were no soldiers at the Santa Cruz Cemetery itself.

As the procession filed in to the high-walled cemetery to lay flowers on Sebastião's grave, the crowd stopped on the road, exhilarated. They had achieved a historic breakthrough. They had pierced the veil of terror. They had walked across town in an act of open protest and lived to speak about it.

It seemed to me and others there that East Timor would never be the same. Young people were clambering atop the cemetery walls and waving banners and flags. I was there with Amy Goodman from WBAI/Pacifica Radio and we were talking to an old man in the street, when suddenly he looked up, pointed, and exclaimed: "The Gestapo!" We turned and saw that the Indonesian soldiers had arrived. They got down from trucks and, holding U.S. M-16s, sealed off the exit route. Then we turned and saw that marching up the same route by which we had come was a long column of Indonesian troops in brown uniforms. They were marching 12 to 15 abreast and were wielding M-16s. There were hundreds, perhaps thousands of soldiers. I never saw the end of the file.

Thousands of Timorese on the road were hemmed in by the cemetery walls. Some at the back could peel away, but most had no escape. I thought at the time: we will just go stand in front of the crowd. The troops will see we're foreign journalists and that will prevent any trouble. Their only choices would be to shoot us and create an international incident, or to stage a massacre in front of us. I couldn't see them doing either one. I was confident that we could serve as a shield for the Timorese, so we went and stood in the middle of the road, 15 yards in front of the crowd. The troops kept marching toward us. The Timorese had nowhere to go.

The troops closed in deliberately. They fired no warning shots and did not tell the crowd to disperse. They simply marched up, enveloped us, and, as they got a step or two past us, raised their rifles to their shoulders all at once and opened fire on the crowd.

Though I knew the history of repression in East Timor and had dealt, after the fact, with many massacres in Guatemala and El Salvador, I couldn't quite believe in human terms that they were going through with this. I thought at first that the soldiers must be firing blanks. But then I saw the people buckling and the blood spilling on the road. They were torn apart by the M-16s. The people we'd been talking to were dying all around us. The street was carpeted with bodies and growing slick with blood.

The soldiers were firing and charging in unison. They leaped over fallen bodies. They aimed and picked off people in the back.

Seconds after they opened fire on the Timorese, the soldiers grabbed me and Amy and began to beat us. They took our camera, tape recorders, and bags; they didn't want us to have any evidence of their actions. They fractured my skull with the butts of their M-16s and put us on the ground. A group of seven to eight soldiers put their rifles to our heads. It seemed they were deciding whether or not to execute us.

They were shouting at us, "*Politik!*" "*Politik!*"—politics—a crime in occupied Timor. They were accusing the Timorese of the crime of politics for having marched to the cemetery, and they were accusing us for being there to see it. We shouted back, "America!" They had asked if we were from Australia. Knowing that in the course of the 1975 invasion and occupation, Indonesian soldiers had executed several Australian journalists, we wanted to make clear that we were not Australian. Being from the United States seemed to make a difference. It was Indonesia's patron—the country that supplied their weapons. When we finally convinced the soldiers that we were from the United States, they took the rifles from our heads. I think they realized that there might be a price to pay if they executed Americans. They had never paid a price for executing Timorese. Indeed, they had been rewarded. The guns and money had kept flowing, as did the Timorese blood.

We were able to escape from the scene and, that afternoon, from East Timor and report the massacre to the outside world. I hoped that getting the word out quickly to a wide audience could prevent further killings. But as Bishop Belo later disclosed, the executions continued for days. Indonesian troops finished off wounded people in their hospital beds, using knives, stones, and lethal injections. At least 271 Timorese died at or around the cemetery on November 12, Constâncio later estimated. (One foreigner, Kamal Bamadhaj, a citizen of New Zealand, was killed.) Several hundred more were murdered in the following days. To this day, the location of their bodies has not been disclosed.

The day after the Santa Cruz Massacre, in a formal speech to a gathering of military graduates, General Try Sutrisno, the Indonesian national armed forces commander, said that the Timorese were "disruptors." "These ill-bred people have to be shot," he said, "and we will shoot them." Sutrisno has since been promoted to vice president of Indonesia.

General Herman Mantiri later said that the massacre was "quite proper" because the Timorese "were opposing us, demonstrating, even yelling things against the government."

Though the U.S. government's public stance was to condemn the massacre, privately U.S. officials were commiserating with Suharto's men and urging them to evolve a strategy of international damage control. Internal State Department documents obtained under the Freedom of Information Act reveal that on December 10, 1991, in a secret post-massacre meeting in Surabaya, Indonesia, U.S. officials reassured Suharto's commanders (including three generals, two admirals, and an air vice marshall) that while Washington "understand[s] Indonesia is under considerable pressure from the world at large," "we do not believe that friends should abandon friends in times of adversity."

On December 24, U.S. Ambassador John Monjo met Suharto's senior adviser, Dr. Widjojo, who "thanked the ambassador for the stance adopted by the USG [U.S. Government] thus far and commented that the reaction of some countries in publicly linking aid levels to the Dili incident was counterproductive."

The State Department and Pentagon, instead, proposed to *double* Indonesia's military aid, and continued to provide Suharto with new U.S. arms. The aid was in the form of IMET (International Military Education and Training) funds. A State Department spokesman said that the IMET training would "expose" Indonesian officers to "democratic ideas and humanitarian standards."

In a twisted way, that statement was unfair to Suharto's army. It suggested that Washington had higher—and contrary—ideas and standards, when, in fact, the United States had been Suharto's senior partner all along. One might ask whose higher ideas and standards would Washington teach the Indonesians? Those of Ford and Kissinger, who approved the invasion and doubled military aid? Those of Moynihan, who blocked enforcement of UN resolutions against the occupation? Perhaps those of President Carter, who sent in planes and helicopters that the Indonesian army used to bomb and strafe Timorese such as Constâncio to force them from their exodus in the hills? Or perhaps those of Vice President Walter Mondale, who intervened to speed up Suharto's fighter plane shipments? Or those of Richard Holbrooke, now celebrated for the Bosnia settlement, who ran Carter's Timor policy and kept the arms, money, and support flowing as Jakarta put the Timorese in concentration and resettlement camps and implemented enforced starvation? Or maybe those of President Reagan, who continued the bipartisan policy, selling Suharto $40 million per year in arms in his first four years in office, then $300 million in 1986?

The Bush administration was joined, in its post-massacre Congressional push for IMET, by General Electric and AT&T, two major investors in Indonesia, who were called in by the regime to lobby on Suharto's behalf. But in a fierce behind-the-scenes battle, all but completely ignored by the corporate press, these powerful forces were defeated by a nascent grassroots movement (which has now become the East Timor Action Network, ETAN) with coalition help from church, peace, veteran's, and human rights groups. Working intensively with student activists (especially at Brown University and the University of Wisconsin), the grassroots forces generated thousands of calls and letters targeting key congressional committees and members at critical times. As someone heavily involved in this campaign, it was quite revealing to see how multi-million dollar bureaucracies could be quickly outflanked and beaten by bursts of committed citizen work.

On an amendment by Representatives Ron Machtley, Republican of Rhode Island, and Tony Hall, Democrat of Ohio and one of the longest-standing Congressional voices on behalf of East Timor, with key assistance from Representative David Obey, Democrat of Wisconsin, and Senator Patrick Leahy, Democrat of Vermont, Congress voted to cut off IMET. Jakarta was rightly stunned. It was the first time that Suharto's U.S. aid had ever been cut for atrocities. This was the first of a string of less-than-total, but politically unprecedented, blows to the Jakarta regime. These included the reversal of the traditional U.S. position on Indonesia and East Timor at the UN Human Rights Commission (when the United States, under bipartisan pressure from some in Congress, switched sides to successfully co-sponsor a resolution critical of the Indonesian regime); helping to block the delivery of F-5 fighter planes; passing the Feingold Amendment through the Senate Foreign Relations Committee (although the amendment by Senator Russell Feingold, Democrat of Wisconsin, which conditioned large weapons sales on human rights improvements in East Timor, never reached the floor, it compelled the State Department to retreat on small arms sales); and winning bans on small arms sales to Indonesia and, in 1996, the sale of armored vehicles.

These victories, which were built on grassroots pressure transmitted through Congress in the face of Bush and Clinton administration resistance, did not change the fundamental fact that the United States still backed Suharto and, *de facto*, the Timor occupation. For the first time, however, they qualified that support and put the issue in contest.

In 1995, Admiral Richard Macke, the commander in chief of all U.S. military forces in the Pacific, privately told members of Congress that the political flak was getting so bad that it would be tactically wise for Indonesia to set East Timor free and thereby quiet Suharto's critics. This was not the official Clinton administration view, but the fact that Macke had reached it indicated that the grassroots strategy of making Suharto and his Washington patrons pay a price was starting to register at the level of pragmatic power calculations.

Predictably, the Suharto regime and the big U.S. firms that profit most from business deals with it have launched a lavishly funded political counterattack. It includes the creation of a Suharto-corporate-U.S. government front and lobbying group—the United States-Indonesia Society—launched in late 1994 with backing from Indonesian intelligence, General Prabowo (Suharto's son in law, known for his role in various Timor massacres), the Lippo Group, Chevron, Texaco, Freeport McMoRan, and a host of former State Department, Pentagon, and CIA officials; a project funded by oil companies and Lippobank to distribute "educational" materials on Indonesia to 10 million U.S. high school students "to increase understanding of a country that has long been a solid friend of the United States and a nation that offers a great number of opportunities for American business"; and, apparently, some of the Lippo Group's massive campaign contributions to Clinton and the Democratic National Committee.

This counter-effort has won some successes in Congress, notably in a partial restoration of the IMET aid in 1995. On October 26, 1995, Clinton welcomed Suharto to the Oval Office. Also waiting were Vice President Gore, Secretary of Commerce Ron Brown, and U.S. Special Trade Representative Mickey Kantor. Clinton offered to sell Suharto 20 F-16 fighters. "He's our kind of guy," an administration official told the *New York Times*, referring to Suharto.

For several months after the Dili massacre, I didn't know if Constâncio was alive. Amy Goodman and I had last seen him on the night of November 11, surrounded by underground lookouts. We were in a dark room lit by a single candle. Constâncio was extremely tense. Part of his face was still frozen from the effects of torture. He was organizing the following day's protest and was under an army death warrant. They were searching for him house to house, but the organizing continued. Constâncio, like so many other Timorese who have been conscripted for heroism, was facing epic choices that no one should have to make. It was the essential dilemma: taking calculated risks that might endanger family and friends to save the larger community. He and Xanana Gusmão didn't expect that the Indonesian army would be so bold as to open fire with U.S. journalists and other foreigners at the cemetery.

But they did, and hundreds died. Timor was further damaged and transformed. It is hard to convey what happened at the Santa Cruz Cemetery, but one legacy was a lasting tension. The tension of loved ones gone and presumed dead, their bodies never found. The tension of wondering what might have happened if one had acted differently. Then for months there was the tension, for us, of wondering if Constâncio was alive. The Jakarta army command had a national manhunt out for him, and speculation and rumor ran wild. Then, one day in New York I was handed a letter. Enclosed was a photo of Constâncio. He didn't write down his name, but he was alive and on the run inside Indonesia.

When Constâncio finally made it out to Portugal and we spoke on the phone, one of the first things he said was that he wanted to come to the United States—for East Timor, the key center of power. Having been bombed by U.S. OV-10s and shot at by M-16s, he wanted to stop the trigger fingers that were still taking shots at his friends. Once in the States, he went on speaking tours, helping to build the movement here.

As this is being written, East Timor has reached the corporate press agenda after being off the map for 21 years. The award of the Nobel Peace Prize to Bishop Belo and José Ramos Horta came just as the Lippo/Riady contributions to Clinton broke open as a presidential campaign scandal.

Even before these developments, though, I think it was becoming clear that the East Timorese were well on the way to winning their freedom. They had successfully made the occupation into an international issue (even if, in some countries, such as the United States, East Timor was still below the corporate press horizon) and had damaged Suharto's world standing. The Dili massacre, in particular, had sparked a wave of global organizing.

It is also beginning to look as if the Timorese may contribute to ending not just their own occupation, but also Suharto's reign. In the past two years, East Timor has become a catalyzing issue inside Indonesia. It has inspired rising pro-democracy forces and has helped to fuel dissident campaigns.

These are remarkable accomplishments for a people who have had to fight for their survival, often armed with little more than the ability, and will, to tell others the facts of their lives.

But the power of facts should not be underestimated. Both the weak and the powerful have often learned that facts can motivate people and set events in train.

Last year Constâncio, Amy Goodman, and I had a chance to confront Henry Kissinger in New York. He was promoting his book, *Diplomacy*, and in the question period Constâncio stood up and asked Kissinger just what he did when he was in Jakarta on the eve of the East Timor invasion. Kissinger at first seemed caught off guard, then thanked Constâncio for his politeness, and wound into an answer that included a documentable lie. Kissinger claimed that during the

Jakarta visit "we weren't even thinking about Timor" and that "Timor was never discussed with us when we were in Indonesia."

Then Kissinger amended his story:

> Nobody asked our opinion [about an invasion]...I don't know what we could have said if someone had asked our opinion...It was literally told to us as we were leaving. When the Indonesians informed us, we neither said yes or no. We were literally at the airport. So that was our connection with it.

Kissinger claimed not only that Washington had nothing to do with the invasion plans, but that it had not even formed an opinion on it.

I was next in the question line and was carrying documents showing that Timor was discussed at the December 6 meeting, and that the documents and my interview with Ford indicated that the United States had given a green light for the invasion. I asked whether Kissinger would facilitate full declassification of the meeting's minutes, and whether he would support the convening of a UN war crimes tribunal on East Timor and agree to abide by its verdict in regard to his own conduct.

Kissinger replied, "[T]his sort of comment is one of the reasons why the conduct of foreign policy is becoming nearly impossible under these conditions."

Unfortunately, his rejoinder was not really true. Foreign policy still goes on roughly as before, regardless of occasional questions or the raising of inconvenient facts. But Kissinger's answer was pointing the way to a deeper political truth: if Americans really knew the facts about the U.S.-backed terror, policymakers' lives *would* be hell. Many of them would be on trial. People would not support massacres like the one that took place at the Santa Cruz Cemetery.

This means that the system is vulnerable. It is a fundamental fact. Another way of looking at this issue is to think that if enough people knew stories like Constâncio Pinto's, then the policy conduct of officials like Kissinger would indeed be impossible.

— October 17, 1996

Constâncio in Dili, East Timor, February 1991

Introduction

On December 7, 1975, a little more than one week after East Timor declared its independence from its Portuguese colonial master, the Indonesian Armed Forces (ABRI) launched a full-scale invasion of the territory located at the eastern end of the Indonesian archipelago, 400 miles north of Darwin, Australia. Out of a total population of about 700,000 at the time of East Timor's brief independence, nearly one-third of the East Timorese population—more than 200,000 people—has died as a result of the Indonesian invasion and ensuing war, politically created famine, and ongoing occupation.[1] Proportionally speaking, East Timor is the site of one of the worst cases of genocide of the late twentieth century.

Despite the levels of human suffering that the Indonesian invasion and occupation brought on the people of East Timor, the West has done little or nothing to prevent Indonesia's aggression.[2] Rather, through military, economic, and diplomatic support, countries such as the United States, the United Kingdom, Japan, Germany, Canada, France, and Australia have greatly facilitated Indonesia's invasion and subsequent annexation of East Timor. In short, Indonesia's geopolitical and political-economic importance to Western interests set the stage for Western acquiescence to Jakarta's desire to conquer East Timor, a tiny territory the size of El Salvador or the U.S. state of Mas-

1

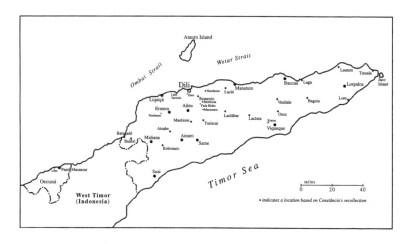

East Timor

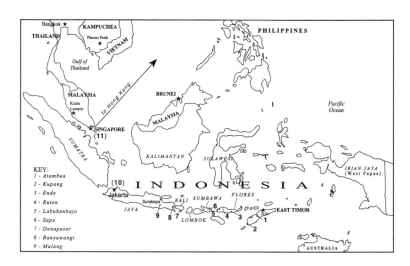

Constâncio's Escape Route from East Timor

sachusetts. Of course, the situation in East Timor has not taken place in a vacuum. To understand Indonesia's invasion and occupation and the West's partnership in this crime, we must appreciate the complex set of historical relations that dragged East Timor from its relative isolation to the center of regional and international power politics.

The Arrival of the Portuguese

At the vanguard of European imperialism, Portugal arrived in Asia at the beginning of the sixteenth century as part of Lisbon's efforts to establish global economic hegemony. Southeast Asia was of specific concern to the Portuguese because of the region's lucrative spice trade. By establishing itself in Asia, Portugal circumvented the Turkic Ottoman Empire's blocking of trade with Asia through the Mediterranean, as well as the stranglehold of the city-states of Venice and Genoa, which until that time were the agents of European trade with Asia.[3]

Long before the Portuguese arrived on Timor, the island was well known for its abundance of sandalwood, a highly perfumed and valued white tree used to make incense and medicinal ointment. Other goods, such as beeswax (important for Java's batik industry) and honey, also interested trading partners and facilitated the territory's integration into trading networks politically centered on East Java and the Celebes (Sulawesi) and tied commercially to China and India. Slaves, captured in wars between Timorese kingdoms, were also a significant trade commodity.[4]

The Portuguese first arrived on the island of Timor around 1511. Limiting their contact to occasional visits to coastal trading missions and posts, a practice established by Chinese and Muslim traders centuries earlier, the Portuguese extracted resources from Timor through treaty arrangements with local chiefs, who would have sandalwood and other commodities, including slaves, brought to the coast by groups under their rule, receiving in return items such as cloth, guns, and iron implements.[5]

Although a viceroy from the Portuguese enclave of Goa (in India) officially ruled the island throughout the sixteenth and seventeenth centuries, the Portuguese exerted little influence over Timorese society. The sandalwood port of Lifau in the region of Oecussi was the site of the original Portuguese settlement on the island of Timor. But not until 1702, with the arrival of a Goa-appointed governor and the building of a fort in Lifau, did the Portuguese succeed in establishing an effective presence on the island. Dutch competition for control of the island, however, ended the Portuguese influence on the western end of the island in the 1700s. Even further east, the Portuguese position was rather weak due to intermittent attacks by various indigenous leaders and their retinues. As a result, in 1769, the Portuguese relocated their capital eastward in from Lifau to Dili, which had better natural defenses to prevent surprise attacks and a harbor more suitable for shipping. Portugal's hold on the eastern half of the island remained somewhat tenuous until the early twentieth century due to strong resistance on the part of the indigenous population. That Portugal was able to maintain a certain order in its claimed territory at all was due to its ability to take advantage of rivalries between different indigenous kingdoms.[6]

Throughout the nineteenth century, the Portuguese and Dutch control of their respective regions of the island continued to be rather weak. Nevertheless, in the mid-1800s, the two imperialist powers began to divide the island on paper. In 1913, the Hague Court established the final border between Dutch (west) Timor and Portuguese (east) Timor. The agreement cut the island almost in half, with the Portuguese retaining the enclave of Oecussi and the islands of Atauro (off the coast of Dili) and Jaco (off the eastern tip of the island).[7]

Like all colonial powers, the Portuguese hoped to transform the indigenous economy from one of subsistence production to one that produced for export largely oriented to the "mother country." Originally Portuguese economic activity on Timor was largely trade-related, benefiting small groups of Portuguese merchants and local elites. By the end of the seventeenth century, "trade was in a relatively flourishing condition."[8] Nevertheless, serious economic development did not take place in Portuguese Timor until almost the twentieth century.

Through the nineteenth century, Portuguese Timor was probably the most neglected of all of Lisbon's colonies, remaining "little more than a trading post."[9] Native resistance and the poverty of Portugal's presence prevented Portuguese penetration of the territory, making it a colonial backwater. As Alfred Russel Wallace, a British explorer who visited East Timor in the late 1860s, wrote,

> The Portuguese government in Timor is a most miserable one. Nobody seems to care the least about the improvement of the country, and at this time, after three hundred years of occupation, there has not been a mile of road made beyond the town [Dili], and there is not a solitary European residence in the interior.[10]

Toward the end of the nineteenth century, the situation in Portuguese Timor began to change rapidly. Challenged by the rapid economic development of its European rivals and threatened by the rise of new colonial powers such as Britain, Germany, and France, Portugal moved to consolidate its colonial empire. This led to increased social and economic development in Portuguese Timor.[11]

As part of stepped-up Portuguese efforts to increase cash crop production among the indigenous population, Governor Afonso de Castro (1859-69) attempted to impose a regime of forced coffee cultivation through local chiefs. Combined with Portuguese distribution of coffee seedlings and rising prices on the world market, coffee production increased and soon became the colony's most lucrative export, replacing sandalwood, which, because of overexploitation and competition, steadily declined, essentially disappearing by the 1950s.[12]

Apart from encouraging cash crop production, Portugal also implemented a number of other measures to further its economic exploitation of the territory and integrate it into the Portuguese empire. To build infrastructure such as roads, for example, the colonial authorities instituted a forced labor program between 1884 and 1890. Beginning in 1908, the Portuguese administration levied a head tax on all males between the ages of 18 and 60, thus forcing peasant families to produce above the level of subsistence and therefore be able to sell goods on the market.[13]

Portugal's heavy-handed attempts to develop a cash crop economy and to build a modern infrastructure soon resulted in political instability in the colony. Various colonial governors' attempts to collect the head tax and the authorities' use of forced labor led to wide-spread resentment and, eventually, to large-scale violence. Under the leadership of the *liurai*, or local chief, of Manufahi, Dom Boaventura, a number of local kingdoms united to fight the Portuguese. A series of revolts ensued over a 16-year period, culminating in an uprising in locations throughout the territory from 1910 to 1912. In 1912, the rebellion threatened Dili itself for a short time, with members of one kingdom entering the city and killing numerous residents, burning buildings, looting the Government House, and killing and decapitating several Portuguese soldiers and officers. Only with the aid of African troops from the Portuguese colony of Mozambique were the authorities able to suppress the revolt, reportedly resulting in 3,424 East Timorese killed and 12,567 wounded, and 289 Portuguese killed and 600 wounded.[14] The defeat of the rebellion marked the end of the so-called pacification of Portuguese Timor. While resistance to Portuguese colonization was to continue, 1912 marks the beginning of effective Portuguese control throughout East Timor.

In the aftermath of the rebellion, the Portuguese continued their efforts to create a modern, export-oriented agricultural economy. The governor punished the defeated Timorese by imposing large-scale forced cultivation of coffee, copra (the dried kernel of the coconut from which coconut oil is extracted), and sandalwood; Portuguese efforts to cultivate sandalwood, however, failed because they did not understand the parasitic nature of the tree. Throughout the next few decades, the colonial authorities continued to employ forced cultivation to boost cash crop output. Despite great efforts by the Portuguese and serious hardship on the part of the Timorese, the material results were rather modest.[15]

Along with their efforts to restructure the territory's economy and boost production, the colonial authorities began to extend their administrative control of the territory in the late nineteenth and early twentieth centuries. As in the early period of the colonial project, the assistance of members of the indigenous elite proved to be of great importance. While force was an important component of Portuguese Timorese society, Portugal's ability to maintain working relations with many of the important local chiefs gave it the ability to maintain its colonial enterprise: "Indeed, it was mostly the Timorese warriors commanded by loyal chiefs who fought the colonial battles, and not Portuguese soldiers."[16]

In addition to co-opting and successfully bargaining with important factions of the indigenous elite, the Portuguese began to create town-based elites, who they called *assimilados*. Although local chiefs played an important role in facilitating Portuguese influence in traditional East Timorese society, the construction of a modern colony required the availability of an educated class capable of filling various occupations in the growing administrative, managerial, and service-oriented bureaucracies. As late as 1950, however, only 568 people were classified as European, with 2,022 Mestiços, or mixed-bloods, out of a total population of 442,378.[17] The colonial authorities thus had to turn increasingly to the East Timorese themselves to manage Portugal's colonial possession, mostly in the areas of education and administration.[18]

Portuguese efforts to modernize East Timor, however, soon came to a standstill as a result of the worldwide economic depression in the 1930s and the Second World War. Despite Portugal's official neutrality in the conflict, East Timor soon became embroiled in history's bloodiest war, leading to devastating results.

World War II and the Japanese Occupation

Imperial Japan's attempt to establish a Greater East Asian Co-Prosperity Sphere marked the beginning of the Pacific War by directly challenging Western domination of East Asia. Despite its benign name, Japan's "sphere" was essentially a colonial enterprise, part of resource-poor Japan's efforts to broaden its sources of raw materials for domestic industrialization and to find markets for its goods. With surprising speed and ease, Japanese forces drove out Western imperial powers and rapidly occupied colonies such as French Indo-China, the Philippines (colonized by the United States), and the Dutch East Indies to gain control over their vast reserves of natural resources, consumer markets, and labor.[19]

In response to Japan's attack on the U.S. naval fleet in Pearl Harbor on December 7, 1941, Western allies decided to use the island of Timor as a forward line of defense against Japan's southward advance. Despite the protests of the Portuguese administration, the Netherlands and Australia, which was only 300 miles from Timor and long fearful of a Japanese attack on its territory, landed troops in Dili and Kupang to block a potential Japanese invasion. Two months later, the Japanese attacked the island. The subjugation of Portuguese Timor, however, proved difficult for the Japanese. With the help of the East Timorese, several hundred Australian commandos held about 20,000 Japanese soldiers at bay for almost one year, killing 1,500 soldiers in the process.

Fearing that order maintained by the Portuguese facilitated Australia's guerrilla war, the Japanese occupational forces greatly disrupted the colonial administration with the use of "Black Columns" of hostile native Timorese, largely from Dutch Timor. The Japanese used the "Black Columns" both to drive out the Australians and to terrorize all those who might cooperate or sympathize with them, including Portuguese administrators, a number of whom were killed. In this situation, most of the Portuguese who had decided not to leave the island sought the relative safety of the internment zones established by the Japanese in the area of Liquiça. By January 1943, the Japanese soon controlled the entire island.[20]

The Japanese occupation was one of the darkest times in East Timor's history. Timorese suspected of aiding the Japanese were often tortured, and many died.[21] About 60,000 East Timorese lost their lives as a result of the brutal Japanese occupation and Allied bombing. The war badly damaged Dili and partly destroyed many of the territory's principal towns and villages.[22]

The Portuguese Return

With Japan's defeat in August 1945, the Portuguese returned to East Timor, employing brutal methods at times and forced labor to reassert their command and rebuild the colonial infrastructure, which lay in ruins.[23] From the end of the war until decolonization, relations between the colonial administration and the East Timorese remained largely peaceful, at least on a superficial level. As before the war, however, Portugal's heavy-handed treatment of its colonial subjects did not endear the colonial administration to many of the Timorese, sometimes resulting in violent confrontation. In 1959, there was a serious revolt in the eastern end of the colony (around Viqueque); the Portuguese quickly and violently suppressed the rebellion, killing possibly hundreds of East Timorese in the process.[24]

Prior to the disaster of the Pacific War, East Timor was the most economically backward colony in all of Southeast Asia. Dili, the capital, for example, had no electricity or town water supply, paved roads, telephone services (except to the houses and offices of senior officials), or wharves for cargo handling.[25] This situation changed little over the next three decades. In the era after World War II, Portugal, under great economic and military strain from insurgencies in its prize colonies of Angola and Mozambique, did not have the capacity to develop East Timor[26]; but it continued its modest pre-war efforts to modernize the colony. As before, this entailed the co-optation of the indigenous elite and the creation of a class of *assimilados*. Many of these people were to play leadership roles in the political parties that sprang up in 1974 in the aftermath of the overthrow of the Portuguese military dictatorship.

The key institution in this process of the creation of pro-Portuguese colonial elites was the Catholic Church. The Church helped to unify the colony and served as an important vehicle for the promotion of pro-Portuguese sentiment, particularly during the reign in Portugal of António de Oliveira Salazar, whose corporatist state, the so-called *Estado Novo*, was Europe's most enduring fascist dictatorship (1926-68). Although the Church had played an important role in the territory since the inception of the Portuguese colonial project, the number of Catholics in Portuguese Timor was very low through the nineteenth century; this was a result of the relatively unaggressive clergy and antagonisms between the Church and colonial authorities, who actually expelled the missionaries from the colony for a period. It was not until after the pacification campaigns that ended in 1912 that conditions in the territory were truly favorable for the development of the Church. But at the outbreak of World War II, the level of conversions still remained unimpressive because of low levels of education in Portuguese Timor, the lack of funds during the 1930s depression, and a lack of motivation among the clergy for missionary work. The harrowing experience of the Japanese occupation and the resulting devastation, however, gave a certain impetus to missionary work in the post-war era, especially in terms of education.

As the primary source of education in the colony, the Church was probably the most significant institution in the colonial state's efforts to assimilate the local people. By 1900 the Catholic Church was running 16 schools for boys and four for girls. By 1952, out of the 39 primary schools within the territory, 33 were run by Catholic missionaries. In the post-war era, church membership increased rapidly, growing from an estimated 60,000 in 1952 to 113,500 in the early 1960s to about 196,570 in 1973 (with the rest of the population practicing animist religions). By the 1970s Catholicism was an almost official state religion that included the vast majority of the elite and the educated as well as substantial numbers of the indigenous population. Increasingly the Church became a Timorese institution. By 1974, 25 out of the territory's 44 priests were East Timorese. While the Church was generally a conservative force in East Timorese society, it did not always conform to the state authority. Certain priests, for example, would sometimes intercede with the authorities on behalf of Timorese to seek redress for abuses of power or to obtain assistance for them. The Church did share, however, the basic assumptions and vision of the colonial regime, generally supporting its social and political goals and the colonial order.[27]

As in all social processes, however, there were unintended consequences of the Church's activities. Many prominent East Timorese nationalists who were to emerge in the aftermath of the overthrow of the Portuguese dictatorship in 1974 were products of the Church's educational system. Many had also attended the Jesuit seminary at Dare, outside of Dili. While most educational institutions in the colony presented matters from the perspective of Lisbon, the Jesuits were often critical of colonialism and the social conditions within the territory. Although the Jesuits were far from revolutionary in their perspectives, they deviated from the conventional education of the colonial system. A number of the seminary's teachers discussed the changes going on throughout Asia, such as nationalist movements as well as more progressive approaches to development; they also helped to engender a sense of Timorese identity among the students by discussing East Timor's colonial predicament and its future, rather than treating the territory and its people as mere objects of history subject to the wave of progress flowing from Lisbon.[28]

Like the Jesuits, the East Timorese were not immune to the influences of the post-war era. In the aftermath of World War II, a powerful wave of decolonization ripped apart former colonial empires. Broad-based national liberation fronts waged war to expel imperialist powers when they resisted. A number of East Timorese who were to emerge as prominent nationalist leaders in the 1974-75 period had been sent into temporary exile to Portuguese colonies in Africa and were influenced by the independence movements taking place in countries such as Mozambique and Guinea-Bissau.

In addition, mass communications gave the East Timorese a new outlet to the world and new ways to exchange ideas. By the late 1950s, public radio had begun broadcasting in Portuguese, Tetum (the indigenous lingua franca of East Timor), and Chinese (ethnic Chinese dominated the colonial commercial sector). A government-controlled newspaper, *A Voz de Timor*, began publishing in 1960. These media, however, were relatively limited in terms of exposing their audiences to "foreign" ideas because they were heavily censored by Portuguese authorities.[29]

A Catholic newspaper, *Seara*, which was free from censorship laws because of its association with the Church, taught Tetum to its readers and sometimes served as a lively forum for the exchange of ideas on a range of subjects, including the morality of violence, traditional marriage law, and the causes of the insufficient economic development of the territory. Some of its contributors, who had established contact with African liberation movements, privately began to advocate East Timor's independence. The Portuguese authorities forced *Seara* to stop publication in 1973, but by that time like-minded dissidents were already meeting clandestinely in Dili.[30]

Despite the post-war socio-economic developments within the territory, Portuguese Timor did not change significantly in the twentieth century. In addition to the territory's relatively poor resource base, Portugal simply did not have the economic strength to do much more than maintain the status quo.[31] Although educational levels rose beginning in the 1950s, 93 percent of the population was illiterate in 1973. With enrollment in government-run schools restricted to children of *assimilados*, Catholic mission schools were the only other option. Thus, as of 1960, primary school enrollment stood at only 6 percent of the total school-age population.[32]

Economically, the indigenous Timorese were very marginalized. Economic development, apart from the small Portuguese business class, and a few *assimilados* and *liurais*, largely benefited ethnic Chinese who, under the protection of Portuguese military installations, began settling in the colony following the "pacification" campaigns at the beginning of the twentieth century.[33] Because of their economic domination and the perception among the East Timorese that the Chinese were exploitative, the ethnic Chinese were often the object of Timorese animosity. From the Portuguese perspective, however, the small Chinese community (of about 20,000 in 1975) played a very useful role in the colonial society by serving as a buffer between the East Timorese and the Portuguese.[34]

Even after centuries of Portuguese presence, most East Timorese lived in relative isolation of the colonial system. In 1974, more than 80 percent of East Timorese still lived in small rural hamlets largely controlled by traditional rulers who were sometimes quite despotic. While the vast majority of the East Timorese population produced for subsistence, a small but significant indigenous urban and rural elite developed within the colonial administration or as part of a modern export-import sector linked to a series of Western metropoles and their colonial possessions, principally Portugal, the United States, Australia, the Netherlands, the United Kingdom, Singapore, and Hong Kong.[35] With the downfall of the Portuguese fascist dictatorship in April 1974, East Timor emerged from its relative isolation into the turbulent world of international power politics.

The Carnation Revolution

On April 25, 1974, the Carnation Revolution, a relatively nonviolent coup d'état, took place in Lisbon, the capital of Portugal. The Armed Forces Movement (MFA), a group of left-leaning military officials dedicated to democracy within Portugal and the decolonization of all its overseas territories, overthrew the fascist government of Marcelo Caetano (which had succeeded the Salazar dictatorship in 1968). News of the coup led to a flurry of political activity in East Timor, specifically among the town-based East Timorese elite. Prior to the coup, an East Timorese nationalist movement was all but invisible, the small opposition to Portuguese colonialism largely centering on a small group of students and civil servants in the colonial administration who would meet clandestinely in Dili.[36]

Within a few weeks of the MFA coup, the East Timorese elite founded a number of political parties, only three of which were to play significant roles in shaping the decolonization process: the UDT (the Timorese Democratic Union); the ASDT (the Association of Timorese Social Democrats, later to become FRETILIN, the Revolutionary Front for an Independent East Timor); and APODETI (the Timorese Popular Democratic Association).

The UDT, the first party to be founded, quickly became the most popular. Generally conservative and pro-Portugal, the UDT's most prominent members represented East Timor's wealthiest citizens, many of whom were senior administrative officials in Dili, leading plantation owners, and some indigenous elites. The UDT started out strongly in favor of a continued association with Portugal, but, in the face of significant opposition among the populace and within its own party to such a position, it quickly evolved to support eventual total independence.[37]

Established very shortly after the founding of the UDT, the ASDT based its program on "the universal doctrines of socialism and democracy" and "the rejection of colonialism." Fully committed to independence, the ASDT envisioned a period of decolonization of eight to 10 years during which the East Timorese could develop the appropriate political and economic structures necessary for national

independence. Populist in its approach, the ASDT program emphasized the need for literacy campaigns, agrarian reform, a Timorese-
oriented education system, and the promotion of local culture.[38]

Founded as result of a meeting of 30 to 40 individuals on May 27,
1974, APODETI was originally called the Association for the Integration of Timor into Indonesia and favored an "autonomous integration" with Indonesia. The group, however, quickly changed its name
to the Timorese Popular Democratic Association (APODETI) for public relations purposes. By far the smallest of the three major political
parties, APODETI's followers never numbered more than a few hundred, but its influence well exceeded its size. APODETI appears to
have been largely a project of Indonesian intelligence. Three of its key
leaders all had been cooperating for a number of years with BAKIN,
the Indonesian army's intelligence service, which had decided in the
late 1960s that, for reasons of national stability and security, Indonesia
could not permit an independent East Timor. Immediately after
APODETI's founding, Indonesia began providing its East Timorese
agents within the party with financial support.[39]

While the UDT began as the largest political grouping, it quickly
began to lose ground to the ASDT. The UDT's initial wavering on the
question of independence, the concentration of its political activities
in the major towns, and the identification of many of its more prominent members with the old elite worked to the ASDT's favor. In the
few months following its creation, the ASDT worked to increase its
popularity, winning the support of a number of key *liurais* throughout the country and solidifying its base in rural areas. At the same
time, popular pressure within East Timor for rapid decolonization
and growing strength of the more radical elements of the MFA in Lisbon led the ASDT to harden its position on independence and to
become impatient toward the other parties' relatively conservative
politics. In September 1974, the ASDT leadership changed its name to
FRETILIN, declaring itself the "only legitimate representative of the
people." Furthermore FRETILIN demanded an immediate declaration of *de jure* independence from the Portuguese and the establishment of a transitional government that would carry East Timor
through a rapid process of decolonization.[40] By early 1975, FRETILIN,

by most accounts, including that of the Portuguese administrators, enjoyed the most popular support.[41]

With the assistance of the MFA administration in Dili, FRETILIN and the UDT joined in coalition in January 1975 to work for independence. APODETI refused to participate in the MFA-led process.[42] Despite the advancement of the decolonization process, the progress was to prove short-lived due to Indonesian subterfuge.

By mid-1974 BAKIN had developed *Operasi Komodo* (Operation Giant Lizard), a plan to integrate East Timor into Indonesia, though preferably avoiding a full-scale invasion. By bolstering the strength of APODETI while simultaneously undermining FRETILIN, BAKIN and its allies hoped to make inevitable the integration of East Timor into Indonesia. Tactics included soliciting international support for integration, disseminating pro-integration propaganda, discrediting FRETILIN, and gathering intelligence within Portuguese Timor, including the identification of potentially pro-Indonesian *liurais* and the assessment of the territory's military defenses. If these tactics failed, a military strategy would be developed.[43]

Civil War

Compounded by Indonesia's ongoing destabilization campaign, relations between FRETILIN and the UDT deteriorated; the UDT withdrew from the coalition in late 1975. Relations continued to worsen in June and July, and reached a head in August. Instigated by false Indonesian intelligence reports of an imminent FRETILIN power grab, clandestine Chinese arms deliveries, and "Vietnamese terrorists" entering the territory to aid FRETILIN, the UDT decided to try to seize power in the territory and thus launched a coup in Dili on August 11, 1975. The UDT quickly captured key installations of the Portuguese administration, including the communications station in the center of Dili and the airport, and soon began to arrest FRETILIN leaders as part of its efforts to consolidate power and marginalize FRETILIN. On the basis of meetings in Jakarta with Indonesian officials, UDT leaders were convinced that Indonesia would not allow East Timorese independence under FRETILIN leadership and probably not even under the UDT. The UDT felt that only by purging the territory of "communist" influence would it have any chance of preventing an Indonesian invasion.[44]

The UDT greatly underestimated FRETILIN's strength. FRETILIN won the support of most East Timorese units of the colonial army and soon regained control of Dili. On September 24, 1975, the brief civil war ended when FRETILIN drove 500 UDT soldiers, along with 2,500 refugees (most of whom were family members of UDT leaders and soldiers), into West (Indonesian) Timor.[45]

When the civil war first broke out in August 1975, the MFA administration made efforts to establish negotiations between the two parties, but the MFA's policy of *apartidarismo*, or political neutrality, and the seemingly irreconcilable preconditions for negotiations between the warring factions paralyzed the local authorities. Lisbon, meanwhile, apart from sending a low-level peace delegation (which Jakarta blocked from traveling from Indonesia to East Timor), did nothing, preferring to wash its hands of East Timor. Well aware of Jakarta's designs on the territory, Lisbon acquiesced to Indonesia.[46]

FRETILIN's *De Facto* Rule and Indonesian Aggression

With the defeat of the UDT and the departure of the Portuguese administration, that had fled to Atauro, an island off Dili's coast, during the conflict, FRETILIN began the task of setting up an embryonic national administration. The new *de facto* government quickly took shape. As José Ramos Horta, one of the founders of FRETILIN and now, in exile, the top diplomat of the East Timorese resistance, commented:

> [In] spite of our shortcomings [the provisional government] was functioning reasonably well. What motivated people to work hard, to volunteer their labor, was the euphoria of the victory and the prospect of a free and independent East Timor within a short period of time.[47]

A number of international visitors commented on the popularity and efficacy of the FRETILIN administration. The former Australian Consul in Dili, James Dunn, observed:

> This administrative structure had obvious shortcomings, but it
> clearly enjoyed widespread support or cooperation from the popu-
> lation, including many former UDT supporters. . . . Indeed, the
> leaders of the victorious party were welcomed warmly and sponta-
> neously in all main centres by crowds of Timorese. In my long as-
> sociation with the territory, I had never before witnessed such
> demonstrations of spontaneous warmth and support from the
> ordinary people of Timor. The FRETILIN administration was not
> without its critics and opponents, but opposition appeared to be
> largely confined to expressions of dissatisfaction rather than hostility.[48]

FRETILIN's strengths lay in its relatively successful implementation of
health care, education, nursery care, and agricultural programs.[49]

Meanwhile, the Portuguese flag continued to fly in front of the
governor's palace in Dili. As part of FRETILIN's efforts to encourage
the Portuguese administration to return, complete the process of decolonization, and ensure domestic stability, reconciliation, and international legitimacy (which was especially important in the face of an
increasingly menacing Indonesia), FRETILIN respected Portuguese
symbols and institutions and called for a peace conference that would
include Portugal and Indonesia. Lisbon's constant postponements,
however, prevented the proposed talks from ever taking place.[50]
Meanwhile, FRETILIN had to deal with increasing aggression from
Indonesia, including military incursions by the Indonesian military in
the regions close to the border with Indonesian West Timor. As early
as September 4, 1975, the U.S. Central Intelligence Agency (CIA)
noted the entry of two ABRI special force groups (of about 200 men)
into Portuguese Timor.[51]

In order to give the appearance of an ongoing civil war, which
would facilitate the acceptance of Indonesia's propagandistic claim
that it was intervening on behalf of East Timorese suffering from
FRETILIN-led brutality, Indonesia maintained a border strategy. This
consisted of frequent incursions with the intent of establishing bases
along the border, as confirmed by the CIA's *National Intelligence
Daily*.[52] Indonesian troops captured a number of towns in the border
region. The aggression culminated in mid-November when the Indonesians mounted a land, air, and sea attack against the town of

Atabae that lasted for about two weeks; Atabae finally fell on November 28, 1975.[53] On that same day, FRETILIN declared independence from Portugal and founded the Democratic Republic of East Timor. Nine days later, Indonesia launched a full-scale invasion of the territory.

The Roots of U.S. Partnership with Suharto

There is little doubt that the United States gave Suharto the green light to invade East Timor. In Jakarta, the day before the invasion, U.S. Secretary of State Henry Kissinger told reporters that "the United States understands Indonesia's position on the question" of East Timor.[54] According to columnist Jack Anderson, President Gerald Ford, who was visiting Suharto with Kissinger, himself admitted that, given a choice between East Timor and Indonesia, the U.S. "had to be on the side of Indonesia."[55] Prior to this event, however, it was clear that the East Timorese could not depend on the West, in which the FRETILIN leadership had originally placed a lot of hope, to help them secure independence. In general, the reaction of the West to the invasion and occupation, apart from pro forma criticisms, has ranged from resignation to outright complicity with Jakarta's brutality. Indeed, a number of countries could probably have easily prevented the invasion, especially the United States, which at the time provided the vast majority of Jakarta's military weaponry.

The involvement of the United States in Indonesia has its roots in the latter years of the Dutch colonial project. Already by the end of World War I, almost one-third of the Dutch East Indies' imports came from the United States and Japan. Significant U.S. demand for strategic resources such as tin, rubber, and oil led to extensive involvement in Indonesia by U.S.-based multinational corporations ranging from Goodyear (rubber plantations) to Caltex (oil).[56] By 1939, the Dutch East Indies was the primary supplier to the United States of 15 key commodities.[57]

World War II drastically altered the power relations in the Pacific. In the aftermath of the defeat of Japan, the United States emerged as the dominant power in the region, a position for which it had striven since the nineteenth century. Soon the Pacific would become "an

American Lake."[58] Quickly stepping into the power vacuum created by the vanquished powers of Europe and Japan, the United States was eager to take advantage of the region's vast resources and commercial opportunities, as some in the U.S. Congress were quick to articulate:

> Trade with China and other parts of the Orient, Australia, New Zealand, the Dutch East Indies, and with many islands of the Pacific will unquestionably develop and expand during the post-war era. These areas not only offer many markets for American products but are substantial producers of raw materials useful to our economy. . . . Our merchant marine and commercial firms should be given the opportunity to take over a large portion of that trade formerly handled by the Japanese and their vessels.[59]

In the post-war era, the United States was in the position to dictate the shape of the global political economy, a situation that did not escape prominent U.S. policy makers.

In a famous top secret foreign policy document from 1948, U.S. State Department Director of the Policy Planning Staff George Kennan laid out what many regard as the basis for President Harry Truman's anti-communist "containment policy" and for post-war U.S. foreign policy in general. Noting that the United States had "about 50 percent of the world's wealth but only 6.3 percent of its population," Kennan advised:

> Our real task in the coming period is to devise a pattern of relationships which will permit us to maintain this position of disparity without positive detriment to our national security....We should recognize that our influence in the Far Eastern area in the coming period is going to be primarily military and economic. We should make a careful study to see what parts of the Pacific and Far Eastern world are absolutely vital to our security, and we should concentrate our policy on seeing to it that those areas remain in hands which we can control or rely on.[60]

Many countries emerging from colonialism, however, were not willing to accept a permanent position of inferiority and subservience in the world political economy, and refused to cooperate with Washington's neocolonial designs. Non-alignment (neither pro-Soviet nor pro-U.S.), nationalism, and indigenous left-oriented movements presented serious challenges to U.S. regional hegemony. From Washington's perspective, all such challenges needed to be contained or eliminated to protect the interests of U.S. capital, as the U.S. war in Vietnam illustrates.

As President Dwight Eisenhower observed in 1954, the principal reason for the United States to intervene militarily in Vietnam was to control the region's natural resources.[61] But Vietnam was just one part of a larger puzzle in which, for some, Indonesia was the centerpiece; following such logic, the U.S. had to maintain each component of the whole within its sphere of influence to prevent a "domino effect" from occurring. In a 1965 speech in Asia, for example, Richard Nixon argued in favor of bombing North Vietnam to protect the "immense mineral potential" of Indonesia.[62] Many American elites saw U.S. aggression in Vietnam as part of a larger effort to contain nationalist and left-leaning movements in places such as Indonesia.[63]

Suharto's Bloody Rise to Power

Much to the chagrin of the West, post-independence Indonesia under Sukarno, the country's first president, became highly nationalistic, anti-West, and a champion of non-alignment and third world solidarity. Sukarno's nationalist strategy of building alliances with both the staunchly anti-communist Indonesian armed forces as well as with the huge Communist Party of Indonesia (PKI) greatly worried Washington. Seeing the Indonesian army as a potential bulwark against communist influence, and thus pro-West, the United States began cultivating the army's favor through military assistance and training programs. U.S. investment in the Indonesian army soon paid off with the overthrow of Sukarno and the 1965-1966 pogrom against the PKI.[64]

In the aftermath of an alleged communist attempt to overthrow the Sukarno government on September 30, 1965, and the murder of six ABRI generals, Suharto, a pro-U.S. general, assumed control of the military and launched "one of the great slaughters of our time."[65] The vast majority of those killed were from the Left: from the PKI and its affiliated organizations of peasants, workers, and women. The Indonesian government claims that the Indonesian population spontaneously rose up in outrage over the PKI's attempted coup, but there is little to no evidence to show that the PKI was trying to seize power. Far more likely is that Suharto used an internal power struggle within the Indonesian military as an excuse to destroy the Left and to take power.[66]

The exact scale of the killings, the great bulk of which occurred from October 1965 to March 1966, is unknown. Amnesty International has estimated that "many more than one million" were killed. The head of the Indonesia state security system approximated the toll at half a million, with another 750,000 jailed or sent to concentration camps.[67] While even the C.I.A. described the massacres "as one of the worst mass murders of the 20th century," many in the West welcomed the overthrow of Sukarno and the emergence of Suharto's "New Order." *Time* magazine hailed General Suharto's brutal seizure of power as "the West's best news for years in Asia."[68]

The United States' role in the killings was far from innocent. The U.S. government supplied weaponry to the Indonesian army in the early weeks of the slaughter.[69] According to a May 1990 States News Service report by Kathy Kadane, the U.S. Embassy in Jakarta supplied the Indonesian military with the names of thousands of PKI leaders who were subsequently killed by the military:

> As many as 5,000 names were furnished to the Indonesian army, and the Americans later checked off the names of those who had been killed or captured, according to U.S. officials. . . . The lists were a detailed who's-who of the leadership of the party of three million members, [foreign service officer Robert] Martens said. They included names of provincial, city, and other PKI committee members, and leaders of the mass organizations, such as the PKI national labor federation, [and] women's and youth groups.[70]

Deputy chief Francis Galbraith clearly articulated the embassy's view of the massacres while reporting to Washington on a conversation he had with an unidentified, high-ranking Indonesian army officer about one month after the mass killings had begun. Galbraith said that he had "made clear" to the officer "that the embassy and the

U.S. G[overnment] were generally sympathetic with and admiring of what the army was doing."[71]

U.S. and Western Complicity in the Annexation of East Timor

By the time of the Carnation Revolution, General Suharto's Indonesia was firmly allied with Western political and economic interests, a fact that would lay the basis for U.S. and Western acquiescence to and cooperation with Indonesia's desire to annex East Timor. As an unnamed U.S. State Department official explained in early 1976, "In terms of the bilateral relations between the U.S. and Indonesia, we are more or less condoning the incursion into East Timor. . . . The United States wants to keep its relations with Indonesia close and friendly. We regard Indonesia as a friendly, non-aligned nation—a nation we do a lot of business with."[72]

According to the State Department, U.S. companies supplied some 90 percent of the weapons used by ABRI during the invasion. When it looked as if Jakarta was actually running out of military equipment in late 1977, the "human rights" administration of President Jimmy Carter responded by authorizing $112 million in commercial arms sales for fiscal 1978 to Jakarta, up from $5.8 million the previous year (an almost 2,000 percent increase). U.S. military sales peaked during the presidency of Ronald Reagan, exceeding $1 billion from 1982 to 1984.

In addition to the sale of weapons, the United States has provided Indonesia with significant military aid. The Ford administration more than doubled its military assistance to Jakarta (to $146 million) in the year following the invasion. Similarly, U.S. military aid increased during the Carter and Reagan administrations, during which the bulk of the killings were taking place in East Timor. More than 2,600 Indonesian military officers have received military training in the United States under the International Military Education and Training (IMET) program since the 1975 invasion.[73]

Following the lead of political and economic elites, reporting on East Timor by the corporate-owned media in the West has been paltry at best. While a number of reports on Portuguese Timor appeared in major newspapers in the months preceding the invasion, major

U.S. media coverage on East Timor actually decreased significantly after December 7, 1975.[74]

The *Los Angeles Times* is a case in point. From August 1975 until the invasion, the paper ran 16 articles dealing with East Timor. After the Indonesian invasion, however, reporting quickly dropped off. In fact, there was not a single mention of East Timor in the *Los Angeles Times* from March 1976 until November 1979, a time when the Australian Parliament Legislative Research Service said East Timor was experiencing "indiscriminate killing on a scale unprecedented in post-World War II history."[75]

The United States certainly has not been alone in its criminal complicity. With few exceptions almost all Western countries are guilty of crimes in East Timor. From Australia, France, and Canada to Germany, Japan, and the United Kingdom, narrow economic and political considerations have informed Western practices toward Indonesia and East Timor since 1975. Constâncio's story vividly shows the human costs of such realpolitik.

I first heard of East Timor in the late 1980s from reading books by Noam Chomsky. By the time I began graduate school in 1990, though, I knew only that something terrible had happened in the former Portuguese colony and that the United States government had somehow contributed to Indonesia's crimes. During my first quarter of graduate school, I took advantage of a course I was taking to write a research paper on East Timorese nationalism. While researching the paper, I became shocked at the scope of what had transpired in East Timor and my own ignorance of such a crime against humanity. At that point, I decided to write my master's thesis on East Timor's struggle for self-determination. The November 1991 Santa Cruz massacre in East Timor was the impetus for me to apply my academic pursuits to political activism and I became involved with the newly formed East Timor Action Network. Since that time, I have dedicated a considerable amount of my activist, journalistic, and academic work to the cause of East Timorese self-determination.

This book is the product of almost three years of collaboration between Constâncio Pinto and myself. I first met Constâncio in April
1993 when Constâncio was in Los Angeles as part of a North American speaking tour of East Timorese refugees, and he stayed at my
home.

But Constâncio and I had inadvertently come into contact months
earlier, even though we didn't realize it at the time, during the sum-
mer of 1992, when I spent almost four weeks in East Timor.

Without a doubt, East Timor is by far the scariest place I have ever
visited. Never before have I sensed such a climate of fear and para-
noia among a population. The Indonesian military presence is quite
noticeable throughout the country. In Dili alone, there are literally
dozens of military installations. I would often see passing trucks full
of young Indonesian soldiers singing military songs on the roads of
Dili and throughout East Timor, probably off to the battlefront.
The ubiquitous presence of military personnel and Indonesia's extensive network of spies and paid or coerced informants (who are often
East Timorese) create an atmosphere where trust is very scarce. On
my second day in Dili, a Catholic priest, himself worried that people
in his own church were spying on him, advised me not to trust anyone.

I was constantly paranoid. There were times when I was followed
and other times when a "friend" would ask far too many questions.
On a few occasions, Indonesian military personnel interrogated me as
I visited towns in the territory. As a result of such monitoring, most
East Timorese I encountered were too afraid to speak with me. As one
passes people on the street, most people do not make direct eye contact, only doing so, if at all, in a very fleeting manner. Some would go
so far as to cross the street to avoid being seen walking near a foreigner and inviting the suspicion of the Indonesian military.

Nevertheless, through my own luck and the brave efforts of individuals working with the Timorese resistance, I came into contact
with various individuals working with the underground movement.
One of them gave me two very large envelopes containing the results
of an extensive survey of the armed resistance and the underground
that they wanted delivered to resistance leaders outside of East
Timor. When I met Constâncio several months later, I showed him

the stack of documents (I had made a photocopy of them in case they became lost in the mail). The cover letter introducing the survey to the various resistance leaders was signed by "Terus," Constâncio's *nom de guerre*. I had carried out the product of Constâncio's last official act as head of the clandestine front before his flight from East Timor in mid-1992.

When I proposed the book project to Constâncio in April 1993, he was immediately receptive. He had already given thought to writing some sort of memoir of his experiences in East Timor, and his speaking experiences in the United States and Canada had shown him how his story could raise people's awareness of the East Timorese struggle.

The power of a personal testimonial to move people and to expose them to larger social dynamics is enormous. *East Timor's Unfinished Struggle* tells one among many compelling stories from the people of East Timor. Yet Constâncio's story is important because it reflects East Timor's history within the context of an unjust world order. We hope that this book teaches people something about East Timor and moves them to work locally, nationally, and globally to facilitate East Timorese self-determination. We also hope that this book moves people to actively challenge the myriad relationships that underlie a world of gross socio-economic inequality, sustained by a politics of great violence, in which situations like that of East Timor are all too common. Only then can we build local, national, and global orders truly based on human rights for all peoples.

—Matthew Jardine

1

Origins of the Struggle

My name is Constâncio Pinto. I was born in Dili, the capital of Portuguese Timor, on January 25, 1963. I was my parents' first of 11 children. Fortunately, all of my brothers and sisters are still alive. Currently they all live in Dili.

I only spent a few months in Dili because my parents moved to the town of Remexio, about 20 kilometers south of Dili, six or seven months after I was born. Fewer than 500 people lived in the town.[1] There was just one unpaved street and the town had no electricity. Most of the land in the area belonged to the Portuguese *administrador*, the head of the *posto administrativo*, or subdistrict; he had a rubber plantation as well as land for fruit trees and flowers.

Remexio had two schools in the town, one government primary school, and one Catholic primary school. There was also a clinic where my father later worked, two shops owned by ethnic Chinese,[2] a church, and the *administrador*'s office and house. There were only a few modern houses in Remexio.

My father, Tomás Pinto, was born in 1938, and my mother, Isabel da Conçeicão Nascimento, was born four years later. My father has two sisters and two brothers, but one of his brothers died before Indonesia invaded East Timor in 1975. My mother has three sisters and four brothers. The Indonesian army killed two of her brothers after they surrendered in Aileu in 1978; the other two, along with her three sisters, are still alive.

Both my parents are from the *concelho*, or district, of Aileu, but only my mother's family lived in the main town, also called Aileu.[3] My father's family lived in the mountains. His family raised livestock and cultivated coffee and rice. My father speaks and writes Portuguese because he went to a Portuguese school run by Catholic priests, but he only completed primary school. Unfortunately he was not able to continue his studies because the Portuguese colonial regime did not allow East Timorese children to continue their studies after they reached the age of 18. Most of those who were able to complete their studies were the children of Portuguese residents in East Timor and the children of *liurais*. As a result, over 90 percent of the population was illiterate at the end of Portugal's colonization of East Timor.[4]

My mother comes from a *liurai* family. A *liurai* is a traditional king. It is a composition of two words in Tetum, the traditional *lingua franca* of East Timor. *Liu* means "over" and *rai* means "land"; so the word literally means someone who controls land.[5] Some *liurais* were rich and powerful, but not all of them. My mother's family led a modest life. They had a few animals and possessed some land and, like all *liurais* to varying degrees, were Portuguese collaborators, helping to uphold Portuguese colonial law. *Liurais* often cooperated with the Portuguese authorities to oppress their own people. My mother's parents did not speak any Portuguese, but my mother understands a little because she went to a Portuguese nuns' school for a very short time.

When my parents got married in the early 1960s, my father was working in Dili and my mother moved there to join him. In Dili, my father worked as a civil servant at the department of public works, *obras publicas*. My parents obtained a little piece of land where my father built a very modest house for us to live. My father worked for *obras publicas* for some years and then resigned. The Portuguese department of agriculture loaned my father some money and gave him a few hectares of abandoned land in Remexio, where my parents became farmers. In Dili, my father worked outside while my mother took care of the children and the household; but in Remexio my mother began to work on the farm alongside my father.

My parents grew corn, manioc, sweet potatoes, beans, green vegetables, and coffee. My mother took care of us and took care of the farm. She managed the people we hired, and worked herself. We had about six people working with us every month at that time. People had to work for wages to pay the *imposto*, the colonial head tax. The *administrador* would send people who needed to earn money to pay their taxes to my father. If they couldn't pay their taxes, they had to go to jail.

The workers had their own land in the mountains, in their *knua*, a hamlet of a few houses. Several *knuas* made up a village.[6] But the products of the land were only for subsistence. So the workers had many difficulties earning money to pay government taxes and had to work for someone who could pay taxes for them. I often spent time with the people who worked for us on the farm, sometimes sharing with them their fresh coffee tea (a drink made from the leaves of the coffee plant), sweet potato, manioc, and fried corn.

I remember that I used to follow my parents to the farm when I was young. I also remember playing football (European football) and *kalek*, a Timorese game. *Kalek* is a wild fruit from the *trepadeira* tree. You had to be able to hit the fruits on the tree by throwing other pieces of *kalek* from increasing distances. It was a lot of fun.

My parents worked hard to support me and my brothers and sisters. I remember my father taught me to write by holding a pencil in my hand and helping me draw my first letters and Portuguese words. My parents also taught us to pray every day. We were a poor family, but I was happy. I used to help with household chores, such as gathering firewood, getting water, working on the farm and in our garden, washing dishes, cleaning the yard, and helping my mother take care of the other children.

At that time my family lived under rather poor conditions. We did not produce that much, and because we did not have a car and couldn't pay for transportation, it was difficult for my parents to get the crops to market. I remember my parents sent some workers to Dili to sell vegetables. The workers had to walk for about half a day to reach Dili. But the revenue that my parents earned from selling vegetables was enough to buy kerosene for candlelight, sugar, salt, and other household necessities. In addition, my parents could also save a little money to buy my notebooks, school uniform, and pencils. They would give me a few *escudos* (Portuguese currency) every day to buy bread and groundnut, which I loved eating.

We bought our basic supplies at the local Chinese stores. The Chinese shops provided most of the necessities of the population. The Chinese in Remexio were rich. They were the only ones in Remexio, apart from the *administrador* and officials in the Portuguese army, who had cars. At that time, if someone had a car, the person was considered rich.

My father ran out of money after a few years of being in Remexio and stopped hiring people. He began to work the farm by himself with my mother's help. My father also began making and selling *tuaka*, palm wine. We made a good amount of money out of *tuaka*. I was almost seven years old at that time and I began to help my parents on the farm.

Soon thereafter, my father got a job at the Remexio *enfermaria*, the clinic, as a nurse's assistant. Our lives improved because my father received a civil servant's salary from the Portuguese government. For the first time in my life, my family had enough money to buy food every day.

My parents sent me to a Catholic primary school when I turned five. There were two teachers, Senhor Zacarias da Costa and his daughter, Judite da Costa.[7] I went to the primary school as a pre-school student, just to listen, for one year before I registered as a student.

My parents always said that the Catholic schools were the best schools in East Timor. In the state schools, which were run by the Portuguese colonial administration, the students had to memorize everything without knowing the meaning. Paulo Freire, the Brazilian educator, has called this style of teaching the pedagogy of oppression. Around 200 students attended the Catholic school in Remexio. The majority of the students came from the mountains. During the school year they lived in town, in houses their parents had built for them. Most of the students lived in group houses depending on what regions they had come from. Students from Manumera, for example, all lived together. Most of the students came from poor families. My father had to pay a small amount of money for me to go to the Catholic school. The state schools were free and were run by the Portuguese government.

We didn't have any priests living in Remexio, but Father Brito was responsible for the Remexio parish and was in charge of the town's Catholic school; he would visit Remexio about once a month. Father Brito was an Indian from Goa, but he was a Portuguese citizen. Besides Father Brito, one of the Portuguese priests, Father João Felgueiras, who was the rector of the Catholic seminary in Dare, would sometimes visit Remexio. Because of the influence of the colonial authorities and the Catholic Church, we respected priests in East Timor as the representatives of God on Earth.

I remember I was very happy the first day that my father brought me to school. At school I played with other kids who I had never seen before. My teacher, Senhor Zacarias, treated me well because he was the *compadre*, the godfather, of my sister Celestina, who was born two years after me. In East Timor, people consider godparents part of their family. My godparents were a Portuguese couple who left East Timor in 1964 to return to Portugal; I don't remember ever seeing them.

At school, I remember learning about Portuguese culture, geography, and history, but I never learned anything about my own country; I didn't even know about colonialism. I thought that everything was fine, probably because we never learned anything about politics in school. In fact, I don't think I ever even heard the word *politics*.

Even though I saw myself as Timorese, I also thought that Portugal was my fatherland, *a minha patria*. This was what I was taught at school. This is the confusion colonialism creates in the minds of the colonized. I was eager to study hard in order to go to Portugal one day. But I never saw myself as Portuguese; I considered myself a Timorese learning the Portuguese language. Portuguese people were white, and I am black. During the colonial period, only white people who came from Portugal and their children, and East Timorese who had Portuguese identity cards, *assimilados*, were Portuguese citizens. *Assimilados* were people who were loyal to the Portuguese colonizers, including people born in East Timor of mixed blood, *mestiços*. Although there were ethnic divisions within East Timor, the experience of

Portuguese colonialism helped unite the people of East Timor, as the frequent uprisings by the Timorese against the Portuguese, such as the Manufahi rebellion in 1912, demonstrated. Even as a young boy, I knew that the Portuguese did not belong in East Timor and that I, as a Timorese, was indigenous to the territory.

Nevertheless, I thought that the Portuguese were nice people. I did not have any ill will toward the Portuguese because I did not directly experience the exploitation that my parents and most other people suffered, but it affected me because of the poverty that almost all East Timorese endured. I did not even know the word *exploitation*. To me the Portuguese were good because the military delivered a bowl of soup every week to the students at my school.

There was a military post in Remexio with approximately 100 military personnel. Most of the officers were Portuguese, and most of the soldiers were Timorese. I would visit the soldiers almost every week because I tried to sell vegetables at the military post. One of my uncles was a soldier there. Every time I went to the post, the soldiers fed me plenty of food, like soup, bread, and meat.

The Portuguese soldiers were real womanizers. Many Timorese women suffered because of the Portuguese soldiers. Most of the Portuguese soldiers and officials married Timorese women, but some of them just made the Timorese women their lovers. Of course, not all of the East Timorese women who married or dated soldiers went to Portugal with their husbands or boyfriends. Many of the women had children by Portuguese men who later abandoned them in East Timor.

Until I was 11 years old, I could say that my life was good. We lived peacefully. My parents were able to get food every day. I did not know anything about politics and I never heard people talk about politics. I did not even know where Indonesia was. I thought Indonesia was West Timor and that the capital of Indonesia was Kupang. No one spoke about the Portuguese critically, at least not until the revolution in Portugal in 1974, probably because people were afraid of the Portuguese secret police and possible repression. I never heard my parents speak against the Portuguese; I only heard them speak about PIDE, the secret police of the Portuguese dictatorship before the revolution.[8] People were really afraid of PIDE.

Sometimes a Portuguese dignitary from Dili, such as the governor, would visit Remexio. I remember that this happened when I was eight years old. The *liurai* forced thousands of people to gather in Remexio to greet the governor with flowers and traditional dances. The people had to spend a whole week in town waiting for the governor's arrival. When the governor arrived, the people, many wearing traditional dress, danced and marched and displayed Portuguese flags. What we called the traditional armies, groups of indigenous Timorese warriors, marched with their swords and drums. As a sign of respect some people laid their clothes on the ground for the governor to walk on so his feet would not touch the ground. I was there as a primary school student, wearing a blue and white uniform. I had to sing the Portuguese anthem *Herois do Mar* in a loud voice. I was like a parrot in the jungle of Remexio.

The Portuguese flag was treated as if it were sacred. When you passed it on the street, wherever you were, you had to stop and salute it. Otherwise one of the soldiers might kill you. People were even afraid to cross the shadow of the flag. If you saw the shadow of the flag, you waited until it passed or you walked around it. I never saw anyone disrespecting the flag. When you passed in front of the administration building where there was a flagpole, you had to take off your hat. And when you passed on a horse, you had to get off the horse and walk it, just because you were passing the administration building. Even as a little boy I did these things. It didn't matter if you were old or young. People also treated the *administrador* with great respect. People treated the Portuguese almost as if they were gods.

The Portuguese used to force people to do manual labor for the colonial administration. I remember seeing the entire road that goes west from Remexio being built by forced labor. People worked very hard and received nothing in return. Most of the people who worked on the construction of the street came from urban areas and could not afford to pay taxes. Even if you paid taxes, you still had to serve the government at least one week a month, or one month a year. The amount of work would depend on the *chefe de suco* where you lived.[9] Several villages made up a *suco* and the *chefe de suco* was in charge.

My father and mother didn't have to do forced labor because my father was a Portuguese citizen.

The Portuguese military did not treat civilians as poorly as the Indonesian soldiers treat the East Timorese today. This does not mean that the Portuguese military did not commit human rights violations. They did, but nothing like what the Indonesians are doing now. Most of the atrocities committed by the Portuguese happened in the beginning of the colonization of East Timor and during the Manufahi revolution in 1912 when Portuguese soldiers killed thousands of civilians who fought against the colonizers under Dom Boaventura's leadership.

The Portuguese would sometimes beat people. They used something called the *palmatoria*. People were really afraid of the *palmatoria*. It's a round, flat piece of wood with a thickness of maybe one inch and a hole in the middle to let the air pass through as you're swinging it. It has a handle so you can hold it and strike the palm of a person's hand. It's really painful. Sometimes they would beat someone's hand until the hand became swollen and was bleeding. If they hit you a lot, you couldn't use your hand for weeks. The *liurais* and the administrators, not the military, were responsible for most of the beatings. I never actually saw any abuses with my own eyes, but many people told me about them and I saw people who had scars on their palms and body from the *palmatoria*. You could get the *palmatoria* for many reasons. Sometimes people got it simply because they could not afford to pay the *imposto*.

Besides the *palmatoria*, there was also the *chicote*, which is a whip that people usually use for horses. It was used on human beings sometimes, whipped across their backs. The *administrador* or the *liurais* would order someone to do the whipping. I didn't spend much time with my grandfather, the *liurai* in Aileu, but I think he must have done such things as well.

I know many old people who say that they were tortured in public, especially during the *arolamento*, the population census. *Arolamento* was also the time for tax collection. During that time the *administrador* would go from one village to the next, registering people's names as well as punishing people who had committed some sort of infraction, such as failing to participate in forced labor.

These punishments were carried out in school as well. In my school, we had a *palmatoria*. When a student did not complete an assignment he or she would receive at least 15 to 20 hits. Sometimes it would depend on the teacher, but the *palmatoria* was used in most schools to force the students to learn the Portuguese language and other subjects. If anyone was caught speaking Tetum, that person would get many hits. We would call the *palmatoria "mandioca seca,"* dried manioc, because manioc becomes like wood when it is dry.

Our lives changed greatly when I was 11 years old and the Carnation Revolution occurred in Portugal. This revolution took place in April 1974 when a section of the Portuguese army overthrew the military dictatorship of Marcelo Caetano, who succeeded the dictator Antonio de Oliveira Salazar in 1968. When people in East Timor found out about the revolution, many started throwing away pictures of President Caetano and Americo Tomás, his prime minister.

I was able to follow what was happening in Portugal through my parents and through radio news. We did not have any newspapers. There was only one newspaper at that time, *A Voz de Timor*, which was run by the colonial government. It circulated only in Dili. Television did not exist in Portuguese Timor. Later on in 1974, I saw a movie about the revolution shown by the local government. I remember seeing Portuguese soldiers arresting Tomás and Caetano and putting them in a car and taking them to prison. My father told me that freedom and independence would soon come to the Portuguese colonies: Angola, Mozambique, Cape Verde, Guinea-Bissau, and São Tomé e Principe, as well as East Timor, because of the revolution. We would be free from the oppression of other countries and we would rule ourselves.

The Carnation Revolution in Portugal changed everyone's life in East Timor. It opened our eyes to the oppression that we had long experienced. But things were very uncertain during the first weeks after things began to change in Portugal. No one knew what was going to happen. But it became more clear when political parties began to form.

My father and mother immediately joined the ASDT, the Association of Timorese Social Democrats, in May 1974. They joined the

ASDT because the party defended independence for East Timor and because Xavier do Amaral, one of the founders of the ASDT, is related to our family. Xavier do Amaral was married to one of my father's aunts. My father and Xavier spent their childhood together in Aileu.

It was hard for me as a little boy to know what my parents felt about the Portuguese. They probably did not support them, but they couldn't say that to me or the other children. It seems, however, that the spirit of nationalism had already been cultivated within my parents because they both became so quickly involved in the ASDT.

My father actively worked for the ASDT in Remexio with the hope that East Timor would soon become an independent country. Because of the strengthening pro-independence sentiment within the population and the influence of certain left-wing, East Timorese intellectuals who had returned from Portugal after the Carnation Revolution, the ASDT changed its name in September 1974 to FRETILIN, the Revolutionary Front for an Independent East Timor.

I knew nothing about politics at that time. Like other kids, I just followed my parents. Because my parents were FRETILIN, I was proud to be FRETILIN. I participated in demonstrations and rallies and went to speeches. The events I attended took place mostly in Remexio, but in Dili as well. I remember that FRETILIN cadres would lead us in shouting slogans: "*Fim ao colonialismo Português!*" (End Portuguese colonialism!), "*Abaixo o imperialismo!*" (Down with imperialism!), and "*Viva FRETILIN!*" I also went to FRETILIN parties, which we called *convivios*. These were not only times for people to get to know one another and build trust and confidence within the party, but also opportunities for FRETILIN to propagate its political ideology and to recruit new members. Even though I was very young, I knew the names of some of the FRETILIN leaders such as Nicolau and Rogerio Lobato, José Ramos Horta, Hamis Hatta, Alarico Fernandes, Rosa Bonaparte, Mari Alkatiri, and Guido Valadares.

My father tried to persuade many people to join the party. My house was one of the places where men and women gathered and signed up for FRETILIN. I still remember how people came down from the *knuas* in the mountains to get their FRETILIN membership cards during the weekly FRETILIN meetings at our house on Sundays. Whenever they saw my father they said, "*Camarada, ukun rasik an mak diak liu*": "Comrade, independence is best." My father and a few others, like two of Zacarias da Costa's sons, who were students in Dili, were the main FRETILIN organizers in Remexio. Zacarias' daughter was a supporter of the UDT, the Timorese Democratic Union. The UDT was the first party formed after the Carnation Revolution and was more conservative than FRETILIN.

FRETILIN, for example, demanded immediate independence from Portugal, while the UDT favored a federation with Portugal as an interim stage to independence. But the UDT didn't have a lot of sympathizers in Remexio. The UDT did come there, but it found little support and never had a rally in the area. The local *liurai* was UDT, but the population was FRETILIN. APODETI, the Timorese Popular Democratic Association, was the only party that wanted to incorporate East Timor into Indonesia. It never came to Remexio and had no supporters there.

Most of the people in Remexio did not know a lot about the FRETILIN political program. What attracted them was FRETILIN's strong commitment to ending colonialism. I didn't even know what colonialism was when I was 11, but I soon learned from FRETILIN that it was bad. Through colonialism, the Portuguese exploited our resources, like sandalwood, and exploited our people through forced labor, poor wages, and other human rights violations. One of FRETILIN's most striking sayings was that for 400 years the Portuguese rode us, the *Maubere* people, as their Lusitanian horses. *Maubere* is a word from an indigenous Timorese language that the Portuguese used to express scorn toward the East Timorese people. But FRETILIN took up the word *maubere* (and *bibere* for women) as a term of pride for the East Timorese people.[10]

From late 1974 through 1975, FRETILIN's strength in Remexio and throughout East Timor continued to grow. Then, in August 1975, a civil war broke out in East Timor because of growing tensions between the UDT and FRETILIN, instigated by the Indonesian intelligence service to undermine the decolonization process. The civil war started under the leadership of Francisco Lopes da Cruz, the head of the UDT. The UDT attacked and took control of Portuguese

installations in Dili and began arresting FRETILIN activists throughout the country. The UDT then tried to capture Remexio, from the
north and the east, because many FRETILIN leaders had fled there. I
heard people shooting but I did not see actual fighting because it was
taking place about four miles away from the town.

As the battle intensified, FRETILIN instructed everyone in the
town to evacuate into the mountains as a precautionary measure.
FRETILIN had a lot of people who could fight; some FRETILIN members who had military experience guarded the town while others went
to the border between Remexio and Lacló to fight against the UDT.

My family lived for about one or two weeks in the jungle in a temporary shelter that we built. During our time in the jungle, my parents
told us stories of what had happened during World War II, when the
Japanese military occupied East Timor in response to the arrival of
Dutch and Australian troops on the island. My father said that this
war would be more dangerous than the Japanese one because
Timorese were fighting each other. There were seven children in my
family, including me, by that time. My father was a nurse, taking care
of sick and wounded people.

In the jungle we heard sad news from Dili: the UDT army, which
was fighting FALINTIL,[11] had killed Senhor Zacarias da Costa in Dili.
He moved to Dili to live with his daughter when the situation became
tense in Remexio. According to the report, UDT militia killed him, but
we don't know who was responsible. It was so sad not only for us but
for everyone in Remexio because he was well known in the town.
Zacarias' family was split into two: one daughter was UDT, and the
rest of the family were FRETILIN.

My family returned to the town in September 1975, when the situation calmed down. FRETILIN was able to prevent the UDT from
reaching Remexio and declared victory over the UDT throughout
East Timor. But when we returned to town, we had no food. Fortunately, when the two Chinese families fled to Dili at the outbreak of
the civil war, they left all their belongings and store supplies.
FRETILIN took control of the stores and distributed the supplies to
the local population. Now we were dependent on FRETILIN. The
Portuguese administration had fled during the civil war to Atauro

island, off of Dili, and didn't return. My father continued to work at the same clinic, but he didn't receive any salary.

FRETILIN took over the office of the head of the sub-district of Remexio and began to organize the town. I don't remember very well what the administration looked like, but I remember that some new books in Tetum began to circulate. FRETILIN put a heavy emphasis on mass education. Apart from that, every week we had a party in the town. FRETILIN also soon opened the local market again and began organizing the army. At that time, we were still using Portuguese currency, the *escudo*.

People were really happy then, but they were also afraid that Indonesia might invade East Timor. They were happy because they were not subjected to any kind of oppression. People considered East Timor an independent country, although independence had not yet been officially proclaimed. I even saw people voluntarily working, cleaning the town and helping to organize things throughout the district. FRETILIN started to reorganize the government, establishing schools and hospitals and opening the markets, though it was difficult to organize a newly independent country within a short time.

Meanwhile, in West Timor, Francisco Lopes da Cruz, the head of the UDT and an agent for Indonesian intelligence, continued to threaten on Indonesian shortwave radio that he and his supporters were going to recapture East Timor from the hands of FRETILIN. Lopes da Cruz had already joined with the Indonesian military to launch military attacks from West Timor. I still remember his saying on the radio, "Brothers and sisters, don't be afraid. The UDT will take over East Timor in 24 hours."

On November 28, 1975, my father and I went to Dili to visit family there. When we arrived, we heard that there was a FALINTIL exhibition in front of the governor's office, so we went there to see it; it was some sort of flag ceremony. We didn't realize at that time that it was the day of FRETILIN's unilateral proclamation of independence, because FRETILIN had decided only within the previous 24 hours to have the ceremony.[12] We saw a lot of people marching in the street. When the marching stopped for one hour, I thought that the ceremony was over; but an hour later, the troops were still there. At that time, there was an announcement that there would be a ceremony for the proclamation of East Timor's independence.

People began filling the whole area in front of the governor's palace; there were about 2,000 people there. The Portuguese flag was still flying. Suddenly I saw FALINTIL soldiers begin to fall into formation along the street in front of the governor's palace. It was about six in the evening. The members of the FRETILIN central committee, Xavier do Amaral, and many members of UNETIM (the National Union of Timorese Students, a FRETILIN youth organization) were there. Then someone began to play a revolutionary song on an organ. Nicolau Lobato and Xavier do Amaral appeared in new uniforms. The uniforms were gifts from Samora Machel, the leader of FRELIMO, the victorious revolutionary party that led Mozambique to independence. The colors looked like those of a tiger. Then some FALINTIL soldiers began to lower the Portuguese flag and raise the East Timorese flag, and Xavier do Amaral pronounced the founding of the Democratic Republic of East Timor.

When the East Timor flag rose to the top of the pole, everyone began singing "Patria, Patria," the national anthem of East Timor. When the flag rose up the pole, it looked beautiful. There was no wind. It was peaceful. After that, soldiers threw hand grenades into the sea. Everyone seemed very happy.[13] I, too, felt very happy and was excited. "Your grandfather is now our president, the president of the Democratic Republic of East Timor," my father said to me. (In East Timor, you also call the uncles and aunts of your parents "grandparents.") "You should feel proud to have a family member as the president of the country." I was very proud.

After the ceremony, everyone went home. I was happy that we had finally won independence from Portugal and that we were forming our own government. I was sitting at an uncle's house, listening to the news from Radio Maubere, FRETILIN's radio station. We were receiving messages of congratulations from the other former Portuguese colonies. We received no reaction from Portugal or from other countries; only Angola, Mozambique, Guinea-Bissau, and Cape Verde immediately recognized our independence.[14] No one slept that night; the city was really noisy. It was a big party. Everyone was walking in the streets, shouting out *"Timor Livre,"* "The Democratic Republic of East Timor," and "Independence!"

Many people thought our problems were over, but FRETILIN declared independence because the leadership knew that Indonesia would soon invade. That's why they declared independence so early. The proclamation of independence had originally been planned for May 1976. People knew about the incursions of the Indonesian military into East Timor because there was news that Indonesia had begun to attack the border. In response, FRETILIN began to send militias to defend the area along the border with West Timor. Many people were killed during the Indonesian attacks. I remember when the Indonesians captured Batugadé, near the border of West Timor, on October 8, 1975. FRETILIN told the population that we should be on alert. In November, my father started joining other adults patrolling Remexio to guard against a possible Indonesian attack. Many people, however, did not believe that Indonesia would invade East Timor; others thought that if Indonesia did invade, we would receive support from many countries. That's what FRETILIN told people. People knew that Indonesia was attacking the border, but it was said that it would take time for them to get to Dili and to take the whole island if they invaded. And if they took more land, then we'd get immediate support from others. That's what people thought or hoped. Even my parents were saying this. But I'm sure that the FRETILIN leaders feared otherwise. Many hoped that East Timor's proclamation of independence would prevent Indonesia from invading East Timor.

The Portuguese didn't help at all. After fleeing East Timor during the civil war, they never came back. While the Carnation Revolution was the beginning of democracy and prosperity in Portugal, it was the beginning of a wave of human suffering and genocide in many of Portugal's former colonies, including East Timor. Indonesia's invasion changed everything forever.

2

The Indonesian Invasion

On December 7, 1975, when the Indonesian military began to drop paratroopers in Dili, people in Remexio thought that the planes flying over Dili were our supporters. Even my father thought this because FRETILIN had said that we would get support from Australia. On December 6, FRETILIN had instructed all men in Remexio to report for an all-night patrol. My father joined the patrol, monitoring Remexio. Because Remexio is high in the mountains and Dili is at sea level, they saw the fighting when it began in Dili. We could see the planes dropping parachutes from the sky. At 5 a.m. on December 7 my father returned home. He woke everyone up and told us, "The Indonesian army has invaded Dili. But don't be afraid. We will have support." My parents looked very worried, but they weren't panicking because Remexio is still far away from Dili.

Early that morning, people began arriving in Remexio from Dili, carrying luggage, backpacks, and children; they were in a panic and were looking for a way to escape the Indonesian troops. The first groups arrived by car, and others later arrived on foot. Even FALIN-TIL soldiers and their families were fleeing. Soon there were thousands of refugees in Remexio. Many people were crying because they had to leave their families, their houses, and all their belongings in Dili. Some people had been wounded by the Indonesian bombardment and the indiscriminate shooting by Indonesian soldiers in Dili. My father, because he worked at a clinic in Remexio, helped to take care of them.

I didn't know what to do. I was only 12 years old. I tried to imagine what the war was going to be like. I had heard stories about the Japanese war, but I didn't know exactly what to expect, especially since I knew nothing about Indonesia. I just followed my parents. We packed clothes, food, and medicine in case we had to evacuate to the mountains. We also began to kill some of our animals, including pigs and sheep.

During the two and a half weeks between the invasion of Dili and our departure from Remexio, we heard stories about thousands of people being killed, women being raped, and people, including children, being rounded up and shot by Indonesian soldiers on the streets and at the harbor in Dili. I remember hearing about how Indonesian soldiers had raped the wife of Rogerio Lobato, a FRETILIN leader, and then shot her to death and threw her body into the ocean.[1] I was really afraid. I was afraid for my own life and for those of my brothers and sisters and my parents. In a war, no one can escape from death. But in the end, we offered ourselves to God, as God predetermines everything. God is the one who would make the final decision on our lives.

We couldn't stay at our home. We had to hide in caves and shelters because the Indonesians bombed Remexio every night. Fortunately, no one in Remexio was killed because the bombs never hit any hiding place. This was not because of the generosity of the Indonesian army; the Indonesians dropped thousands of bombs in Remexio, but they were not effective.

We spent most of our time hiding in our shelter, one mile from our house, until December 25. Because the Indonesian military was very close to the outskirts of Remexio, we fled our hiding place that afternoon and headed south toward Bereliurai. A few hours later, while we were fleeing, the Indonesian army captured the town of Remexio. We went up and down the hills pushing our two horses, one pig, and one sheep with our rucksacks on our backs. There were at least 100 people with us. When the Indonesians captured Remexio, everyone fled to different places.

When we left Remexio, we didn't know where we were going. We didn't even know the names of the villages where we went. The walk was really difficult. My parents and the older children carried my younger brothers and sisters as well as the lightest things, such as clothes. The horses carried the medicine and food. We stayed overnight in the jungle and we had a very, very bad time. We had only a little food that we brought from home. We had to eat wild food, like leaves, and there was not enough water for us. We slept on the ground.

I was worried about what would happen if the Indonesians arrested us. I thought that they would certainly kill us. I was always imagining that the Indonesians were coming from one side or another, or coming over the hill. It was scariest at night when you could not see anyone. Sometimes trunks of trees looked like soldiers. There were no guerrillas with us because they stayed near Remexio trying to prevent the Indonesians from advancing beyond the town. I had two hand grenades in my rucksack, but I didn't know how to use them.

I didn't think that the Indonesian army would conquer the area around Remexio because FALINTIL, even though it was not as well armed as the Indonesian army, was there. Many FALINTIL fighters had received training from the Portuguese, and the fighters had many light arms that are very helpful in guerrilla warfare.[2] I was confident at that time that FALINTIL could hold the Indonesian army in Remexio. But the Indonesians had sophisticated weapons and helicopters to drop their soldiers into combat.

One of the most dangerous aspects of the attack was the Indonesian army's use of rockets. The shells they fired would explode twice—first when they were launched, and then when they hit something. In a panic, people would run after the first explosion. When they would hear the second explosion, they thought that the Indonesians were nearby, so they would turn back and run into the Indonesian soldiers.

It took two days for us to reach Aikoko, a small, isolated hamlet of three houses near Bereliurai. We arrived in the late afternoon. By that time, my family had split from the rest of the group, which went toward Manumera. The local people in Aikoko helped us by giving us food and places where we could rest. The people knew my father because my father worked at the clinic that served the entire region. The people in Aikoko were farmers who raised crops and some animals. They knew that we were fleeing from the war, so they helped us. We stayed there for a few days and then we left for Bereliurai.

We went to Bereliurai because it was the closest and safest town to Remexio and the population there was very pro-FRETILIN. Many other families who were fleeing passed through Bereliurai, but they did not stay there. There was no church there. The majority of the population of Bereliurai were animists; they believed in natural spirits and the power of the *liurai*.

It was a big change for us to be in such a small village with people we didn't know, but everyone there was really helpful. When we arrived, they gave us food to eat and mats to sleep on and then offered us a modest house made of bamboo with a roof of thatched grass in a *knua* on the outskirts of the village. The house belonged to the local FALINTIL commander; he had another house in Bereliurai.

We lived in the Bereliurai area for more than one and a half years. The conditions were difficult. Apart from my family, there were only a few other refugee families in the village. At the beginning, we were dependent on the local people. We were lucky to have a house, but we had to get food. Sometimes we could buy food; other times, we had to ask people for food. We also began to cultivate land, grow corn and legumes, and raise animals.

Militarily, Bereliurai was a threatened area; it was the border between the resistance and the Indonesian army. But we were confident that FALINTIL and the difficult terrain between us and the nearest Indonesian military positions would protect us.

Bereliurai is about 15 or 20 miles from Remexio, but it was much safer. When the Indonesian Armed Forces (ABRI) took over Remexio on December 25, they occupied the town for only one day and then left. Remexio was not a good place for the Indonesian army to stay because the town is surrounded by mountains and there is only one narrow and steep road in and out of Remexio. But we couldn't go back to the town because ABRI would sometimes return. In some ways, Remexio was a neutral zone. The FALINTIL fighters were on the outskirts of the town and they tried to prevent the Indonesians from advancing.

From Bereliurai we could sometimes see the guerrillas and the Indonesian army fighting each other. Bereliurai was also very close to Talibela, where one of the Indonesian army posts was located. Talibela was a building on the top of the hill on the way to Aileu. The Indonesian army occupied it to protect military movements from Dili to Aileu. Every day the East Timorese and Indonesians would call to each other by shouting. Sometimes when there was no fighting, either FALINTIL or the Indonesian army would challenge the other to battle. They would say, "Let us meet tomorrow!" And the next day FALINTIL and the Indonesians would fight each other.

The Indonesian military dropped hundreds of bombs every day in Bereliurai. Beginning in early 1976, it never stopped. The Indonesians fired mortars and rockets from Dili, from Talibela, from the road to Aileu, and from the air, using OV-10 Bronco fighters manufactured in and supplied by the United States. Though the bombs were destructive, many more people were killed on the front lines. Some civilians were killed by the mortars, but not many. The mortars usually landed in empty places, in fields and in the jungle, but they still caused a lot of suffering. There was one incident that I particularly remember. A woman who was over 60 years old lost one of her eyes when a piece of shrapnel from a mortar hit her. The mortars also killed a lot of animals and destroyed many farms.[3] This, of course, created food shortages. There were mortars that landed in people's fields and didn't explode. As a result, people were afraid to work their fields and they had to abandon their farms. Some of the unexploded shells are still there today.

We built underground shelters to protect ourselves; every family had its own. Whenever there were bombings from the sea or from the road to Aileu, everyone would go into the shelters. Even though some of my brothers and sisters were very young, they knew who our enemy was. Every day when we heard the American OV-10 Bronco jets flying over head, my brothers and sisters would immediately run to the shelter to protect themselves.

Many of the people in Bereliurai had lived in the village for their entire lives, so they already had established farms where they cultivated food and raised their animals. Everyone in the village also worked together in two big, collective gardens run by FRETILIN. We called them *hortas communais*; we grew manioc, corn, and other basic foods. The food from the gardens was given both to people who were unable to grow food and to the guerrillas. We also created a reserve food supply in case of an emergency, such as a surprise attack by the Indonesian army. Typically people worked on their own plots of land as well and gave food to support the guerrilla fighters on the front lines.

FRETILIN ran Bereliurai. There was a FRETILIN secretary and a FALINTIL commander there. FRETILIN had a *sede*, an administrative seat, that was just a simple house, in a *knua* on the outskirts of the village, where children and adults would gather to learn how to read and write. Every week all the people in Bereliurai would have a meeting there to discuss the state of the war. We would hear reports about the military and political situation from other regions as well as speeches to inspire us to continue the struggle. Almost 500 people would attend these meetings.

Because there was no clinic in the village, my father helped people with the little Western medicine that we brought from Remexio. We distinguished between traditional, Chinese, and Western medicines. Traditional medicine was what we could gather from nature, such as medicinal leaves, roots, herbs, seeds, and flowers; Western and Chinese medicines were those medicines we imported from Portugal and China. At the time, my father was working as the village nurse. With the medicine we brought from Remexio, my father was able to help the guerrilla fighters who were wounded on the front line and treat people suffering from diseases. Disease was widespread because of the poor conditions and the lack of medicine. Many people died from diarrhea, dysentery, and tuberculosis. Most of the people that my father treated would often give him food as compensation.

Because Bereliurai was at the front line, FALINTIL was very well organized there. It was important to make sure that the Indonesian army could not cross Bereliurai. FRETILIN activists tried to educate people about the struggle and to show them how to support the guerilla fighters on the front line. They instructed people how to build shelters to protect themselves from the Indonesian bombing.

FRETILIN activists also worked to politicize people, as they did throughout the liberated areas, by encouraging people to continue the war and by teaching them about the struggle and politics. Many FRETILIN activists, including my father, also worked to convert people to Catholicism. This was not a FRETILIN policy, but it was not prohibited either. Only about 10 people in Bereliurai were Catholic prior to Indonesia's invasion, but within a year and a half most of the population had converted to Catholicism because of the influence of my parents and other Catholic refugees, and the prestige associated with the Portuguese. When people came down from the jungle from 1977 to 1979, almost everybody was Catholic.

FRETILIN had special programs for women, such as the FRETILIN women's organization, OPMT, the Organização Popular da Mulher Timor.[4] My mother wasn't a member but she cooperated by working with women in the village. The OPMT would help other women, make crafts and baskets, and also cook for the guerrilla fighters and take food to the front lines. Of course, these women were also ready to use weapons when necessary, and many women guerrillas died fighting in the front lines. The OPMT had its own political program. OPMT activists often delivered speeches on women's issues. They also challenged some East Timorese traditions like polygamy and berlake. Berlake was a form of bride price that men had to pay to a woman's parents before they could be married.

FRETILIN outlawed both traditions in the Manual Politico, the party's political manual, because they were seen as acts of exploitation. Although the manual was distributed by FRETILIN activists, mostly before Indonesia's invasion, and widely read and discussed, it was difficult to make changes in the relations between men and women in a short period of time. Nonetheless, women in the liberated zones had more freedom than they had before. Women participated as equals in political discussions, gave constructive criticisms in public meetings, and talked about how to continue the struggle. OPMT members were also active in educating children.

As the struggle continued, women and men in East Timor became conscious that everyone should participate in the effort to fight against the common enemy, the Indonesian military. Men and women treated each other as brother and sister. Today in East Timor, men and women, no matter what age, call each other *irmã* (sister) and *irmão* (brother). All of the East Timorese who have escaped to Portugal and to Australia continue to consider everyone as brothers and sisters. These terms, however, probably sound strange to those East Timorese who left before the invasion.

In early 1976, when I was 13 years old, I began working with FALINTIL, not as a guerrilla fighter, but as someone who helped to bring food from the territory occupied by the Indonesians. I did this for the guerrilla fighters and for my family. At that time, the food situation was difficult, especially for the refugees, because they had just started to grow food and there was not enough food for them from other sources. But there was plenty of food in the occupied zones; many refugees had left behind their farms with their crops unharvested, so we would cross the border and go into the occupied or contested territory.

We didn't go into the Indonesian-controlled areas by ourselves. Guerrilla fighters who already knew the front line would guide us. Sometimes we would enter the Indonesian areas when it was dark and gather food by moonlight. Often we couldn't get food during the day because it was too dangerous. If the Indonesian military had found us, they would have immediately killed us.

We gathered bananas, corn, sweet potatoes, and other vegetables. It wasn't really stealing food because the food belonged to us. We went to farms that belonged to people who had fled to Bereliurai. Sometimes we would go two or three times a week, sometimes only once a month. It depended on the situation.

One day, the Indonesian military almost killed me. We were going to get some food in place called Kaboraluta, about 11 miles from Bereliurai. I went there with two men, one about 30 and the other around 40 years old, and two women, who were both about 18 years old. I was the youngest in the group. We had one rifle and one pistol. Unfortunately, we didn't know that the Indonesian army had already occupied the front line that had been under the control of FALINTIL earlier that day. As we approached the front, I heard someone make the sound of a deer. We didn't know if it was the enemy or guerrilla fighters that were giving signals to each other. It sounded like a deer, though it's very rare that you hear that sound. I told my friends that I had heard a strange sound. But my friend José said, "That is our comrades. Come on." We continued walking, but very cautiously. At a distance of about 30 feet, I saw an Indonesian soldier hiding behind a tree. I saw his cap moving while he was preparing his position, and I immediately shouted to everyone, "*Inimigo!*" (The enemy!). As I was shouting, the Indonesian soldier also shouted loudly saying, "Surrender, FRETILIN, communists!" He immediately began firing at us. Fortunately, there were a lot of trees, so it was difficult for him to get a clear shot, and everyone managed to escape. While I was running, I heard bullets flying past my ears and I was thinking that I was going to be killed. Soon the Indonesians were also firing mortars. There were a lot of people shooting at us. When the first soldier opened fire, every soldier who was in the area kept firing at us, not just shooting with M-16s but also with grenades and mortars. They chased us for about a half mile, but they were afraid to go further because of the FALINTIL fighters.

The incident took place about three or four miles from Bereliurai. People in Bereliurai could hear the shooting. When we got back to Bereliurai, we let the people know what had happened and told the guerrillas so they could fight back against the Indonesian army. More than 10 Indonesian soldiers were killed in that battle, and we lost one commander, Sargento Manuel. He was killed in Remexio while chasing some Indonesian soldiers. The Indonesian army cut his body into pieces and stole his gun.

By 1977, the situation had changed; we stopped going to the occupied lands for food because there wasn't any more food there. Fortunately, after one year in Bereliurai, people were able to grow enough food to feed themselves, as well as the FALINTIL fighters. Almost everyone had a small plot of land to grow corn, manioc, sweet potatoes, and vegetables. In addition, we also had the communal gardens.

My family depended on the food we grew in Bereliurai.

In January 1977, I joined FALINTIL as a guerrilla fighter on the front line so I could fight for my country. It was not because I wanted to prove that I was no longer a young boy; at that time I already felt like a man. War makes young people become adults very quickly.

I was not the only 14-year-old in FALINTIL; there were others as well. There were even boys as young as 12 that joined their brothers or their fathers on the front line. There were no young girls on the front line, though they also supported the guerrilla fighters. If there were confrontations between the Indonesian military and the guerrilla fighters, the young girls would often take food from the village to the front lines.

It was not a difficult decision for my parents to let me join FALINTIL because they trusted the commander of my unit. The *commandante* was the one who gave us accommodations and land in Bereliurai. He spent most of his time on the front line with his fighters. I already knew many of the guerrillas; some of them were my friends. They were mostly between 15 and 18 years old; but there were also guerrilla fighters in their twenties and thirties and some as old as 45.

The *commandante* accepted me to be part of one of his platoons. "If you are willing to join us," he said, "please come. We are not forcing anyone to join, but it's the obligation of every Timorese to fight, to defend the country." Then he set up the schedule and he assigned me to a *seção*, or section, of nine people. There was one other person who was my age in the *seção*. My *seção* was part of a platoon of about 30 people. A platoon was part of a company, and there were about three platoons to a company. At that time, there were no women in my company, though there were some women FALINTIL fighters in other areas.

My *seção* commander had been a member of the Portuguese militia and had received several months of training. FALINTIL actually had a military base where people received instruction. It was in Fada Bloko, about 12 miles from Bereliurai. But I received very little formal training. I was given a light gun and shown how to shoot, but only theoretically, because we couldn't afford to waste ammunition.

FALINTIL preferred that we practice on the front line. They taught me basic tactics, such as how to escape from ambushes, protect others on the front line, and retreat. We were told not to run away without knowing where we were going and without protection, and not to shoot without necessity. The instructions were very basic. I followed orders from the older guerilla fighters. In general, most of the FALIN-TIL fighters had little to no military experience and received very little formal training. Nevertheless, they were successful fighters because they knew the terrain very well and were fighting to protect their homeland.

We generally had access to only two types of weapons—Mausers and G3s, both left by the Portuguese. There were also some semi-automatic weapons and mortar launchers. I carried a Mauser. It was a German rifle used during World War II. It is a long-range weapon and carries only five bullets. I would go to the front line for one week and then return home for one week while another *seção* replaced me. And then I returned to the front line for another week.

On the front line, the nearest *seção* was about six miles away, but it would depend on the terrain. Each of us always had to be in some sort of shelter, like a trench, or hide in the trees. My *seção* was responsible for about three miles on each side of our position on the front line. But we had also small posts in between, and in areas controlled by guerrillas we could keep in contact with others. It was easy to transfer letters to other groups. We were in constant communication. We didn't have radio communication; we would just send messages from person to person through *estafetas*, or messengers. *Estafetas* could be guerrilla fighters or civilians who were members of Arma Branca, the civilian auxiliary to FALINTIL. The Arma Branca was composed of older people and also some young boys and girls. We used this messenger system throughout the country to communicate with each other. It sometimes took a long time for a message to arrive, but the system was very reliable and secure.

Of course, we also had soldiers who stayed in the villages. We didn't put the whole army on the front line. We were not only responsible for the front, but also for the areas behind the lines. We had many types and sizes of FALINTIL organizational groupings to confront the Indonesians.

In 1976 and 1977, FALINTIL guerrilla fighters were usually distributed into many pockets, or fronts, depending on how many fronts the Indonesian army had. There were not many people in each front, sometimes only two or three, to confront 15 or 30 Indonesian soldiers. Because of that, we didn't need to involve so many guerrilla fighters in one battle. Sometimes only 20 or 30 people were enough to confront a company of Indonesian soldiers. We also had a special force, the Brigada Choque, that we could rapidly deploy to areas where other FALINTIL guerrillas needed assistance. The members of the Brigada were the best-trained fighters of FALINTIL; many of them had served in the Portuguese colonial army. This special force was based in Fada Bloko and had about 100 soldiers.

When I first went to the front lines, I was a little timid. I just followed an experienced guerrilla fighter and obeyed his instructions. If the Indonesians came, we had to shoot. I was really nervous. In the evening, when I heard shooting from the area controlled by the enemy, my body would shake. I couldn't control myself. But after a while I calmed down and convinced myself that it was no use for me to be afraid. After a week on the front line, I became accustomed to it. I was not afraid anymore, but I was always very careful.

I went to the front line with eight soldiers. We would spend almost all our time waiting for the enemy. The front line was about three or four miles from Bereliurai. In back of us, about three kilometers from Bereliurai, we had a shelter. The reason the shelter was so far away from the line was because we had most of our ammunition there. We wanted to keep it away from the enemy in case there was a surprise attack.

One person would stay at the shelter at all times. I remember one day during my first week when I was at the shelter. It was cold and raining. I was sitting there alone in front of a fire listening to the birds singing and I started thinking about my life. I was thinking back to my hometown, Remexio, and my life before I was in that tent. I was thinking about my school and how I came to be there, and about how hard my parents' lives were. At that time my parents were in a very bad situation. They didn't have enough food, so I would sometimes have to bring them food from the front line. I was thinking about this and how people in Australia and other countries were really free and how they could enjoy their childhoods at my age. That made me sad and I began crying. I was thinking about the struggle of many other countries for the liberation of their people from oppression—such as Angola and Mozambique, places we had heard about from Radio Maubere—and those who had been killed by the Indonesian army because of our struggle. I realized that it was now my turn to continue the struggle.

I spent most of my time on the front line. We would stay there day and night, waiting for the Indonesian soldiers. However, we would rotate every couple of hours. We would have between four and six people on guard all the time. We called guard duty *vigilancia*. The others would take naps. But it was hard to sleep on the ground; it was cold and we couldn't have a fire because it was too dangerous. If the Indonesians saw smoke, they would immediately launch mortars and radio Dili to have them send missiles.

During my first week at the front, I didn't actually have any confrontations with the Indonesian army because FALINTIL had adopted a defensive strategy. We wanted to save ammunition, so we didn't launch any surprise attacks against the Indonesians.

None of my friends in my *seção* was killed. We were very lucky. We had a very good commander. The closest I ever came to being killed by an Indonesian soldier was one day when one of my friends, who was deaf, came to the front line with me. We went close to the Indonesian military post at Talibela to observe the situation there. An Indonesian soldier was on patrol, walking in front of a tent. He was playing very loud music, and it seemed that he was thinking about his family or his friends or his hometown.

There were four of us, and we split into groups of two and took up positions. At that time, the FRETILIN Central Committee had a strict rule stressing the importance of saving ammunition. Whoever spent one bullet without any result faced severe punishment. One bullet was supposed to result in the death of one Indonesian soldier and the capture of one rifle. Given the punishment that I might face, I hesitated before shooting the Indonesian soldier, even though I could see him clearly. As I was trying to decide whether to shoot him, I suddenly heard my friend shooting. We were about 100 feet away and my friend started to fire. He shot at the soldier, but he missed. The soldier went down into a shelter and he and other Indonesian soldiers started to fire at us. We immediately ran away through the trees. We fired one bullet and the Indonesians fired for two hours. They just kept on firing. For two hours, we heard the sound of their guns firing, and the explosion of mortar, hand grenades, and rockets. Just one bullet and the Indonesians fired what seemed like millions of bullets. My deaf friend survived that day, but he was killed in 1978 during the encirclement.[5]

I remember the first time I shot a rifle. It was not at a person, but at a deer. One night I had an interesting dream that was related to hunting. Early in the morning, I woke up and tried to tell everyone in the shelter about the dream. After I told them, everyone tried to guess what it meant, but no one was able to figure it out. As usual, those who did not go on patrol during the night had to switch with those who did. I called a friend of mine and we went on patrol. On the way to the front line I told my friend to walk slowly and pay attention. Because of my dream, I had a feeling that we would see some wild animal, either a boar or a deer. As we walked toward the front line, I saw deer footprints. We followed the tracks for about one mile and suddenly the deer smelled us. When the deer appeared from its hiding place and tried to escape, I hit it in the head with my first bullet. We returned to the shelter and told our friends to take care of the deer. We celebrated that day. We ate some of the meat and sent some of it to our families and to my parents in the village. When I shot the rifle I didn't hear the sound of the gun, but I felt it kick strongly against my shoulder. I could only hear the echo afterward. After that, I became confident in my shooting.

I'm not certain if I ever shot a person because in the front lines everyone would shoot into the enemy area. I never engaged in a big battle. I always had bad luck. Most of the battles occurred when I was sick or retired from the front line. One incident that sticks in my mind was when a friend of mine, Koli, shot an Indonesian officer on a slope of a hill. They saw each other and laughed for a while before firing. It was sad. First the Indonesian officer fired at Koli and the bullet cut down a branch of a eucalyptus tree, which fell on him. It was then Koli's turn and, sadly, his bullet took away the life of the poor Indonesian soldier. It is possible that the Indonesian soldier's family is still waiting for him to return to Indonesia.

The first time I ever saw anyone killed in battle was in July or August 1977, when the Indonesian army infiltrated the outskirts of Bereliurai and shot a friend of mine. He was hit by mortar and shot in his legs and chest. He was the only one killed in the attack because the FALINTIL guerrilla fighters stopped the Indonesians from going into the inner village. That was a very crucial time. It was really difficult because the Indonesians burnt the whole area. There was no green grass left for us to hide in. The Indonesians burnt some houses down and also the jungle around Bereliurai. They wanted to make it difficult for the guerrilla fighters to hide or fight back.

I usually spent two weeks of every month on the front lines as a guerrilla fighter. I would then spend two weeks at home working on the farm. Sometimes I would visit ill people with my father. I also participated in political education meetings and religious activities. Every Saturday morning I would join the Bereliurai population and walk to Manumera to participate in large political rallies with speeches by senior FRETILIN leaders. Manumera was a village close to Bereliurai; it was about five times bigger, and served as the FALINTIL headquarters for the *sector norte*. At that time, FALINTIL had divided the country into three zones.

At the political meetings we would hear people talk about how to organize and continue the struggle. Most of the talks were inspirational. The leaders tried to encourage people to maintain their courage and assured us that we would win. There would also be political education about the ideology and policies of FRETILIN, about the evils of polygamy, and about the differences between democracy and feudalism, and capitalism and socialism. We were taught that in capitalist countries like the United States, the rich become richer at the expense of the poor. In the same manner, powerful and rich countries exploit poor countries. Socialism meant cooperation and equal distribution of wealth within and between countries, and democracy meant that everyone had the right to speak, to criticize, to participate in decisionmaking, and also that everyone had the responsibility of being self-critical.

Every weekend we had a party. We didn't have alcoholic beverages at the parties; coffee was our primary drink. We would also eat manioc or popcorn. That was enough to make everyone happy until the next morning. We played traditional East Timorese music that we call *koremetan*, and everyone would dance. Sometimes we just had a harmonica and one bottle with a fork to accompany the harmonica. The parties were important in our lives. We all needed to have fun, to replace our suffering and pain with happiness; everyone needed to have energy to bear the burdens of the coming week.

In August 1977, FALINTIL launched a major military operation. Every August 20, we celebrate the anniversary of the founding of FALINTIL in 1975 to fight the UDT and its ally, APODETI, during the civil war. So on August 20, 1977, FRETILIN planned to commemorate that day by retaking Dili from the Indonesians. It was a daring plan. FRETILIN had sent FALINTIL to Dili on many fronts, while others occupied important towns such as Aileu, Remexio, Manatuto, and Tibar. I joined the guerrillas and went on the operation as a nurse. Unfortunately, the operation failed. According to the plan, Talibela was to be the main point from which to send signals because it is in a high position.

Commander Karlele was appointed to occupy Talibela. The operation was set up for one in the morning. Everyone was supposed to open fire when they heard noise from Talibela at one, but Karlele was probably a traitor. At midnight, while the guerrilla fighters and I were on our way to Kaboraluta to take our position and block the Indonesian army coming from Aileu, Karlele gave the signal. But he gave it before Talibela was occupied. There were already some guerrilla fighters in Dili, but they had to retreat because of the early signal. In spite of that, we did not retreat. We continued to go to Kaboraluta, which was about six miles from Bereliurai. It was quiet when we arrived in the area. At six in the morning we sent a platoon to occupy the road. Unfortunately, the street had already been occupied by the Indonesian soldiers during the night. Because of that, Manuel, one of the guerrilla fighters, was killed as he entered the road.

The Indonesians fought us all day, firing on our hiding place with bazookas and mortar. We had to wait until 10 that evening to escape. It was a big disappointment for FALINTIL. We had hoped to take over Dili for a couple of days to show that the resistance was still strong. Luckily we lost just one guerrilla fighter.

In mid-1977, I stopped fighting as a guerrilla, but I did not stop participating in the struggle. I became a nurse for the resistance. Being a nurse was one of the most important tasks of the resistance. At that time, we began to have serious difficulties getting medicine and people began to suffer from many kinds of diseases, such as diarrhea, dysentery, tuberculosis, pneumonia, and fungus. Most of the medicine we used was traditional medicine. We did not have a doctor, and the number of nurses was very limited. Because of that, FRETILIN needed to create a course to train more people to be nurses. I had to ask permission from the commander, but the decision came from the head of the FRETILIN in Bereliurai. I trained intensively for one month with some experienced nurses. I received the training at RENAL, the Reabilitação Nacional, or National Rehabilitation, located in a *knua* called Nundamar, east of Remexio. RENAL was also where FRETILIN trained people for political leadership and imprisoned people who broke the law. About 1,000 people lived there. The village was also the center for the Central Committee of FRETILIN.

At RENAL we studied the symptoms of various diseases. We also studied the use of different types of medicine, Western and traditional. We learned how to perform a minor operation to remove bullets from people, but we also learned about a traditional medicine that could remove bullets from the body without an operation, unless the bullet had hit a bone. The wounded person needed to drink an herbal liquid every day for one to three weeks until the bullet exited the body. If someone was seriously wounded, we treated them with antibiotics, penicillin, or tetracycline, supported with traditional medicine.

I was happy with my job as a nurse. It was inspiring to visit people's houses and hear of their desire for the liberation of East Timor, and to hear of their suffering and happiness. I also treated injured

FALINTIL fighters. I never delivered any babies. There were women who did this, but most of the Timorese women delivered their babies at home using traditional medicine and methods.

From RENAL, I began to go from village to village to treat patients. I went all over the Remexio district and also traveled to parts of Lacló and Aileu. On a typical day, I would go from house to house to find people who were sick. I would listen to their complaints and, after finding out the symptoms of the illness, I would tell them what traditional medicine they should take.

My first trip was with a senior nurse. He was there to make sure that I gave the right prescriptions and medicine to people. But later on, after I had received sufficient training, I worked alone. The length of my visit in each village depended on how many patients there were. If there were many, I would stay three or four days. If not, I would stay for only one or two days and then move on to another village, going up and down the mountains and hills. I was always escorted by a member of the Arma Branca as I went from one village to another. I was always well protected.

Many people knew traditional medicine, but very few knew Western medicine, so it was important to have nurses to help prescribe drugs. For example, we used chloroquine and quinine diluted with Vitamin B complex to fight malaria. We got the drugs from hospitals in Dili and Baucau and from towns that Indonesia hadn't been able to invade and occupy at the beginning of the war. As soon as Indonesia invaded, FRETILIN raided all the clinics throughout the country. We also sometimes obtained antibiotics and vitamins from contacts who worked at Indonesian clinics and hospitals in Dili.

At RENAL, there was always a group of people who recorded all the traditional medicines. They took us to the jungle and showed us many types of trees that could be used to cure different types of illnesses. We never ran out of traditional medicines because the raw materials for producing them were all around us.

Even though I often had to treat people who had been shot in the war either by bullets or by shrapnel, I never had a patient who died in front of me from a war injury. I did see a patient die in the clinic where I was working when I was taking the course to become a nurse. Of course, people frequently died because of dysentery, diarrhea, and tuberculosis. Malnutrition was a serious problem contributing to these diseases. People died almost every day, but children had the highest mortality rate. We tried to save as many people as possible. Sometimes we arrived in a village and people would tell us that someone close to them had died just a few hours or minutes ago. There wasn't enough food at that time because people were always having to move from one place to another and were sometimes unable to grow food. There were too many people in small areas. Of course, I felt sad when I saw my comrades suffering. They suffered because of their love of their country and the people of East Timor.

Through mid-1977, we all still thought that we would drive the Indonesian army from East Timor soon. The size of Indonesia and its large population did not frighten the East Timorese people. I didn't hear anyone expressing hopelessness. Everyone was hopeful and determined. At that time, FALINTIL controlled most of the areas of East Timor. The Indonesian army controlled only the main towns, such as Dili, Baucau, Lospalos, and Same, and the roads between them. FRETILIN controlled most of the countryside, so about 80 percent of the population was in liberated territory. The liberation and independence of Angola, Mozambique, Guinea-Bissau, and Cape Verde inspired all the East Timorese people. We always thought that if those countries could free themselves from colonialism, we could as well. We heard about these countries often from Radio Maubere, which played every day. It played music, news about the situation in East Timor, and news from abroad. It was a powerful political tool for FRETILIN.

The political situation in the jungle seemed to be stable during the first year or so of the war, but later some political problems within FRETILIN began to emerge because of differences in opinion, lack of trust, personal ambitions, and the stress caused by the war, especially as Indonesia increased its military pressure.

3

Life in Remexio

In September 1977, the situation in the mountains became really bad. The Indonesians began an encirclement campaign. It was a massive military operation. In Remexio, for example, which was a small district, the Indonesians used 10 battalions. The objective was to surround an area and push people to the center and kill or capture them. The operation included intensive air strikes and bombardment day and night. The Indonesians applied this strategy from region to region. After they dominated the central area, they moved to the eastern part of the territory—Baucau, Lospalos, and Viqueque. The encirclement operation ended in the Baucau region in early 1979.[1]

Around the time of encirclement, my father and I were working in Nundamar, where RENAL was located. One weekend my father and I asked permission to visit our family. Two days after we arrived, the Indonesian army took over Fada Bloko, FALINTIL's main regional base; that marked the beginning of the encirclement in the Remexio region. Fortunately we were there to take care of our family during the evacuation.

As soon as the Indonesian army captured Fada Bloko, FALINTIL immediately abandoned Bereliurai. The Indonesian army was only about three miles away and everyone was in a panic. Everyone just tried to save his or her own life. That was the beginning of our long pilgrimage. We headed toward the east, along with hundreds of other people. As we moved, the Indonesian army constantly pursued us. Children, women, and men were dying on the way. Day and night we continually ran without knowing where we were going; we just followed the crowd. There was no time to bury those who died on the way. It rained almost every day at that time of year. We did not have raincoats or any real shelter other than the trees. Everyone and everything got wet and would dry only when the sun came out.

We could carry only a few things, such as a little food, some clothes, and medicine. My brothers and sisters were crying all the way. Things were so crazy that, at one point, I almost killed my youngest sister. At a certain location we were really close to the Indonesians. We were on the slope of a hill and everyone had to be silent. Suddenly my sister Rosalina started to cry loudly. I pulled a handkerchief from my pocket and put it into her mouth to stop her crying, and I almost smothered her.

We ate extremely little while we were on the run. We hardly had any time to rest, to prepare food, or to take a nap. During the first week, the guerrilla fighters were able to delay the Indonesian soldiers who were chasing us and prevent them from overtaking us. The guerrillas would choose particular places to stop and fight the Indonesians to give the population time to move. But soon the power of the Indonesian military proved overwhelming and FALINTIL could no longer fight the Indonesians on a large scale. The soldiers had to split up to take care of their families.

It was a time of incredible suffering. Food shortages, diseases, and killing were all around us. The Indonesian army was always hunting us. We didn't know how we could cope with the situation. We didn't even know how to cry. We were eight children altogether and two of us were very young. When we fled Bereliurai, I was 14; my sister Celestina was 12; my brother Francisco was 10; my sister Eduarda was nine; my brother Filomeno was seven; my sister Rosalina was four; and my brothers Ladislao and Tito were three and one. We always had to carry the youngest ones, in addition to food and clothes, on our shoulders, even as we were going up and down the mountains and running from intense air strikes. I knew that my parents were very sad about the condition of their children, but they never said anything to us about their feelings. They only encouraged us to pray.

About one month after the encirclement began, we ran out of food. I was really afraid that some members of my family would starve. We wanted to return to Bereliurai to get food from our own garden, so I joined with about five other young boys and went to Bereliurai. It took three to four days to get to there because we could only walk at night.

We didn't have any guns with us. The village was under occupation, so we had to sneak in at night. We took all the food we could carry and then left immediately for Taroke, a village near Lacló, about 20 miles east of Remexio, where we were hiding. Everyone had big sacks of food on their backs.

Halfway back to Taroke, at six in the morning, we almost fell into an Indonesian army ambush. We were walking along a river bank and the Indonesians were up on a hill 150 feet away; there were about 30 Indonesian soldiers, but fortunately we saw them first. As soon as we saw them we ran and they immediately opened fire on us. After running for one mile, we stopped and checked everyone. Luckily, all of us had escaped and no one had thrown away any food. Because the Indonesians were up on the hill and we were on the riverbank, it was difficult for them to chase us right away. The only reason we survived was because the Indonesians did not see us first. The whole time I was running with that huge sack of food on my back I did not even think to throw it away so I could run more easily. If we had thrown away the food, our families and friends would have died of starvation.

Before the encirclement, the Indonesians used U.S.-made OV-10 Bronco fighter jets. I was very familiar with that airplane. FALINTIL described all the different planes to us. But new fighters came with the encirclement—including U.S. F-16s. For the first time, the Indonesians used those airplanes to drop napalm bombs on civilians, as well as for air strikes. It was not that Indonesia didn't have this technology before. It was a question of timing. They wanted to wipe out everyone in the jungle. I also think that they knew we were running out of weapons and ammunition.

I never saw the Indonesians use napalm, but I spoke to many people who suffered from this strange bomb and who explained to me how it worked. Just by the description, we came to the conclusion that it was like the napalm bombs the U.S. government used against the people of Vietnam. When it explodes, nothing escapes: human beings and trees were all wiped out. Even the leaves of trees were burned off.[2]

It seemed as though we were constantly on the run. We stopped sometimes in liberated places for a few days at a time, but never for more than a week. We got food, mostly manioc and vegetables, from abandoned farms, but because so many people went to the same place, the food on the farms was very scarce. We also ate coconuts, wild beans, and leaves from banana trees and from particular types of eucalyptus trees.

A few weeks after we left Bereliurai, we found shelter in another village about six miles away. The guerrillas joined us there to protect the people. But the Indonesian military also moved toward that area. One day two of my brothers and I were at a nearby riverbank with about 30 guerrilla fighters. We didn't know that the Indonesian army was already close and was planning to attack us. Ten minutes after we joined the guerrilla fighters, we heard a strange shooting sound coming from the hills near the camp.

A group of 15 Indonesian soldiers began shooting at us and attacking us with hand grenades. We were lucky that they shot a FALINTIL soldier who was up the hill on patrol first. The noise of the shot warned us and allowed us to spread out. The Indonesian soldiers came to the riverbank, threw grenades into two barrels of food, and began firing all over the place. There was a big battle between the guerrilla fighters and the Indonesian soldiers, who then escaped. After one hour, everyone joined up again in the same place. No one was killed and only one of us was injured. Luckily, the Indonesians abandoned some medical supplies. I used some terramycin to treat the one who was wounded. The medicine was really strong. After one week the wound was cured. Later the Indonesian military came back and bombarded the place. During the night, they threw flares into the sky and sent OV-10 Broncos that killed hundreds of water buffaloes with their bombs. Fortunately, people were spread out and hiding in safe places and no one was hit.

While we were on the run, I couldn't take care of people on a regular basis because of the difficult circumstances. We couldn't even get enough medicine from the jungle; in many places it was not possible to find the right plants and trees for traditional medicines. We tried to use some of the Western medicine that we had, but thousands of people died of starvation and diseases. I saw this every day when we moved from one place to another. We walked among the dead bodies. Often people did not have time to bury their dead family members. I saw the bodies of a lot of children and parents and old people who died of starvation or disease as a result of the lack of food and medicine. I also saw a lot of children crying because their parents were killed by the Indonesians or because their parents had abandoned them. Parents abandoned their children because they were afraid that they would slow them down, because their crying would put everyone else's life in danger, or because there was no more food to feed them. The smell of rotting human corpses was everywhere. Some of the corpses seemed to have been there for days; others looked as if they just died a few hours before we arrived. As I say this, I can smell the dead bodies again.

We couldn't help anyone. How could we? We were also trying to escape from the Indonesians. There was no time for us to help each other. It was sad seeing the abandoned children. I still hear the crying of those children. I couldn't help those children or babies because I had to save my own life and those of my other family members. We left those abandoned children with the hope that someone else would take care of them, but I don't think anyone did. Everyone feared for his or her own life. In my own family we had three children to carry.

Death was not news for the East Timorese at this time, but we were all afraid of being killed. Everyone thought that he or she was going to be alive for only another one or two days. We didn't know what was going to happen. We just tried to survive.

My family was suffering. Some of my brothers and sisters and I were really sick from malaria and diarrhea. We were close to starving. Sometimes we had only a piece of manioc to eat for the whole day, and at other times we would go a whole day without eating anything. Luckily, my parents were physically strong enough to take care of us.

My parents always asked the children to pray, to pray to God and ask Him to save our lives and to bless the medicine that we were taking. My parents always said to the children, *"Tutua sei tulun o hanoin maromak"* (God will help you. Think of God). My parents always believed that our family's life was in God's hands. They believed that God would save our family in whatever circumstances of the war. My family was very lucky. God protected us. None of us was killed or injured during the war, though we did lose close relatives.

During the encirclement, all we could do was to stay hidden, looking for food at night and studying the possibilities to move around. By early 1978, the whole FRETILIN structure was broken down. We didn't see any political activists walking around to educate people. When the Indonesian army took over the villages there were no more coordinated guerrilla activities or communications. Even the guerrilla fighters were split up. Radio Maubere was no longer operating, either.

When we hid, we always hid in the forest. There were no more *aldeias* (villages) around; the Indonesian army had burned them all down.[3] Each family hid by itself. We were more secure if we separated into many places in a given area, rather than all camping in a small, restricted area. There were a few hundred people with us altogether.

Several months after the encirclement had begun, we headed back toward Bereliurai because we couldn't get enough food. About one month after the Indonesians had captured Bereliurai, they abandoned it. They continued to chase people toward the east, so we tried to go around them. We were successful. While the Indonesian soldiers were moving east, we were going toward the west. We returned successfully to Bereliurai. By that time there were about 150 of us from the original group that had fled from Bereliurai. We were lucky: only 10 people from our group had died since we had left; unfortunately, we never had time to bury them.

Again, I saw many dead bodies on the way; some of them were already bones, skeletons. Seeing this made me think that this would also be the fate of those of us who were still alive, that no one could escape from death. One day, after the sun had set, everyone stopped for a while. I tried to find a place to rest. While I was looking for a spot, I found an old woman sleeping face down. The place was nice and I also tried to rest there. Around six the next morning I woke up because we had to continue our journey. I tried to wake her up and tell her that we had to move ahead. When I touched her body it felt like a stone. She was dead, but I felt nothing.

When we got back to Bereliurai it was empty. Everything had been destroyed. All the houses were burnt down, the gardens abandoned. We could only hear wild birds singing. There were no roosters, no cows, and no human beings. The Indonesians burned the fields when they first occupied Bereliurai, but some manioc, sweet potatoes and other root crops, and banana trees survived the fire.

We had to be very conscious of everything we did in Bereliurai. We tried not to leave any evidence of human activity because the Indonesian military was close by. Almost every morning Indonesian soldiers did exercises along the trail to the village while we were hiding along a riverbank.

Unfortunately, a family that was hiding nearby made a big mistake. One day they found an abandoned cow and killed it. After they killed the cow, they tried to dry the meat as soon as possible. During the day they dried the meat in the sun; but when the evening came, they continued drying it by using a fire. Unfortunately, they didn't extinguish the fire and, early in the morning, it produced a lot of smoke. The smoke immediately attracted the Indonesian army to their shelter. Some Indonesians arrested them and took them to Remexio without anyone knowing. The big group was still hiding with us in the same area. The Indonesian army later used that family to find the rest of us hiding in Bereliurai, including me and my family.

Around midnight on September 2, 1978, we heard some strange movement of people up on the hill. It seemed as if someone was throwing rocks at us. We were really afraid that night. My whole family couldn't sleep. We just kept praying. We knew that we were going to be arrested, but we couldn't predict what would happen to us. I was crying. I began to think that, after almost three years of suffering, we were near our last moments, that all of us would probably be killed at the same time and buried in the same grave. The next day, at six in the morning, the Indonesian army began to fire at our shelter from various points, simultaneously calling on us to surrender. They then sent someone from the arrested family to our shelter to persuade us to surrender.

One of them met with my father and said, "Don't be afraid. They will not do anything to you. We have already been arrested. I have come with the Indonesian soldiers to take you to the town." In spite of the message by that person, we didn't trust the Indonesians. We were afraid because they had already killed a lot of people. The enemy is always the enemy. The Indonesian soldier is not our brother. He is our enemy who had already killed tens of thousands of our people.

There were about 150 of us, but only around 50 people were at the riverbank. The majority of people there were FALINTIL members, but they didn't have any weapons. They had given their weapons to other FALINTIL guerrillas. There was only one FALINTIL fighter with us who had a gun, a Mauser with five bullets.

Around 30 soldiers surrounded us. The first ones to approach us were East Timorese who had been trained by the Indonesians. I was confused because they spoke broken Indonesian. But later on some Indonesians joined them. They spoke Indonesian and they looked very different from the East Timorese soldiers. That was the first time that I had seen an Indonesian face. Actually, I had seen some Indonesians before, but they had been either far away or were dead.

It was scary to look at Indonesians the first time they arrested me. I was afraid of what they were going to do to me and my family, so we did exactly what the Indonesians told us to do; we feared that it was going to be the end of our lives. The two youngest, my brothers Ladislao and Tito, were very sick and were crying all the time. They looked as if they only had bones. We were all very weak and extremely thin. Today, every time I see starving people on the television it reminds me of what I looked like when we were captured.

The Indonesians had some East Timorese interpreters. But the interpreters spoke Indonesian very poorly. The first words the Indonesians spoke to us were, "Don't be afraid." The Indonesians also showed us their skin and said, "Look at our skin color. We are the same. We are brothers and sisters. Why do you run away from us?"

This didn't make us feel better. It is difficult to trust your enemy the first time you meet. Twenty years after the invasion, we still don't trust the Indonesian soldiers. They are our enemy. When they lay down their weapons and recognize the independence of East Timor, they will immediately become our friends.

So the Indonesians took us to Remexio. We had to walk. Before we left, they searched everyone's clothes, baskets, and packs. Some people were forced to take off their clothes so the Indonesians could see if they had guns or not.

The Indonesians told us, "Be frank and tell us who you are. Don't tell any lies. If you are guerrilla fighters, tell us that you are guerrilla fighters. We feel sad when we see East Timorese getting killed." I told them I was a nurse. My father did too. My mother said nothing. Fortunately, none of the women in our group experienced any abuse.

When we arrived in Remexio, it looked very different. It was the first time I had been there since the invasion. The environment was totally insane. The town was crowded with East Timorese civilians and Indonesian soldiers. The Indonesian army had repaired some of the buildings to use for its military base and police headquarters. Thousands of people were there without any food, medicine, shops, or religious activities. Soldiers would take baths naked in public. I felt as though I were a foreigner in my own country. The landscape in Remexio was the same—the hills and rivers, the roads I used to walk, and the church on top of a hill where I used to pray. But the language and practices of the Indonesians were strange to me.

When we passed by the place where we grew up, the farms that we had to abandon were occupied by other people. Our old house no longer existed because the Indonesians had burned it down. As we arrived in the town, it seemed as if the Indonesians had ordered everyone to stand on the edge of the street. Many people who had been arrested before us greeted us. I knew some of them. As I passed, I heard a woman shout: "That is the nurse, Constâncio. He is still alive!" She had heard that I had been killed.

It was, of course, emotional to see people, especially friends, whom I hadn't seen for a long time. But I didn't feel happy. We didn't know what was going to happen to us. People couldn't talk to us at that time; they seemed very afraid. They knew my family, but they avoided talking to us.

When we arrived, we were taken to a military base, KORAMIL, and our bags were searched once again.[4] They took away anything that was valuable. The Indonesians took my nursing tools—syringes, tweezers, needles, and medicine—and they took my mother's bracelets and rings. None of us protested. The most important thing for us was to save our lives. After that, the Indonesians delivered us a few pounds of food. Then they gave us some rice. We cooked it by ourselves in our own pot.

The Indonesians took my father for interrogation. We were afraid that the Indonesians were going to kill him. Prior to our arrest, we had heard that many people had been tortured badly, their faces sliced by razor blades, their bodies exposed to electric shocks or burned by hot irons. My father was gone for four hours. The Indonesians didn't mistreat him. When my father returned, he said that the army interrogated him about his political activities to find out if he was an important leader of FRETILIN. He told them that he was a nurse, not FALINTIL. My father was the only member of my family who was interrogated. People from other families weren't so lucky. Some people were taken into a room and subjugated to interrogation and torture; some were "disappeared." The Indonesians were looking for FALINTIL and FRETILIN cadres.

After my father came back, the Indonesians sent us to a house that we had to share with a family of five or six people. We didn't know them, but they recognized us because they had been our patients in the jungle. The house was one of many built by the Indonesians for East Timorese who came down from the mountains. The houses were very small and had two rooms. Each house had a zinc roof, bamboo walls, and a dirt floor. There was no land.

In many ways, life was worse in the village than in the jungle because so many people were there. The whole town had become a concentration camp.[5] People were not allowed to look for food in the outlying areas of the town. People could grow food in the town, but there was not enough land for most people. We got some food from the military, but our family of 10 was given only 22 pounds of rice for a whole week. If we wanted vegetables, we had to buy them or find them ourselves. But how could we look for vegetables if we were not allowed to leave the town? There were also no places where we could buy food in Remexio. There were no shops. There was only the Indonesian military. The Indonesians grew a small amount of vegetables and brought food from Dili, but we couldn't afford to buy it from them because we didn't have any money and there was almost no work in Remexio. When we came back to Remexio, we still had some Portuguese *escudos*, but the money was worthless. We couldn't even exchange *escudos* with *rupiah*, the Indonesian currency.

At least in the jungle we lived in freedom and friendship. In the town, there was no freedom: we lived like fenced-in sheep. The town was like a prison. There were regulations against people leaving the town and there were soldiers everywhere. There were certain areas of the town where we were forbidden to go; if someone went to any of these places, he or she could be killed. The soldiers searched people's houses day and night, threatening people not to think about returning to the jungle, trying to persuade people to tell their families and friends who were still in the jungle to surrender, and forcing people to learn the Indonesian language and attend the flag-raising ceremony every Monday morning.

People's houses were treated as the houses of the army. The Indonesian army came to people's houses whenever they wanted, even if they had nothing to say or ask. FALINTIL fighters were often killed after their capture. The Indonesian soldiers would come and get them at their houses and take them away for interrogation and torture, especially after a clash between FALINTIL and the Indonesian army in the jungle. Many of them were never seen again.

The soldiers used to come to our house on a daily basis, asking questions about the FALINTIL and FRETILIN leaders. "Have you heard anything about FRETILIN? Have you had any contact with the guerrillas? Do you know other people still hidden in the jungle?"

These were the main questions. They would threaten my family and the other family that lived with us, but they did this to everyone.

I remember the Indonesian Red Cross came two or three times to Remexio to deliver corn powder and clothes to the population. Ironically, the Indonesian army took some of the clothes and later sold them to the population. I don't know if the Red Cross also brought medicine to Remexio. I only saw Indonesians working for the Red Cross. East Timor at that time was still closed to foreigners.

As a result of food shortages, poor housing, and lack of medicine, many people died in Remexio. An average of 10 to 15 people died every day from starvation and diseases like diarrhea, dysentery, and tuberculosis.[6] My two youngest brothers, Tito and Ladislao, almost died at that time because they suffered so badly from diarrhea and dysentery. We didn't have medicine as we had had in the jungle to cure them. There was no clinic in the town, only the army pharmacy. There were no public health services for the East Timorese. Even the Catholic Church did not have any pharmacy or health services, and we didn't have any nuns and priests in Remexio at that time.

We didn't bring my brothers to the army pharmacy. My parents were afraid that the Indonesian army might use some medicine that would kill them. It seemed to us that the more the Indonesians gave medicine or treatment to people, the more people died.

While I was living in Remexio, the army ambushed a group of guerrilla fighters near the town of Remexio and killed two of the them. The Indonesians arrested between eight and 12 of them and took them to Remexio. A couple of hours before they arrived, the army called the population to wait on the sides of the roads to look at the arrested guerrillas. All of them had their hands tied behind their backs and were paraded into town by the army. The army had beat them along the way. I saw blood on their heads, faces, and all over their bodies. I recognized a friend of mine in the group. He was in bad condition. I felt sad that I was not able to do anything to save their lives or to protect them from the horrible treatment perpetrated by the Indonesian army. The Indonesians took them to the military base of battalion 410, the same battalion that arrested us.

At battalion 410 headquarters, the Indonesians beat the captured guerrillas badly, torturing them in public. The soldiers kicked them and beat them on their heads and all over their bodies while they were tied up. They beat them with their hands and rifle butts, and kicked them with their boots. I don't know how long the torture lasted because we weren't allowed to stay there and watch the military torture the guerrilla fighters for a long time. The army occupied a building formerly owned by a Chinese businessperson. It was very close to the street. So when people walked down the street, they could see the Indonesian soldiers torturing people.

I felt very angry to see the guerrillas being tortured, but I couldn't help them. I don't know what happened to them afterward. Some of them disappeared. Later on, I met one in Dili who survived. Some of them were taken away to a prison in another district. The Indonesians probably forced them to go back into the jungle to search for other guerrilla fighters.

It was common for the Indonesian army to use people this way to find places where people and guerrilla fighters were hiding in the jungle. The Indonesians still use this system today. From the beginning, the Indonesians have used the strategy of having East Timorese kill each other. Many East Timorese have been forced to join the Indonesian army, including battalions 744 and 745 in East Timor, and battalion 741 in Singaraja, Bali, and other military units such as Hansip.[7]

I still remember when the military forced the population in Remexio to gather in September 1978 to listen to a speech by Francisco Xavier do Amaral, the former president of FRETILIN and my father's uncle, who was then a prisoner of the Indonesian government. It was the second time I had seen Xavier since the beginning of the war. I had seen him months earlier in 1977 when he was being detained by FRETILIN.

The pressures of the war caused problems within the FRETILIN leadership, leading to a conflict between the FRETILIN central committee and Xavier. This division in the resistance paved the way for Indonesia's encirclement operation. FRETILIN's leadership arrested Francisco Xavier at that time because he was planning to surrender to Indonesia and negotiate the status of East Timor. We learned this after Xavier's arrest. Some FRETILIN leaders, like Nicolau Lobato, thought that Xavier's plan was a betrayal and that he needed to be punished, but I think the arrest of Xavier was the biggest mistake that FRETILIN ever made. At that time, people saw Xavier as the main resistance leader in East Timor. Many people thought that he was the only one who could put an end to the suffering in East Timor. Most of the FALINTIL and the population were really demoralized when FRETILIN arrested Xavier, probably because there had not been any previous explanation about his case. Suddenly people saw Xavier rounded up with his assistants and made to walk from the south to the east. He was presented in public; his assistants had been badly beaten. I saw Xavier for the first time after he was arrested and taken to Fada Bloko in 1977. In Fada Bloko, people shouted at Xavier, "Traitor! Traitor! Polygamist! Polygamist!" Xavier replied, "No, I never betrayed my people. Yes, I committed polygamy." Ironically, people were shouting at Xavier without knowing why he had been arrested. Xavier was moved between FALINTIL units for several months, but Indonesian troops captured him on August 30, 1978, during a battle in the Remexio area.[8]

The Indonesians brought Xavier along with some ABRI generals to Remexio for propaganda reasons. We all had to go to that meeting. We lived in such a small town, you would get in trouble if you didn't go. When the people had gathered, the Indonesian army told people through a megaphone, "Xavier do Amaral, your president, is about to arrive. Come close so you can see him."

The Indonesians allowed Xavier to speak in Tetum; he was very weak at that moment. He was taken to Remexio only about one month after his capture. I still remember what Xavier said: "I am Francisco Xavier do Amaral, the former president of FRETILIN. Because of many ideas and many egos, many people have died. Today, I am here before you, alive. You can do whatever you want to me. I'm ready to accept responsibility for all the human suffering in East Timor." Xavier never said that it was right to integrate into Indonesia. At the end of his speech, he said, "We will win" in Mambai, another language spoken in East Timor, in the area from Dili to Maubisse.

After Xavier's speech, I remember people saying that the suffering that they had faced was due not to Xavier but to the people's desire to defend our right to independence. We can't say that FRETILIN did not make any mistakes, but neither we can we blame FRETILIN for the tens of thousands of people killed by the Indonesian army. Also, if Portugal had not abandoned East Timor and had instead tried to restore peace and complete the decolonization process in East Timor, it might have prevented Indonesia from invading.

The Indonesians organized parties every weekend to entertain and indoctrinate the population in the concentration camp. At the parties they would teach people Balinese, Javanese, and Timorese dances. They would also teach people to sing the Indonesian anthem and other Indonesian songs. The parties were not fun. People went there because they were forced to go. They were parties of the enemy. While people were dancing, they were also thinking about their safety, their family members at home who were suffering from malnutrition and disease, and the people who were dying every day. This was the environment at that time. No one was happy. There were lots of young women who went to the parties, some possibly forced to serve as "entertainers" for the Indonesian soldiers.[9]

The Indonesians didn't force people to go the party, but because of the possible consequences of not going, everyone would go, even for just five or 10 minutes. The most important thing was to show your face. Also, in the daytime, the army would ask people their impressions of the parties. Of course, people always said that the party was excellent, *bagus sekali.*

The Indonesians also emphasized political education. The main goal was to teach people the five principles of Indonesia's state philosophy, *Pancasila,*[10] and how to sing the Indonesian national anthem. People didn't even understand the meaning of the five principles of *Pancasila,* but it was important to learn them by heart. In addition, there was a primary school in the camp where we were taught the Indonesian language, as well as the *Pancasila.* I became a student there. The first day I remember learning how to greet people in Indonesian. The salutations were the first words we had to learn. The teachers were East Timorese who had no qualifications. They spoke Indonesian badly. They knew only the Indonesian alphabet, how to count, and how to greet people in Indonesian. They could also recite the *Pancasila*. Another thing I remember was participating every Monday morning in the flag ceremony; we were forced to march and sing the Indonesian anthem. I didn't like it, but I had to keep that to myself. The most important thing was to save my head.

One morning, a police officer who helped run the school asked me if I wanted to work for the police. He promised to give me whatever I wanted. "We will give you food and clothes and a little money for your expenses, and we will buy you books for school. And also you will stay with us." I was fortunate. If the police hadn't offered me a job, the army might have forced me to work for them. The Indonesians forced many boys my age to go to the mountains. The Indonesians used the boys as horses to carry ammunition and backpacks for the Indonesian soldiers. In the camp they had to carry water for the soldiers. A job with the police was much safer.

Without asking permission from my parents, I immediately made the decision to work for the police. I was afraid of going to the jungle with the military, and I thought that I could help my family through this work. I also wanted to learn the Indonesian language. Understanding the language of the enemy is a very important weapon in the struggle for national liberation. The FRETILIN leadership had always told us that if we were ever captured, we should continue the struggle in the towns. After school I went home and told my parents about my decision. My parents agreed with it and hoped that I would help them find some food and some money. Unfortunately, the Indonesians gave me only a plate of rice with some vegetables daily and nothing else. I couldn't help my family.

I began to work for the Indonesian police the same day that I accepted the job. The police station was close to the house where we lived. My first evening, two policemen taught me some Indonesian phrases: "*Selamat pagi, bapak*" (Good morning, sir); "*Namamu siapa?*" (What is your name?); and "*Apa kabar?*" (How are you?).

I woke up early every morning and picked up two buckets. I walked about one mile, filled them up, and brought the water back to the police. The water was for the policemen to wash their faces, brush their teeth, and make tea for breakfast. After breakfast, I would attend school. Then I would return to the police station afterward and eat some white rice with dry fish and get some more water for the police. At six in the evening, I would begin to cook rice; the police would cook the vegetables. During the evening, I would study Indonesian. For two months I stayed at the police station and worked. The police gave me a little bed in a tiny room at the station.

The police often asked me questions about life in the mountains and how we survived in the jungle. "Why did you follow FRETILIN? You East Timorese don't have any cars, any manufacturers, any companies that make shoes or nice clothes. You don't have good food." The Indonesians asked me why we wanted to be independent. I told them that we wanted the same thing that the Indonesians wanted for themselves, the right to self-determination.

Two weeks after I began my job, the rest of my family left for Dili. The Indonesian military allowed people to leave Remexio and establish themselves in other Indonesian-controlled towns. My family left because life in Remexio was perilous, my younger brothers were very sick, and we had relatives in Dili. I couldn't tell the police that I had to go with my family because I had just started to work for them; I thought that they would be angry if I quit. So I decided that my family should go ahead without me, and I would travel to Dili later.

After my parents left, my relationship with the police began to change. One afternoon when I returned from school they gave me a sack of dry fish and said, "This is for you. Starting today we will not give you vegetables. You can fry this dry fish to eat with the rice." I tried to survive on the dry fish and white rice for some days, but then I felt I was going to be sick.

I was really afraid because my parents were away. One Saturday afternoon, a friend of mind came from Dili; fortunately, he had met with my parents. My father sent a letter and asked me to join them as soon as possible. My father also said that the Externato de São José school was still open and he wanted to send me there.

On Sunday I went to church in the morning to pray with the community. There was a catechist in Remexio. We prayed every Sunday. I went there to be close to the population and to see some people I knew. I returned to the police station late. When I arrived, one of the commanders was waiting for me. He was very angry. "Where have you been?" he demanded.

"I've been at church," I replied.

"But church was over one hour ago," he said. "We gave you nice clothes, shoes, and food. You have to be at home on time in order to cook, to clean the yard, and to fill up water in the bathroom and in the toilet." They didn't save my plate of rice, so I didn't have any lunch that day. I became really angry, but I kept quiet and began formulating an excuse to go to Dili. Three days later, I decided it was time to go to Dili and join my parents. My excuse was that my mother was very sick and I had to go see her. One morning I woke up at six and tried to clean up everything in the house and bring water for the police. At 11, I told the commander, "I received news that my mother is very sick, so I want to see her." For some reason he allowed me to leave. Then I asked the police to give me some sort of travel document that had their signatures on it in case someone bothered me on the way. They wrote a letter for me and I took it to Dili.

When I asked to leave, the commander gave me 200 *rupiah*. That was the first time I had seen Indonesian currency. I compared the currency with Portuguese money. In the colonial period, 100 *escudos* was a lot of money, so I thought that 200 *rupiah* was worth even more. I was very happy. I didn't spend the money until I reached Dili because I really wanted to give the money to my parents.

I walked from Remexio to Dili, joining people who were going to Dili to visit or sell things. It's about half a day's walk. I left Remexio at nine in the morning and arrived in Dili at six or seven in the evening. I knew where my parents were because I had received a letter from them as soon as they arrived in Dili saying that they were in the same place that my grandparents had lived before the invasion.

I was worried that Dili would be very different after three years of the occupation. I had heard in Remexio that everything had changed; when I arrived in Dili, however, things were the same as before. I didn't see many new buildings and many of the streets still weren't paved.

When I arrived home, I was really happy to see my parents again and to see that my brothers' health had improved. My family received help from some Catholic nuns in Balide and from my grandparents. For the first time in three years, I ate bread. It tasted really good. It reminded me of when I was a kid in Remexio; we used to eat bread and butter for breakfast.

Then I told my parents, "I have 200 *rupiah*. Take this money and buy whatever you want. Buy some bread for breakfast and other things."

My parents and brothers and sisters laughed at me. "How can we buy so many things with only 200 *rupiah*?" they asked. "What we can buy is two rolls of bread for breakfast and nothing else." I was upset. That was my salary for almost two months of hard work.

That first night, my uncle took me to a public television post that was outdoors in an old market. We had never seen a television before. I admired it. How could it be possible that people could talk and sing in the television? We saw a show about Balinese dance. We watched the TV for a couple of hours and returned home.

The buildings and streets in Dili were the same as they had been before, but life in Dili had changed. It was terrifying. Indonesian soldiers were everywhere, on every street corner. The army was the law. Any time there was a conflict—for example, a land dispute or a marriage dispute—battalions 744 and 745 were in the middle of the conflict. The person who had a relative in the army always won the conflict, even if she or he was wrong. Not only were battalions 744 and 745 in Dili, there were also infantry, marines, and commandos. During the night, armored military cars and tanks patrolled the city.

Across from my house at the military cemetery, the Indonesians buried five to 10 soldiers every day. I was happy to see that at least some Indonesians were dying in return for the tens of thousands of East Timorese that they had killed. But I was sad, too, when I realized that most of the Indonesian soldiers who were killed were very young and didn't really understand why they had come to East Timor.[11]

4

Making a New Life in Dili

When we moved to Dili, we moved in with my father's parents. Living conditions in Dili were better than in Remexio. My grandparents helped us a lot with food, clothing, and medicine. We were also helped by some Catholic nuns. But often there still wasn't enough food for everyone; sometimes we would go almost a whole day without eating anything.

My grandparents had lived in Dili since the Portuguese colonial period. My grandfather, Bernardino, worked for SAPT,[1] a Portuguese company that owned a coffee plantation in Fatubesi, Ermera, southwest of Dili, and controlled coffee prices in East Timor. But P.T. Denok, which was owned by Benny Murdani,[2] the Indonesian general who led the invasion of East Timor, took over SAPT after the invasion. Today P.T. Denok is doing exactly what the Portuguese colonialists did, running the same coffee plantations and controlling the prices.[3] The price that Timorese farmers receive for their coffee is even lower today than it was during Portuguese rule.

My grandparents told us about the first days of the Indonesian occupation, when Indonesians soldiers shot many people in the streets without reason; the military also rounded up East Timorese, including many Chinese (Indonesia has a long history of anti-Chinese sentiment),[4] took them to the port area of Dili and to Licidere beach, and gunned them down indiscriminately. The army forced other Timorese, including my grandparents, to collect the corpses, to burn some, and to bury others. The Indonesians killed about 2,000 people in Dili in the first few days of the invasion.[5]

My grandparents stayed in Dili after the Indonesian invasion because they were too old to leave. My grandfather returned to his job at SAPT, which was then P.T. Denok. My grandmother, Cristina, worked at Balide Church in Dili and later worked for some Catholic nuns as well.

No one in my family spoke Indonesian well. Today my parents still don't speak Indonesian very well. When we came to Dili, I felt the same way I felt when the Indonesian army arrested us and brought us to Remexio, like a foreigner in my own country. In the street, I would often hear people speaking Indonesian. Indonesian was the official language in every public institution. If I wanted to go to the store, I often had to speak Indonesian because the Indonesians already controlled a considerable part of the merchant economy. But having to hear and speak the Indonesian language was just a small part of the oppression that we all experienced.

In East Timor in the late 1970s, all types of human rights abuses happened on a daily basis, including arbitrary arrests and executions, disappearance, and torture—much like today. Everyone lives in fear. We have all suffered from the physical and psychological repression in the streets, in schools, in public institutions, and even in churches. In the first few years of the Indonesian occupation, people's houses were subjected to searches almost every week. The Indonesian army would come to my house and search it without asking the permission of my parents or grandparents. As in Remexio, people's houses were like military headquarters: the soldiers could go in and out as they wanted. Sometimes they would go to someone's house at four in the morning and break down the doors. They didn't care if people were sleeping. They would interrogate and threaten people, ask for identification and search every corner of their house.

In general, the soldiers were looking for weapons, ammunition, and evidence that someone was involved in the underground movement or with the guerrilla fighters. The army was also interested in

Portuguese books, magazines, and newspapers and any international newspapers or magazines that discussed the problems in East Timor. They also searched for Portuguese flags and military uniforms. I've never seen a polite Indonesian soldier in my life. They always act like animals; they are trained to be like that. When they searched people's houses, they would mess up everything; sometimes they would even steal people's valuables, such as gold necklaces, earrings, and bracelets.

The Indonesian military monitored people's houses every day and every night. People were not allowed to listen to foreign radio broadcasts. At night, soldiers not only searched people's houses and spied, they also circulated around the city. In the late 1970s, tanks and armored cars circulated all night in Dili. The military forced civilians to do guard duty every night. People were not allowed to have meetings in groups, sometimes even within their own families. People who were just talking about films they had seen were subject to arrest and imprisonment. The most frightening place for people at that time in Dili was Lake Tacitolo, on the city's outskirts. The Indonesians have executed thousands of people there. Many people have been dropped alive into the lake from helicopters.

These were the circumstances under which my family had to make a new life in Dili. A little after I arrived in Dili in late November 1978, my father and I found jobs working for a construction company to support our family. We worked on the road in Dili that goes from Timur Timor University[6] toward Santa Cruz Cemetery. We made 500 *rupiah* each per day, which wasn't even enough to feed our family.

During that time we collected empty asphalt drums for the construction of a hut for our family because we wanted to move out of my grandparents' house. Fortunately, before we finished our work, we were able to collect more than 500 drums. We cut the zinc drums in half and flattened them, using the metal for the walls and roof of the house. With those drums we were able to build a very modest house for my family in Balide, Dili. We moved there in 1980 and lived there for three years.

In mid-January 1979, I enrolled as a student at the Colegio do Externato de São José secondary school, the only Portuguese Catholic school in East Timor at that time. Externato was an old school that was established during the Portuguese colonial regime. I knew about Externato from my father, who had been a student there and encouraged me to enroll. It wasn't difficult to get into Externato. We didn't have to take any specific tests or present good behavior certificates from the police, unlike at the state secondary schools. All we had to do was to provide birth certificates and school certificates that showed our level of education.

My father helped me pay for my schooling. A few months after I entered Externato, he began working on his own, treating patients as a visiting nurse; he stopped working construction in May or June 1979, but I continued the work until 1980. I saved some money that I earned from the construction work to buy notebooks and other school materials.

I am very appreciative to my parents for their contribution to my studies. In spite of their many difficulties, they still helped to pay for my education. At home, they always encouraged me to study and keep up with my homework, and they always allowed me to study with friends at school.

Going to school was a big relief for me at that time. Because Externato was Catholic and Portuguese, I didn't need to adapt myself to a new environment around the school or learn another language. The education provided by the school was better than the one at state schools: Externato was the only school in East Timor that tried to preserve the Portuguese language, the Catholic religion, and East Timorese culture and identity. It was the only private Catholic school that did not get any financial and material support from the government or from non-governmental organizations; instead it survived on the contributions of the parents who sent their children to study there.

Externato was run by Father Leão da Costa, who served as director, and Father Domingos Cunha, the vice director. Except for the history and Indonesian teachers, all the teachers were East Timorese or Portuguese. There were about 500 boys and girls in the school. The students were friendly. My classroom was in a converted chicken coop with old desks and lots of mosquitos. At first I thought that I couldn't keep up with the other students because they spoke Portuguese better than I did. After one month, however, I found the school-work was manageable for me, and my friends began to ask me for help in arithmetic and other subjects.

At Externato, I joined a football team, the choir, and the theater group. Our performances often inspired the audience because some of them would touch upon the political situation in East Timor. I still remember that in one of the plays my character was a prisoner. I had no idea that this would become a reality many years later when I was arrested by the Indonesian army. Outside of school, I spent a lot of time with the Catholic scouts, a group for young people that was run by the Catholic Church. The Catholic scouts are similar to any other scout organization; for example, we often went camping. The major difference between us and Pramuka, the Indonesian scouts, was that we worked closely with the Church and we had nothing to do with the Indonesian government. The majority of the Catholic scouts' members were students from Externato.

Externato de São José was a place where I could at least maintain my identity and my culture. It was like my second home. I spent most of my time at school, and I would even sleep there sometimes. The school offered very good courses, especially in languages such as Portuguese, English, French, and Indonesian. In history we studied East Timor from the time of the arrival of Portuguese missionaries. We also learned about the Timorese tribes and kingdoms.

During my second year at Externato, I continued to work at home and in construction during my vacations. On a typical day, I would wake up about five or six in the morning. We would have bread, coffee, and milk for breakfast. As every child in a poor family, I always worked at home. I took care of my brothers and sisters, found firewood to prepare food, shopped, washed dishes, and carried water (we didn't have running water in the house).

My mother had three more kids while we lived in Dili, making a total of 11 children. Though having such a big family may seem very difficult from a Western point of view, children are considered a treasure in East Timor. Also, children provide security for the family, as they will one day get jobs and take care of their parents and extended family. I played with my younger brothers and sisters when-

ever I had time at home. I also encouraged them to study. Tradition-
ally in East Timor, the children must respect the eldest brother. My
eldest sister, Celestina, who was born two years after me, had to work
really hard at home. She spent most of her time with my parents. She
helped my mother take care of my younger siblings, as well as helping in the kitchen and the yard. In East Timor, girls usually spend
more time at home than boys. Families restrict the movement of girls.
Boys can hang around outside the house; girls can only go out for a
very short time, and they must have the permission of their parents or
their brothers must accompany them if they want to go out for longer.

After finishing my morning chores, I would study and then go to
school. School started at one in the afternoon and lasted until five
p.m. The main reason we started school so late was because we didn't
have full-time teachers. All the teachers at Externato had to have
other jobs to support themselves.

Externato was a good source of information for what was going on
in East Timor. The students always exchanged news. I followed the
East Timor situation through shortwave radio networks such as the
BBC, Radio Switzerland, Radio Netherlands, the Voice of America,
and the Australian Broadcast Corporation. I also followed other conflicts in the world such as the Western Saharan and the Palestinian
struggles for independence.

I didn't know anything at that time about the existence of the East
Timorese underground. Some people from my family, however, including my uncles, had already been working in the underground
movement. In 1980, even Xanana Gusmão, the head of the resistance,
wasn't well known.[7] I first heard about Xanana in 1981, when the
army began the *pagar betis*, the "fence of legs," operation.[8] During the
operation, the Indonesian military mobilized almost all men from the
ages of 15 to 45 in every neighborhood in Dili to go to the jungle and
capture the remaining guerrilla fighters. I was scared because I didn't
have an Indonesian identity card. I had refused to get one. At that
time, it was dangerous for anyone who didn't have an ID: he or she
would be suspected of being a FRETILIN member. Fortunately, I had
a good friend in the local government office, and I quickly obtained a
provisional ID. The military mobilized most people, but I was exempt

because I was working for the priests and was a student at Externato. Even though the school was not well respected by the Indonesians, it still had some influence and successfully petitioned the military authorities for an exemption for all Externato students. By 1981, my father was already working in the hospital in Dili and looked too old for military service, as well. My brothers were all too young. So, fortunately, no one in my family was forced to participate.

The objective of the "fence of legs" operation was to arrest or exterminate the remaining FALINTIL guerrilla fighters and the population with them in the jungle. So the Indonesians mobilized enough people to be able to sweep across the territory from the perimeter to the center. All the lines moved to the center, with the Indonesian military at their backs, pushing people forward. The operation took a month. Hundreds, maybe thousands, of people—civilians and guerrillas—were killed in the mountains. The Indonesians even killed women who were pregnant. They would cut babies out of women's wombs and smash little babies on rocks and trees. This information came from those who joined the operation. The Indonesian military even killed those who surrendered to them. My friends who had to participate said that the operation was stopped because the army claimed Xanana Gusmão had been killed during the operation. From Indonesia's perspective, if Xanana was dead, the war was over; but Xanana was still alive. This was when I first learned about him.

Around the same time as the "fence of legs" campaign, Adão Mendonça, my mother's brother, disappeared. On June 11, 1981, the guerrilla fighters attacked one of the military posts near Dili. My uncle was involved in organizing the operation. Unfortunately, the operation wasn't successful and the Indonesians quickly began to terrorize the population.

Everyone was scared to talk because they were afraid of being arrested by the Indonesians. The Indonesian army immediately began to search and monitor everyone's house, and to arrest those who they suspected of being involved in planning the attack, including two people from my school, Venancio Mau Seran, a teacher and a former member of the FRETILIN central committee, and Edmundo, a student. No one has seen them since.

During this particular crackdown, some Indonesian soldiers came to my uncle's house in China Rate, a neighborhood in Dili, and picked him up. The army told my aunt that they just wanted to ask my uncle some questions. When the commander of the military headquarters in Becora called him, he and his family thought that he would soon return home. He went to the military headquarters with nothing more than the clothes on his back.

My uncle had been a member of FRETILIN; he was in charge of the whole district of Aileu. The Indonesians arrested him and his family in 1978 or 1979 and then took them to Dili. They forced my uncle to report once a week to Indonesian army headquarters in Dili, as they did with many other FRETILIN central committee members who were arrested in the jungle. Many prominent FRETILIN cadres were not so lucky; the Indonesians killed them as soon as they were captured. Your fate often depended on where, when, and by whom you were arrested. The Indonesian military harassed my uncle from the time he was arrested until the day he disappeared. The military beat my uncle during the frequent interrogations. His family also suffered from psychological repression.

When the Indonesians arrested my uncle again in 1981, no one could inquire about his whereabouts. Even Bishop Martinho Lopes wasn't able to get information from the military about him. We asked people in Atauro, the island near Dili that the Indonesians had turned into a huge prison,[9] as well as in Bali and Jakarta. No one knew where my uncle was. He has never returned home. The Indonesians might have executed him. He left behind his wife, Maria de Fátima, and three children.

My life continued despite the war. In 1980, I stopped working in construction and began to work for Father Leão and Father Cunha. My uncle, Silverio Martins, my mother's cousin, had started working for the priests five months earlier. We helped to clean the house and sometimes cooked. The job enabled me to pursue my studies. For almost two years I paid nothing to go to Externato. Father Leão and Father Cunha paid my tuition in exchange for my work. I didn't live at the priests' house, but I slept in a little room at Externato along with my uncle. Sometimes I slept at home, but I spent more time with the priests than with my parents. Father Leão and Father Cunha were like my second parents.

Even though Externato de São José wasn't a political institution, the Indonesian army considered it and treated it as a political institution from the time it was reopened in 1976. Because of this, the two priests who ran the school and the students suffered from all kinds of repression. The Indonesian army threatened to close the school several times. This repression by the Indonesian army in fact helped to politicize Externato. Interestingly, many of the leaders of the underground of the new generation emerged from the school.

While I was happy to be a student at Externato, my Indonesian language skills suffered as a result of not going to an Indonesian school. We learned basic Indonesian at Externato, but Portuguese was the language of instruction. Indonesian was like a secondary language. When I came to Externato I continued to think that the Indonesian language was important, but because Portuguese at Externato was mandatory, I concentrated on it more.

While my Indonesian wasn't as good as I wanted it to be, there were other advantages of attending Externato. The Indonesians didn't pressure us to join Pramuka, the boys' and girls' scout group of Indonesia. The students who went to a government school had to join Pramuka or participate in Pramuka activities at school. We didn't have to join because Externato was an independent school. At Externato, most students joined the Catholic scouts, we never had any Indonesian flag ceremonies, and we didn't have to attend special events at the governor's palace. On Indonesian holidays, like Hari Integrasi (Integration Day),[10] or Indonesian Independence Day, we didn't attend the ceremonies. Externato did not follow the Indonesian school calendar. In late 1985, however, as Externato came under increasing pressure from the Indonesian military, the school began to adapt its policies to fit Indonesia's. For example, the school began to observe Indonesian holidays and to require all students to take Indonesian final exams. Father Leão and Father Cunha made these changes to help the school survive.

While the school was able to maintain a certain independence from Indonesian activities for a long time, it was much more difficult for individuals or families to do so. My family, for example, had a second-hand Indonesian flag that we raised on important days, such as July 17, the day of the illegal integration of East Timor into Indonesia, and August 17, the anniversary of Indonesia's declaration of independence from Dutch colonialism in 1945. If we forgot to raise the flag, the RT (the local government aide)[11] would call up to us from the street with a megaphone, "Hey, that house up there, raise your flag! Raise your flag immediately!"

Generally, I wasn't very cooperative with the Indonesian authorities. I tried to escape every single official Indonesian activity. In the end, however, I realized that I had made a mistake by being openly rebellious and that pretending to be a good Indonesian citizen is a good way to protect your life and to continue to fight for the independence of East Timor.

Some Indonesian activities, however, were difficult to avoid. Almost all East Timorese had to do *gotong royong*, community self-help work, a form of forced labor, one or two weekends per month or whenever an Indonesian dignitary was coming to visit.[12] The chief of the village, the *kepala desa*, would come by with a megaphone and call everyone to clean the streets with the military for one or two hours. I took part in this work only once because I was usually involved in some sort of school or church activity that I could use as an excuse. But the rest of my family did this work every week. My parents always said that if we did not participate in those activities, the Indonesians would suspect us and cause us trouble.

In addition to *gotong royong*, the Indonesians forced the population to take part in nightly patrols. I was forced into doing it many times after I stopped working with Father Leão and Father Cunha. You were supposed to perform patrol duty once a week. At night the Indonesians put us at checkpoints throughout the city. We had to stay alert all night. They assigned me to a checkpoint in Kaikoli that was infested with mosquitos. Every half hour a jeep or an armored car full of troops passed to check up on us. We didn't understand why we were patrolling. To guard against FRETILIN? The Indonesians have thousands of soldiers, including native East Timorese who they have trained to help them. But they still force civilians to perform guard duty. If I didn't go, I had to pay someone to go in my place. Fortunately, I was able to avoid patrol duty after I obtained a job as a teacher in 1986. Usually teachers could escape patrol duty by arguing that they had too much work.

In August 1985, I had the opportunity to attend a big Indonesian exhibition in Jakarta. Indonesians always tried to persuade the East Timorese that Indonesia was wonderful by showing us how nice and modern Jakarta was. As part of this effort they brought students from all grades and ages. The KNPI, the National Committee of Indonesian Youth (Komite Nasional Pemuda Indonesia), sponsored the trip. In 1985, I was one of the two students chosen from Externato to go to Indonesia. The Indonesians hoped that when the students came back to Dili, we would tell people that Jakarta was a beautiful city and that we thought that it was a good idea for us to join Indonesia rather than fight for independence.

The trip to Jakarta was my first time flying on a plane and my first time outside of East Timor. It was exciting. We first flew from Dili to Kupang, West Timor. It was the first time I had seen Kupang. From there we flew to Bali. It was amazing to me how comfortable it was to fly on the plane. In Bali, we changed to a bigger plane, a DC-9. We arrived in Jakarta at nine in the evening. Jakarta's a huge city. It looks beautiful at night. One of my friends said that it looked like hell. When you look down to Jakarta, lights of different colors are everywhere. There's no end; it's infinite. I had never seen anything like it in my life. My first thought was that people in Jakarta didn't think about war. The war in East Timor did not affect them. My friends and I still thought about the war in East Timor; the suffering never disappeared from our thoughts.

After we arrived at the airport, we went to a nice hotel. The Indonesians paid for everything. In the morning, I rode on a fancy bus for the first time. It was the first time I had felt air conditioning. Our guides took us all over Jakarta. Our group of 25 East Timorese joined with people from delegations from West Papua, Sumatera, and other Indonesian provinces. The Indonesians treated us like dignitaries; our bus even had a police escort, so we passed right through red lights.

We went to the military museum, but there was no section on the war in East Timor in the museum. I was not surprised. The Indonesian government does not want people to know that there is a war in East Timor in which it has lost many soldiers and in which it has killed more than 200,000 East Timorese. One display related to East Timor that I saw in the museum was an old Portuguese machine gun. The inscription read, "This was donated by the Portuguese government." I'm sure that it was stolen or captured from East Timor, from FALINTIL, when the Indonesians invaded Dili. I saw this and was really surprised. Why would they put this gun in the museum? The museum also had an old map of East Timor that showed a division between the Bello people and the Wehale people.[13]

After visiting the museum, we went to many exciting places, including Keong Max, a movie theater center that is well known in Asia. It was the first time I had seen a big screen; it was as big as an entire wall. I watched some movie and it seemed that when the car in the film moved, I was moving too. We then went to some industrial areas and saw some textile factories. Then we went to the national monument to see where the first president, Sukarno, declared the independence of Indonesia from the Dutch in 1945.

We had a very fun week. I had never seen most of the modern inventions in Jakarta, like escalators and elevators, in East Timor. I had learned about them in school, but it was my first time actually seeing and trying them. I also went to a planetarium where we could see stars. Outside it was daytime, but when you went inside, it was like night. I was struck by how advanced the technology was in Jakarta. I was always asking questions. I actually wanted to stay in Jakarta for a few more days and find out more about Indonesia.

In Jakarta I saw not only the beautiful buildings but also tremendous poverty; outside of the war, I had never seen such poverty in Dili. If I dropped a piece of bread, for example, immediately a crowd of children would run and try to pick it up and eat it.

At the end of the week, our guides asked everyone to give his or her opinion of Jakarta. The Indonesians asked everyone to write down what they thought. One question was, "What do you think about Jakarta?" Seeing Jakarta had made me mad. If Jakarta is so modern, why can't East Timor be like this as well? I wondered. I wrote that I couldn't compare Jakarta with East Timor because they were so different. If I had been to Melbourne, Australia, or some other big city, maybe I could compare it with Jakarta.

I knew they wanted me to say that Jakarta was a beautiful city, but as an East Timorese, I had a different impression. In spite of all the new things I saw, I wasn't very impressed. I was thinking about why East Timor or Dili couldn't be like Jakarta and have modern buildings. I didn't want the poverty, but I saw the majority of the people in Jakarta living in better conditions than those in East Timor.

Everyone had to sign their name to the questionnaire and say where he or she came from, but I never heard anything from the Indonesians about my answers. They may have been unhappy with my response, but they didn't say anything after I returned to East Timor.

The trip made me feel more East Timorese than Indonesian. It was as if the Indonesians were asking me, "Are you happy after I destroyed your home and stole your belongings? Now I'll take you to my house and show you all of marvelous things that I have." Seeing Jakarta made me hate Indonesia even more. If the Indonesian army had not invaded East Timor, then East Timor would have a much higher quality of life. People would be happy, and we would not have people living in the street.

As soon as we returned to Dili, we met with the KNPI, the group that sponsored the trip. They asked us to tell the story of our Jakarta trip to the students at our schools. When I returned to school, my friends asked me, "Constâncio, how was Indonesia?"

"It was great, a big city," I told them, "but I hated it. Jakarta belongs to the Indonesians, not to us. I'd rather see East Timor than Jakarta."

The KNPI people didn't try to get me involved in the organization. Perhaps they were afraid that I would tell people negative things about Indonesia, about all the poor children I saw in Jakarta.

5

Joining the Underground

I became involved in the underground movement while I was a student at Externato. The year 1983 was very important in my political development. During that year, a cease-fire and negotiations took place between the resistance and the Indonesian military. They were the result of diplomatic contacts in 1982 between Xanana Gusmão and the other FRETILIN leaders in the jungle and various Indonesian military commanders, and the increasing number of effective FALIN-TIL attacks throughout the territory.[1] This first and last negotiation took place between Xanana Gusmão, Colonel Gatot Purwanto, and the governor of East Timor at that time, Mario Viegas Carrascalão,[2] near Ossu. Xanana Gusmão became really well known at this time as a result of the publicity surrounding the negotiations.

The meeting brought hope to the people in the villages, and towns for a peaceful and internationally acceptable solution to the East Timor crisis. News reached Dili that some guerrilla fighters were even coming to play football in Dili. I was so excited that I skipped a math class one afternoon and went to the football stadium to wait for the guerrilla fighters. When I arrived at the stadium, there were other people there as well. I waited for one hour, but nothing happened. News later reached Dili that the negotiations broke down with no further agreement. The negotiations terminated with a short message by

Xanana Gusmão addressed to Mario Carrascalão: "You are responsible for the people in the occupied towns and villages, and I am in charge of the people in the jungle."[3]

There was no news about the negotiations reported on Indonesian television or in the newspapers from Jakarta sold in Dili. We heard about the negotiations through the underground network. The cease-fire lasted a few months, but the levels of repression in Dili and other major cities did not change much. At that time, Indonesia's intention was to arrest all the guerrilla fighters and reject any proposals from FALINTIL.

Some people were very skeptical about the negotiations, but I think the majority of people in East Timor were happy and thought that the war was going to end and that they could soon see their friends and relatives who had been in the jungle for years. Many people traveled from Dili, Baucau, and other towns and villages to meet with the guerrillas. But then in August the Indonesians announced the end of the cease-fire.

The Indonesian military was furious because its plan to persuade Xanana Gusmão and the guerrilla fighters to surrender failed. In Dili, those who had any sort of contact with the guerrillas during the cease-fire were arrested and subjected to all types of torture. After the negotiations broke up, the Indonesian army immediately planned a massive military operation in the jungle; before it happened, however, the military dropped and posted thousands of pamphlets all over the country appealing to the guerrilla fighters to surrender. The military promised that it would do nothing to any guerrilla fighter who surrendered. The guerrillas could come directly to military headquarters or, if they were afraid, to their family's house first and report to the military headquarters later. But people didn't believe the promises of the Indonesian military and told the guerrillas not to surrender.

After the cease-fire broke down, FALINTIL launched a preemptive attack on various Indonesian army positions in Lospalos and in Viqueque. In retaliation, the Indonesians massacred hundreds of civilians in Kraras and Viqueque, and in Lore, near Lospalos.[4] The breakdown of the negotiations prompted me to join the underground movement. The killings and arbitrary arrests and disappearances made me very angry. The continued atrocities made me even more determined to involve myself directly in the underground movement in Dili.

I felt a sense of urgency. I felt the same way in 1979 when Nicolau Lobato was killed on the front line,[5] a time when the people of East Timor suddenly lost hope. Our leader was killed and it appeared that the struggle might end. Lobato was the president of FRETILIN at that time; he had replaced Francisco Xavier do Amaral and was the first vice president of East Timor. When the cease-fire broke down in 1983, many people again felt that there was no hope. That's why I began thinking that young people in the towns should play a more active role in the resistance movement, especially as the older people continued to suffer from the destruction caused by the Indonesian military. Indonesia had destroyed numerous underground organizations. In 1981, Indonesia was able to destroy almost the entire underground network throughout the country. With the end of the cease-fire, some friends and I decided that the younger generation had to step forward and support the resistance.

I had thought of involving myself in the underground movement earlier, when I first returned to Dili; but when I returned from the jungle, I concentrated mostly on my studies. My education was important to me, and at this time I had never met anyone who was directly involved in the underground movement. As my friendships at school became stronger, I would discuss political issues with my most trusted friends. A good number of students at Externato had spent three very difficult years in the jungle or had stayed in Dili after the Indonesians invaded East Timor and had had terrible experiences. We shared our experiences with each other.

Following the resumption of Indonesia's war in late 1983, I decided to make a serious effort to find out if any of my peers had connections to the resistance. Even though I was already close with many of my fellow students, I had to be careful. I was always suspicious and they were suspicious of me. There were groups of my peers who were already involved in the underground movement, but I was not yet a trusted friend of any of them. Then I began to make friends with

José Manuel Fernandes and Donaciano Gomes. José Manuel and Donaciano were members of the Catholic scouts; I became one of the heads of the organization at the Balide Church in Dili. When they saw that I was a trustworthy person, they invited me to go to the meetings of the underground movement. At that time, José Manuel and Donaciano were both 19 years old; I was 21.

It was not easy to get involved in the underground because the networks and groups were small, and people were very secretive about their organizations. Such caution was necessary. Even if you were already part of one organization, you didn't know other organizations because each had its own channels to the armed resistance. Students, civil servants, merchants, churchpeople, and women's groups all worked discreetly and separately.

By 1983 my uncle Silverio Martins and I had stopped working at Externato and moved out of the school. I went back to my parents' house. My uncle stayed at a small kiosk that he had opened with Father Leão's help. A few months later, he and I rented a small piece of land on which we built a house; we used the front part of the house as a café. We sold coffee, bread with butter, and *pisang goreng* (fried banana). Many young people from Externato and St. Joseph's senior high school, which was in the same complex, came to my house to drink coffee, play guitar, and socialize. Soon the house became a meeting place for young people, including political activists. Sometimes José Manuel came to my house to drink coffee and play guitar. From there we started discussing politics. Later on, José Manuel brought Donaciano, Domingos, Donaciano's brother Lucas, and some others.

The first time I met members of the underground, José Manuel and Donaciano brought me to a meeting in Dili with an older man named Toko. He had been a member of the resistance in the jungle. "The underground movement is something that is very delicate," he told us. "You have to be determined and responsible for your own actions." We had several meetings with Toko, who was a member of a cell of people in their forties, many of whom had already been imprisoned. We shared our experiences and talked about the strategy of the underground movement—how it could continue and how we could better organize it. These meetings encouraged us to become more active.

After this first meeting, Toko became our counselor. I still remember what he said to us in our second meeting: "To be a freedom fighter is not easy. One has to sacrifice his own life, his family life, and maybe even give his wife or husband to the enemy to protect the country and the people." For a few months, we had meetings just with this comrade; then Toko put us in contact with Commander David Alex Daitula, the FALINTIL commander for the Baucau region; Mau Hudo, the vice chairperson of FRETILIN; and Taur Matan Ruak, the chief staff commander of FALINTIL.

The underground was well structured. Its members worked to send messages about East Timor to family members and friends in Portugal and Australia and tried to support the resistance in the jungle. They would send the guerrillas food and supplies. The assistance sometimes included ammunition or money, but information was the most important resource for the guerrillas. We provided information on all sorts of matters, most typically on Indonesian military activities in the towns and throughout the territory, human rights violations, and developments on the diplomatic front regarding East Timor. We would get the information from shortwave radio and from people within the Catholic Church. Psychologically, the information that we provided was very important for the guerrillas. It let them know that they were not alone, that the world had not forgotten about East Timor.

One day, I was sitting with six of my friends—José Manuel, Donaciano, and others who are still active in the underground in Dili. We decided to form our own *nucleo,* or cell. My friends appointed me as the head of the group. David Alex endorsed the formation of the organization and gave us the name 007. We liked the name because there were seven of us and because some of us had seen some James Bond movies. James Bond's films were shown in Dili during the time of the Portuguese. Though I had never seen one, I had heard stories about them from friends.

We formed 007 because we wanted to make the underground more effective by getting more young people involved and by building ties with already established underground groups. Toko thought it was a good idea as well; there was no problem at all when someone wanted to leave a group and found their own cell. One group would give birth to many other groups in the underground movement. Because of that, there were groups all over the city. Each group worked independently of the others. While this independence allowed for a diversity of action and made it almost impossible for the Indonesians to eliminate the entire underground, it also prevented the underground from planning any sort of coordinated, large-scale actions. We hoped that 007 would help to build links between the underground groups, while maintaining the decentralization of the underground that was necessary for security reasons.

It was my decision to join the underground resistance. My parents didn't even know that I was involved. No one in my family knew because I couldn't put their lives at risk.

Everyone who engages in the struggle for liberation is a member of the resistance. In this sense, the vast majority of the East Timorese people are members of the resistance. Within the formal resistance structures, the tasks differ from one person to another. There are people who are in charge of supplying food to the resistance, making political propaganda, directing communications inside and outside of the country, and serving as couriers. My first task was to persuade friends to join our group. I also began to contribute some information and help collect clothes, medicine, and food to send to the jungle.

After we formed 007 in early 1985, we began to work directly with David Alex, the commander of the guerrillas in Baucau. We also began to expand the organization to get more people to become members. To organize other cells, we would only talk to friends we already knew would be willing to join. We began with seven people and started to recruit others. Each of us recruited another six people; along with the original member, these six constituted a new cell. The new members of the cell would not know each other; they knew only the founding member. In this manner, if the Indonesians ever arrested one member of a cell, it was possible for the other members to survive. This process of growth continued by asking each new member of the underground to form at least one new cell of six other people. We also began to link up with cells that already existed throughout the country.

Within one year, we had cells in Dili, Aileu, Manatuto, Baucau, Same, and in all the towns along the main roads, including Oecussi, which is in the middle of West Timor.[6] Our group eventually became one of the largest organizations in the underground, and it was made up primarily of young people. As we began to organize and link up with existing groups, we also tried to help the guerrillas, especially David Alex and the FALINTIL fighters under his command. His unit was the only guerrilla group we had contact with. There was no centralized network for all the different underground groups. Each had its own connections, with David Alex, Mau Hudo, Xanana Gusmão, or other guerrilla fighters in the jungle. We provided David Alex's group with food, medicine, clothes, and military equipment, as well as information.

By 1987, 007 and all its associated cells had grown to such an extent that we decided to form a new organization in the underground, which we called Orgão Oito, or Organ Eight. The original members of 007, plus several leaders of other cells across the country, coordinated the organization. The leadership of Orgão Oito was collective.

It is important for the resistance to understand the political, economic, and social changes taking place in the world. It has always been difficult to get newspapers and magazines that write specifically about East Timor. There were attempts by various networks to smuggle information to the outside world, but it was really difficult to get information out or to get information from the outside world into East Timor. Sometimes we would get news from Portugal, but usually only once or twice a year. We couldn't buy any newspapers that favored or even discussed our situation, and Indonesian radio broadcasts and newspapers suppressed any information about East Timor. It was as if East Timor didn't exist at that time in the Indonesian media. We used to listen to international radio broadcasts like the ABC of Australia and the BBC in Portuguese, but it was illegal for anyone to listen to foreign radio broadcasts in East Timor. If the army found someone listening to a shortwave radio, it would immediately arrest that person and subject him or her to torture. Many people listened to these broadcasts anyway to keep the spirit of the struggle of the East Timorese people alive.

Most of the information that I provided the resistance was on the diplomatic struggle abroad, especially on the United Nations, the Portuguese government, and solidarity movements for East Timor around the world. I also provided information to the resistance about Indonesian plans. We had people who worked closely with the Indonesians as double agents who could provide us with accurate information about Indonesian military operations, so we sometimes knew Indonesian plans in advance. For example, if I heard from someone that Indonesian military activities were going to increase in certain areas, we would channel the information to David Alex and he would send the information to other parts of the country where there were guerrilla bases. I would also offer my opinions about the struggle and how to improve the organization of the resistance and the underground in the towns and villages. Through an extensive network of *estafetas* (messengers) we were able to communicate effectively within the resistance.

Many women were active in the underground, and there were no limitations to their participation. Women had the same rights as men. Some met with the guerrilla fighters in the jungle to discuss matters of the resistance. I worked with many women.

Because the participation of women in the underground movement is very high, many women have been arrested and subjected to severe torture and rape by the Indonesian army. Nevertheless, more and more women have joined the underground. The example of these women who have struggled and suffered continues to inspire people throughout East Timor. Women work in the same line as men in East Timor, sometimes doing things that men cannot do.

For men and women alike, the underground is very dangerous. The Indonesian military often destroyed any underground groups within six months or one year of their establishment. The army uses various methods. They bribe people and torture suspected members of the underground movement. Many East Timorese men and women have suffered from all kinds of torture, such as getting their faces sliced with razor blades, their bodies burnt with cigarettes, and their genitals subjected to electric shock. The Indonesians sometimes pull out people's fingernails and toenails. They employ all these forms of torture to extract information. Because of this incredible brutality, people sometimes provide information to the Indonesian army.

The Indonesian army uses very sophisticated security strategies that they learned from Japan, the United States, and Australia. In every village there are some intelligence agents, whether military intelligence or civilians. There is a *kepala desa* (head of the village), a *binpolda* (a policeman), and a *babinsa* (the local military authority) in every village. In certain villages, the *babinsa* has more power than the head of the village. There are also soldiers who sometimes disguise themselves as merchants selling things from house to house with the purpose of listening to people and uncovering political activity. All of these agents provide information about civilians to the police and the military, and are responsible for the stability and security of the village.

Some East Timorese also work for intelligence. Some are forced to join, often after their release from prison, but others are bribed by the military or have supported Indonesia from the beginning. When the Indonesians ask you to work with them, you can't refuse without putting your life in danger. Sometimes the Indonesians force you to arrest your own friends, your own comrades. The people who work for money are the largest group, but most of them are not pro-integration; they work because they are poor and need the money to survive. Some intelligence agents are very smart and play around with the Indonesian army; they become double agents, working for the resistance while they pretend to work for Indonesia.

Despite the pervasive presence of Indonesian intelligence, the underground was still able to accomplish quite a bit. It became a lot easier to deliver supplies to FALINTIL in 1984 when the Indonesians allowed free circulation of people in and out of Dili for the first time, perhaps because it was confident of its level of control over the territory. Before that, everyone had to ask for a travel document, a *surat jalan*, from the local KORAMIL to leave the city. We used various means of transportation to carry things into the jungle. Military checkpoints and Indonesian soldiers were positioned throughout East

Timor, but the soldiers could easily be bribed with a little money and a pack of cigarettes. There were always good and bad times for us to move. When opportunities arose, we acted immediately. The Indonesians never caught anyone who worked with me carrying things to the mountains until 1993 when they caught our comrade Samoduk bringing food to Commander David Alex. I heard that before they killed him the Indonesians fixed his arms and legs to a tree as if he were Jesus Christ on the cross.

To help the guerrilla fighters in the mountains, we had a special group for fundraising. We collected money only from people we knew very well. Some people even sold their few valuables—perhaps a gold ring, a watch, earrings, or a bracelet—to help the guerrilla fighters. Even laborers and street vendors who made very little money contributed financially to the resistance.

I remember the first time I took things to the resistance. I was scared that if the Indonesians arrested us, they would immediately kill us or send us to prison. But it was not really that risky, because we only had food, medicine, and clothes. The dangerous things to transport are ammunition or other military supplies. If we were caught with food, medicine, or clothes, we could say that we were visiting our family in Baucau or doing business in the area.

The first time we brought supplies to the resistance, we went from Dili to Baucau, which is about five or six hours away by bus. We could carry only as much as the other passengers so we wouldn't attract any attention. When we stopped at the edge of Dili at an Indonesian military checkpoint, soldiers asked us for identification, but we didn't have any problems. When we arrived in Baucau, we dropped off our delivery at the designated location, and other *estafetas* took it to the mountains, so we would not know how they delivered it to the resistance. Such precautions were necessary for the safety of the organization. We stayed overnight and went back to Dili the next day. We couldn't stay longer without raising suspicions.

The people in Baucau who had contacts with the resistance were poor. They didn't have money to buy extra food, so we had to buy food and medicine in Dili that was not available in Baucau. At that time, you couldn't get even one tablet of aspirin in Baucau. Luckily we had some friends who worked at the hospital in Dili who could provide us with medicine free of charge.

I never carried ammunition from Dili to Baucau. We had specific people who already knew how to do that. Rifles were almost impossible to buy in Dili or anywhere else in East Timor. If we could buy rifles in Dili, we could increase the number of our guerrilla fighters. Most of the weapons that the guerrillas obtained were weapons they captured from the Indonesian army during military operations. That's why the resistance has a number of U.S.-made M-16 rifles, the same weapon used by the Indonesian army. We did buy some hand grenades and ammunition, however, but not in great amounts. We could buy only one or two hundred bullets and a couple of hand grenades at a time. We bought them from the Indonesian military. I can't explain how we did this because the underground still relies on this supply source.

Only a handful of people from the Indonesian army supplied or sold us ammunition. Only one person knew the identity of the person involved so no one else could get into trouble. I never met with the person who sold us the ammunition, but I knew the person who purchased it. The sellers weren't sympathetic to the resistance; they sold weapons for money. Ammunition cost 1,500 *rupiah*, about 80 cents in U.S. currency, for each bullet; a hand grenade cost 25,000 *rupiah*.

When we formed 007 in 1985, I was still a student at Externato, but I was no longer staying and working with Father Cunha and Father Leão. There was too much schoolwork. My father was working as a nurse at the hospital in Dili and he had a good income at the time, so he could help me. Also, when I stopped working for the priests, I used my free time, holidays, and vacation to earn some money for myself by working construction. By the time we founded 007, I had moved out of my parents' house again and moved in with my Uncle Silverio in the Santa Cruz section of Dili. My parents' house was on top of a big hill very far from school, but my uncle's house was very close to Externato and it was easier for my friends to visit me there.

I graduated from Externato in 1986 and began teaching Catholic religion classes to primary school boys and girls. Even though Externato was independent of the Indonesian government, primary school teachers of the Catholic religion could receive a government salary, in addition to the small salary they received from Externato, if they were civil servants.

Through the Department of Religion, the Indonesian government employs religious teachers for public and private schools. I applied to the department to be a religion teacher and was accepted. It was really difficult for me to get that job. I had to get a certificate that I wasn't involved in any anti-Indonesian political activities, and had to take the *Pancasila* test and prove that I could parrot the five principles. I had to bow to the Indonesians and praise Indonesia's development in East Timor. As I did this, I thought, "Now I am bowing to the Indonesians, but I will be able to kick them later."

After meeting the requirements, I became an employee of the government of Indonesia. As a Catholic religion teacher, I worked at the Diocese of Dili in the catechist department and taught at Externato de São José. In Externato there were only two of us who were Indonesian civil servants.

I was also invited to teach basic English to secondary school students at Cristal, a private high school. I taught there for about two years. Then, because I had learned some French at Externato, I was invited to give basic French at SMA II, a state high school. These were all part-time jobs, but they made me well known as a teacher. Wherever I would go, people would always say hello to me.

I taught French at SMA II for just one year, and then quit. I made a good salary from Cristal, the government, and Externato—around 500,000 *rupiah* a month, the equivalent of $200 in U.S. currency at the time, which is fairly good for an East Timorese living in Dili.

In 1989, I was invited to teach a basic English course for people at the Hotel Mahkota in Dili. The hotel was preparing to open and it needed some workers who could speak English. P.T. Denok, the huge company that controls coffee and sandalwood in East Timor, owns the hotel.[7] I worked at the hotel for only three months and earned 600,000 *rupiah*. I was happy with all the money I was making. I could help my family, and I also gave money to buy food and medicine for the guerrilla fighters.

At all my jobs I would not only teach but find out who the students were and whether or not they were activists.

I always told my students to learn English. It is a very important language, especially for the resistance.

6

Emergence of the Underground

Until 1989, the activities and the very existence of the underground were not public. But President Suharto's visit to East Timor in November 1988 helped to change things; his visit turned out to be very beneficial to the resistance.

Suharto was visiting because of a national gathering of the Indonesian scouts in Dili for Pramuka national day. The Indonesians mobilized almost the entire population of the city and told everyone to fly the *merah putih*, the Indonesian flag,[1] in front of their houses. Soldiers went through the streets early in the morning with megaphones and called people to greet Suharto, and to bring their Indonesian flags and their traditional instruments for entertainment. The army provided trucks and other vehicles to transport people. People in my family went, but I didn't. If no one from my family had gone to greet Suharto, the army would have immediately suspected us.

Security was really tight. Soldiers were everywhere, walking in the streets and on every corner throughout the city. Many former political prisoners were arrested and jailed. The military monitored people's houses and interrogated and intimidated many people. There were also many soldiers who circulated in plain clothes, disguised as merchants, taxi drivers, food vendors, cobblers, and clothes vendors. They hid their weapons under their clothes and in their bags. But the

East Timorese knew that they had weapons. Just by their appearance, people knew that many of the vendors were soldiers in disguise.

People were not happy with Suharto, but no one could say that they didn't like the murderer of more than 500,000 Indonesians in 1965 and 1966 and 200,000 East Timorese since the invasion.[2] People could only praise Suharto as our leader, the father of development, and the pioneer of the family planning program. If we said anything to the contrary, we would have been in trouble.

People had to stand on both sides of the road all the way from the Comoro airport to the center of Dili waiting for Suharto; it's a long stretch of road and it was hot. But almost no one saw Suharto when he visited. He never came down the road. The army took him in another direction. Suharto was in East Timor for just a few hours. He was probably afraid of going to East Timor, but I think he was confident that his army could protect him.

One important thing came from Suharto's visit: he "opened up" East Timor by declaring it open to foreign tourists and investors. Until 1989, the East Timorese people lived in almost complete isolation from the international community.[3] The resistance was optimistic that the opening would help internationalize the East Timor problem. We knew that most of the Western tourists who would come to East Timor would not be happy about the situation in our country. We hoped that the majority of them would have already heard about our problems and would try to investigate the situation further.

The opening of East Timor was part of an Indonesian political strategy to show the world that there were no human rights violations and that everything was stable in East Timor. At that time, the Indonesians were confident that the underground movement had been largely eliminated and that everything was under control. It was basically the politics of showing off. They wanted to show the international community all the "development" they had brought to East Timor: the new roads and buildings built over the bones and blood of the East Timorese people.

The opening of East Timor was also necessary because of the planned visit of Pope John Paul II to East Timor in October 1989. We heard about it a year before the visit when it was announced in every church. The visit was big news and a message of hope for the people of East Timor. People were very happy when they found out that the Pope was coming to East Timor because well over 90 percent of the East Timorese population is Catholic. For most East Timorese the Pope is the representative of God. At the same time, however, many people were also afraid of the Pope's visit because they thought it would result in increased repression by the Indonesian military.

Nevertheless, my friends in the underground and I were happy. Although we were worried that the Pope's visit might constitute a form of recognition of Indonesia's annexation of East Timor, we immediately began thinking of how we might take advantage of the Pope's visit. We saw the Pope's visit as one of the most important opportunities in the history of our struggle to influence international public opinion. Orgão Oito consulted with David Alex and discussed among ourselves how we could protest the Indonesian occupation; we agreed with David Alex that a demonstration would be the most effective way to embarrass Indonesia internationally. We knew that when the Pope visited East Timor, dozens of reporters and television crews would cover the events. We were concerned, however, that it would be difficult to hold a demonstration because people were not yet brave enough to speak out publicly against the occupation and the repression. None of us, since the time of the invasion, had ever participated in any sort of demonstration, but we knew about the potential effectiveness of demonstrations through we what learned from international shortwave radio and even from Indonesian public television about struggles in places such as South Korea, Israeli-occupied Palestine, and Europe.

David Alex had instructed us that I couldn't be one of the people to lead the actual demonstration because at that time I had too important a task: I was in charge of communicating with abroad. Because of that we decided that José Manuel, Donaciano, Francisco Lelan, and a few others should lead the protest. I helped to plan the action, but my public role was to be very limited.

Three months before the Pope's visit, we lost contact with David Alex because the army had begun an intense military operation covering the whole territory in preparation for the Pope. The military tried to push the guerrillas far away from the villages and towns to keep them busy in the jungle. Soldiers were all over Dili. There were even tanks and other military vehicles. The Indonesians wanted to do as much as possible to prevent any incidents during the Pope's visit. But they didn't actually threaten people or go to people's houses to tell them not to demonstrate. They were confident that nothing would happen.

Indonesia hoped the Pope's visit would lead to the Vatican's recognition of the integration of East Timor into Indonesia. As a result, there were conflicts between the Indonesian church and the East Timorese church over the visit.[4] The Catholic Church in East Timor wanted to make sure that the Pope's trip was not a political trip, but merely an apostolic one; it didn't even want to fly the *merah putih* in Tacitolo, the site of the Pope's mass. It wanted to fly only the Vatican flag as a symbol of neutrality. Some priests and nuns didn't even want the Pope to visit East Timor because they thought his visit would legitimize Indonesia's illegal annexation. Most people, though, didn't think about the possibility that the Pope's visit would lend legitimacy to the Indonesian occupation. Not even my parents thought about that. The debate about the political implications of the Pope's visit wasn't public; it remained primarily within the Church.

Thousands of Indonesian soldiers were present in Dili in the days leading up to the Pope's visit in early October 1989. On every corner there was an Indonesian soldier. Sometimes soldiers just entered people's houses without permission and spent the night. In many instances, soldiers camped out on the verandas of people's houses. They did this in the towns and suburbs of Dili, Aileu, and Ermera.

On the day of the Pope's mass, October 12, 1989, the military blocked off the whole area of Tacitolo. Tacitolo has only two entrances, from the west and from the east, so it was easy for the Indonesians to control access. As people entered the area, soldiers searched their bags. We were not even allowed to bring in a bottle of water. The soldiers didn't allow any bottles or sticks either. I went to the mass as the leader of the Catholic scouts of the Balide church, accompanied by 400 scouts for whom I was responsible. Despite the security, members of the underground who were also members of the

Catholic scouts were successful in bringing banners into the area. The banners said, "Welcome John Paul II," "Long Live East Timor," "Free East Timor," and "Indonesia, Get Out."

When we entered the area where the Pope's mass was going to take place, I was frightened because I was the one dealing with the military about the positioning of the Catholic scouts. We were supposed to be in the front, close to the altar. However, the military wanted to put us behind the crowd and put the Indonesian scouts, Pramuka, in front. When we arrived, the Indonesian commander told me that we had to go to the back of the crowd.

I told him that we had the right to stay in front of the altar to help the priests and the nuns as we usually did during mass. "No, we already have Indonesian scouts there," he said, "so you have to go stay behind the crowd." I continued to insist otherwise, but then he threatened me. "If you don't put the Catholic scouts behind the crowd," the commander said to me, "I will put them there myself." The situation was tense. Immediately I changed my strategy.

I decided to play with time because the Pope was about to arrive. If we had been in the front the half hour before the mass, the military could have moved us behind the crowd. But if we occupied the front at the last minute, as the Pope was arriving, the military would not have time to move us. I advised all the scout chiefs about the plan. As the Pope arrived at the main entrance of Tacitolo, all the Catholic scouts moved up toward the front row. It wasn't difficult to walk to the front because people knew who we were. We had uniforms, so every time we tried to move somewhere, people would say, "Please go ahead." Immediately we went to the front, close to the altar, where there was plenty of room. I told everyone, "Stay there and keep quiet. Don't move."

There was a huge crowd of people at the mass. It almost seemed as if all of East Timor were there.[5] Actually, however, there would have been many more people in attendance if there had been sufficient transportation and if the Indonesian military had not restricted movement in the days leading up to the mass; outside of Dili, it was extremely difficult to get to Tacitolo if you weren't part of a group organized by the Church or the Indonesian government. Unfortunately, the Church wasn't successful in preventing Indonesia from decorating the whole area of Tacitolo with Indonesian flags and images of Suharto. Suharto's picture was to the right of the altar and the Pope's was to the left. Even though everyone was excited to see Pope John Paul II, the mass was long and it was very hot. There was no water for people, so a lot of people fainted during the mass.

Our plan for the demonstration was to wait until the end of the mass. Everyone was concentrating on the Pope as he began to give his final blessing. Even the intelligence agents were paying attention to the Pope. I was near the altar, near the front of the crowd, 10 to 20 yards from the Pope. When the Pope gave his final blessing, a bunch of young men who were with me took off their Catholic scout uniforms, ran to the front of the altar, and began shouting, "Long live the Pope!" and "Long live free East Timor!" They opened three or four banners. The demonstration happened very suddenly. There was not enough time for the intelligence agents to react and stop the demonstration once it began. People in the choir who were singing *Cristus Vencit* continued to sing, but some of them simultaneously shouted out slogans. Other people in the crowd began shouting slogans as well, including myself; others ran away. People thought that there would be violence and so everyone tried to escape. Things became crazy. Intelligence agents and people in the crowd began throwing chairs at each other. I was in the middle of the crowd searching for other Catholic scouts to make sure that they were okay. The Indonesian military immediately grabbed the Pope and took him away. The Pope didn't say anything; he didn't have time.

The demonstrators stopped after just a few minutes because the Pope left immediately. The demonstrators tried to escape into the crowd. Everyone was running away. The intelligence agents couldn't tell which people had been demonstrating. How could you stop hundreds of people running in the same direction? The Indonesians would have had to kill them all. A few others escaped immediately to the site where all the Catholic scouts were camping; it was in Comoro, near the airport, about a half mile east of Tacitolo.

Since it was the first time that we had demonstrated, people were afraid; most didn't have the courage to participate. We thought that when we took this action, everyone would participate in the demonstration. But when it happened, only a few hundred people, just a small group in the center of the crowd, largely individuals from the Catholic scouts and from various underground organizations, took part. The people in the periphery, for the most part, were afraid and ran away. It was a chaotic situation. The army, it seems, lost control. What happened was a big embarrassment for them. Thousands of soldiers were there, not in uniform, but dressed as civilians and carrying pistols and walkie-talkies. But they couldn't do anything. What could they do?

All of us in Orgão Oito were very happy about the demonstration because we accomplished our goal of embarrassing the Indonesian government and letting the international media know that people in East Timor rejected Indonesia's occupation. It opened the eyes not only of the international community, but also of the East Timorese. The demonstration greatly excited people in East Timor and encouraged them to participate in the underground movement.

After the demonstration, we immediately went to our camp. Donaciano never even returned to the camp; he immediately went home. When we returned we made sure that everyone quickly went inside their tents, especially those who took part in the demonstration. Soon the military came to our area and walked around the camp. They already suspected us of being involved in the demonstration. At the same time, Indonesians in civilian dress, probably intelligence agents, came to the tent area and asked about the people there, just pretending that they were visiting the camp. One of them asked specifically for José Manuel; fortunately, he was hiding in a tent. That night I sent José Manuel into hiding. The next day we left the camp and returned to our houses. I told all the Catholic scouts to be alert in case anything happened to any of us.

Indonesian intelligence immediately began looking all over the city for José Manuel and other participants in the demonstration who had been identified. After a few days, José Manuel felt insecure in his hiding place so he decided to seek refuge at Bishop Carlos Ximenes Belo's house in the Licidere section of Dili; a number of other demonstrators also sought refuge there. Bishop Belo had been the head of the Catholic Church of East Timor since 1983. Later on we heard rumors that the military was also looking for Donaciano and me. I told Donaciano to be alert and to keep as low a profile as possible until the situation calmed down. Donaciano, however, was very curious and he visited José Manuel at the bishop's house several times during the day. I told him not to go there very often because he would end up being captured by Indonesian intelligence, but he didn't listen and one day he almost ended up getting arrested by the Indonesian army at his home. Luckily he wasn't there when they came. After this close call, he had to join José Manuel in hiding at the bishop's house.

José Manuel, Donaciano, and the others agreed to leave the bishop's residence after a couple of weeks when the military promised Bishop Belo that the demonstrators would not be harmed. "You can take them to the police and interrogate them," the Bishop said, "but don't do anything to them. You have to promise not to torture them." The army, of course, tortured them in jail and for several days did not allow Bishop Belo to visit them. Fortunately Bishop Belo intervened to save the lives of Donaciano and José Manuel. Even though he had allowed the Indonesians to arrest the young people hiding at his residence, the army was still very angry with him, as he represented a strong challenge to the military. As a result, an East Timorese family, well known as Indonesian collaborators, gave Bishop Belo a cake as a gift in December. Fearing that the cake might contain poison, Bishop Belo gave some of the cake to his dog. The dog immediately died.

When the Indonesians arrested Donaciano and José Manuel in November 1989, I was really afraid that they were going to come after me because I knew through people who worked close to the police and the army that the Indonesian military suspected me. The Indonesians asked Donaciano and José Manuel a lot of questions about me and my activities at Externato. I had asked them while they were hiding in the bishop's house to be courageous if they were arrested and to tell the army that they were the only people who were in charge of the underground. This was the strategy we used to save other activists and to continue our underground activities. In our group we had already promised to each other to be responsible, in whatever situation, for our own actions. Fortunately, for me and the others in the organization, José Manuel and Donaciano had the strength to accept complete responsibility for the demonstration at Tacitolo and completely denied having knowledge of any political activities on my part.

When the military finally released Donaciano and José Manuel in late February 1990, it was clear that they had been tortured badly. According to Donaciano and José Manuel, two or three soldiers often hit them, kicked them with their boots, and beat their heads with rifle butts and pistols. Then the Indonesians applied electric shocks to their backs, their ankles, and their toes. They did this many times. Donanciano and José Manuel also told me that some soldiers applied electric shocks to their tongues, mouths, and ears. Sometimes the Indonesian soldiers would make them sit in a special chair that was electrified. They would put the person in the chair and plug it in for five or 10 seconds. Sometimes the person would be thrown from the chair by the force of the shock.[6] The Indonesians never put Donaciano and José Manuel on trial. But after their release, José Manuel and Donaciano had to promise not to do anything to undermine the Indonesian government and to report each week to the army.

After the Pope John Paul II demonstration, David Alex sent Orgão Oito a letter telling us that he wanted to meet the founders of 007. Unfortunately, Donaciano and José Manuel couldn't go because they were in prison. So I went to meet David Alex in Baucau with the other founding members—Kiak, Lucas, Tetun, and Abut. We left Dili for Baucau on the morning of December 31, 1989, and arrived in the afternoon. We followed the instructions from our two guides, who were responsible for setting up the meeting. That evening, we left the town of Baucau and went to a meeting point far away, up in the mountains, about a three-hour walk. It was not a resistance center, but an area that was sometimes controlled by the Indonesian military. The resistance doesn't have any headquarters; it moves around all the time.

When we went to the meeting place, we were scared. No one said anything on the way. We went to a riverbank and sat there and waited. We tried to sit apart just to avoid talking to each other and also so some of us would have a chance to escape if any Indonesian soldiers attacked us. We waited for two hours and then David Alex came, along with 30 fighters. The guerrillas immediately put security around the area while we met with David Alex and six other FALIN-TIL members.

When David Alex arrived, he was looking for me. "Where is Terus? I want to see him." Terus, which means "suffering" in Tetum, was my *nom de guerre*. I chose the name as a reminder of the daily suffering of the East Timorese people.

I was really happy to finally meet David Alex. We embraced, of course. But it was very sad to see the guerrilla fighters living in the jungle, facing so many difficulties. Most of them looked very, very thin. Only a few looked strong. Many appeared to be suffering from malnutrition; but all of them were very high spirited and were determined to continue to fight.

David Alex was really happy about the demonstration at the Pope's mass, its effects within East Timor, and its impact internationally. We discussed the tactics and strategy of the underground, the mechanisms of the organization, and how to maintain and improve our communications with FALINTIL and abroad. We focused on the upcoming visit to Dili of John Monjo, who was the U.S. ambassador to Indonesia. We had a contact in the governor's office who worked with the underground; all the news about visitors who come to East Timor passes through the governor's office, so we always knew in advance when important guests were coming. David Alex suggested that we have a demonstration if possible during Monjo's visit, though he had reservations. He asked me not to involve myself publicly; I could discuss and plan the demonstration with the others, but I could not participate in the actual demonstration. We also discussed how the clandestine front could better support the guerrillas. The military had launched a big operation in late 1989, and FALINTIL was under intense daily pursuit by the military as a result.

After our discussions, the whole group had a party. It was New Year's Eve. We ate deer meat that the guerrillas brought us. The meat was really good. We also drank sweet wine and ate cake that we brought from Dili. We ate, drank, and talked until three in the morning.

It was still dark when we ended the meeting. After embracing and wishing each other good luck, we separated. We then moved to another place and tried to nap. One hour later, we set out for Baucau. On our way home, we walked slowly and took our time. We passed by Indonesian military posts along the road, but no one asked us anything. At that time, people could visit their families in Baucau because of the holiday. As we approached Baucau, people were outside celebrating the New Year. People were still dancing. We began to talk with East Timorese people, pretending that we were coming from a New Year's Eve party.

As we were leaving our meeting with David Alex and the FALINTIL fighters, they had told us that they were planning an action in the next few days in Baucau, and that if we were going to Baucau, we should leave right away. So when we arrived in Baucau the next morning, we immediately caught the bus and returned to Dili. Two days later, David Alex and his comrades attacked the Indonesian military headquarters on the outskirts of Baucau, in the new part of the town. Unfortunately, the guerrillas killed a Javanese student who was selling coffee and milk. The young man shouted out "FRETILIN! FRETILIN!" when the fighters asked for milk and coffee to drink. They didn't want to kill him, but they had to. The objective of the attack was to get armaments from the Indonesian army headquarters and food from certain shops. The guerrillas stayed in Baucau for only a few hours and then retreated into the jungle. The news of that attack reached Dili the same day.

When we arrived back in Dili, we began planning for the visit of U.S. Ambassador Monjo. We contacted other groups, especially the youth groups and students in Dili, encouraging them to take part in the demonstration. We prepared banners and a letter to deliver to John Monjo. We wanted him to hear the voices and see the faces of some of the victims of the United States' complicity with the Indonesian invasion and occupation.

The morning Ambassador Monjo arrived in Dili, January 17, 1990, I went to the hills on the outskirts of Dili to participate in a forestation program that was sponsored by the Indonesian army. Every student was asked to go there. At that time, I was working at Externato as a religion teacher. It was the first time Externato de São José students had participated in a government activity. Under increasing pressure and threats from the Indonesian military, Father Leão, the director of the school, decided that Externato should begin to participate in such activities; it was probably a tactic on Father Leão's part to reduce pressure from the military. So a group of us from Externato went to the forestation program. By doing so, we also hoped to avoid raising any suspicions that we would hold protests during Monjo's visit. We finished with our work at noon, and many of the young people who participated in the forestation program ran to the Turismo Hotel, where Monjo was staying, to join the demonstration.

The demonstrators were hiding near Bishop Belo's house, which is very close to the Turismo. A little after noon, the demonstrators jumped over the wall of the bishop's house and immediately ran to the hotel to try to meet with Ambassador Monjo. About 80 or 90 students occupied the entrance and forced Monjo to come out of the hotel. Many of them covered their faces with T-shirts or scarves. Not everyone, however, masked their faces. Members of Orgão Oito and other underground groups participated. We had prepared a petition to read in front of Monjo, and two young women were supposed to offer a present to him. The purpose of the demonstration was to occupy the Turismo Hotel and block the exit until Ambassador Monjo said something to secure the safety of the demonstrators.

Immediately, the police came and surrounded the demonstrators. But the demonstrators had the opportunity to present flowers to Monjo and talk to him. They asked him for the U.S. government to support the resistance's proposal for negotiations in East Timor, the withdrawal of the Indonesian military from the country, and the holding of a referendum on self-determination in East Timor. We wanted the United States to put pressure on Indonesia to withdraw its military from East Timor because we knew that if the United States could give Indonesia the green light for the invasion of East Timor, it could give the red light to Indonesia's occupation.

The East Timorese people closely follow what's happening in the international arena. They always hope that wealthy and powerful countries such as the United States, Britain, Australia, France, Germany, and Japan will change their policies toward Indonesia and begin to support East Timor's right to self-determination. Because of that, any time East Timorese young people meet a foreigner in East Timor, they ask the person to tell Alexander Downey, the Australian foreign minister, or Bill Clinton to stop sending military and economic aid to the Suharto regime. We know that the wealthy industrialized countries are legally committed to the protection of human rights according to the United Nations Charter. As the war and genocide went on in East Timor and these countries continued to support Indonesia with military, economic, and diplomatic assistance, however, it became very clear to us that they do not uphold the principles of the United Nations. These countries place their economic interests above fundamental human rights. The Gulf War clearly showed us that. The United States would not have taken action against Saddam Hussein unless it had economic interests in Kuwait. The United States and its allies took action against Iraq because of Kuwait's oil reserves. If Kuwait had not had oil, the United States probably would not have even thought about the issue.

After receiving the flowers and listening to our petition, the ambassador assured the demonstrators that nothing would happen to them. Monjo asked for guarantees from the Indonesian officials present that they would not persecute the demonstrators and would allow them to go home in peace. Of course, he didn't say anything about self-determination. The United States still has never said anything about self-determination.[7] But after Monjo left the Turismo Hotel, the military and the police rounded up the demonstrators and beat them black and blue. The demonstrators joined together and embraced each other as the Indonesians struck their bodies with whips and rifle butts and kicked them with boots. Some of the demonstrators escaped by jumping over the fence and going into the bishop's house or by hiding in nearby houses. There were rumors that we weren't able to confirm that the Indonesians even shot one of the demonstrators as he was trying to escape; reportedly, he and one other protestor died as a result of their injuries.

Some of those who fled ran past an Indonesian air force base located behind the Turismo. When the demonstrators ran toward the base, some members of the Indonesian air force told the demonstrators to run as fast as possible to escape. Even some members of the Indonesian armed forces are not happy with what their government is doing in East Timor. It will take more time for them to speak out, but I think it will happen one day.[8]

I went home after working in the forestation program because David Alex had prohibited me from participating in the protest. I met later that afternoon with some young people from the underground who had participated in the demonstration to find out what had happened at the Turismo. Some of their shirts and pants were ripped from when they climbed the fence around the hotel to escape. They said that many people were beaten, including one of the members of Orgão Oito, Augusto Mausere. He was the one who held the megaphone and spoke to John Monjo. Agostinho, another person at the Turismo, hid in a house of someone he didn't know when he fled from the demonstration, and an Indonesian woman there immediately called the police. The police arrested him and then beat him until his head and face were swollen like a basketball. The Indonesians arrested many of the demonstrators afterward and sent them to prison, where they were tortured. Other demonstrators are still being hunted today. They are still in hiding, afraid of persecution by the military.[9]

The demonstrations during the visits of Pope John Paul II and U.S. Ambassador Monjo were part of a whole series of anti-integration events that took place beginning in the late 1980s. Some people outside the country called it the East Timorese *intifada*. I didn't involve myself publicly in these events; my role was always secret.

Some of the more important events during this period were the raisings of the FRETILIN flag at the Santa Cruz cemetery, in Becora, in the suburbs of Dili, and many other places in East Timor. Sometimes the resistance printed flyers and posted them clandestinely in prominent places in Dili. There was graffiti written on the walls, often in Portuguese: "Integration, No!"; "Get out of here, Indonesia!"; "Viva FRETILIN!"; and "Long Live East Timor!" Sometimes the propaganda was in Indonesian. Other times FRETILIN would write something and we would photocopy it and disseminate it to other people in the underground movement. Because Indonesian intelligence monitored the use of photocopiers, we would only make five or six copies at a time and then distribute them to other people who would make more. The easiest way to disseminate messages at that time was with a tape recorder. We could duplicate the cassette at home in whatever quantity we wanted. It wasn't as risky. We would pass the tape around. Then people would make copies by themselves.

There were many groups in the underground movement, independent of Orgão Oito. These organizations would sometimes take independent actions. On December 31, 1988, for example, someone from an underground organization blew up the Indonesian military arsenal in Taibesse, Dili. I was at a midnight mass at the Balide Church when it happened. The explosion was enormous.

There were also spontaneous actions taken by individuals outside of the underground movement who were unhappy with Indonesia and wanted to do something to express their anger. One of the most well-known examples was when a number of young children started to ask Indonesian people when they were going back to Indonesia. "*Kapan pulang?*" they would say. ("When are you going home?")

There is an interesting story about the origins of this campaign. One day in 1989, before the Pope visited East Timor, two kids who were both eight years old went to a public telephone booth on the street. Because the telephone was high, they couldn't reach it. One sat down and the other one stepped on his shoulders and called the police and asked, "*Kapan pulang?*" The police station knew immediately where the call was coming from. One of the police officers tried to fool the kids and prevent them from hanging up. Meanwhile two police trucks were dispatched to arrest them. When the police arrived, one of the two kids escaped. They took the other one into the police station and interrogated him. "Who told you to do this?" they demanded. "Did your parents to tell you to do this?"

"No," the kid said. "No one told me to do this."

"And who else do you know?" the police asked.

"Well, I have my friend," he answered. The police thought that this friend was an older person. They escorted the kid to his village; it was in Bidau, near the center of Dili. They made the kid lead them to his friend's house. "Here's my other friend," he said. So they arrested the other kid and took him to the police station. And after several hours of interrogation, they both said they just thought of doing it themselves. The Indonesians eventually released them. People say this is how the "*Kapan pulang?*" campaign began.

7

Founding the Executive Committee

In June 1990, a few months after the Monjo demonstration, Mau Hudo, the vice chairperson of FRETILIN at that time, requested a meeting with Orgão Oito. Our earlier contacts with him had been restricted to messages sent by tape cassettes and letters. Mau Hudo, whose real name is José da Costa, wanted to consolidate FRETILIN activities in the underground movement. FRETILIN dealt with political matters in the jungle and the towns, while FALINTIL dealt with military matters.

When we arrived at the agreed upon location in the Baucau area, Mau Hudo was already there with 30 guerrilla fighters. FALINTIL was able to operate within the area in spite of the fact that we almost walked into an Indonesian post on the way to the meeting. That night, the guerrilla fighters made a fire and cooked where we met. Even though I trusted the judgment of the guerrillas, I was really scared because people could see the fire very easily. If something happened to us, then we would have had to join the guerrillas. There would have been no way to go back to the city.

Mau Hudo was well dressed, like a leader in the jungle. I really admired his courage as a fighter and his sharp mind as a political theorist and strategist. Mau Hudo was a very quick thinker. I will never forget one thing that he said. At one point, Mau Hudo wanted to smoke. We had brought some cigarettes with us and I had Indonesian matches with me. I gave him my matches. The first strike didn't produce fire. I remarked sarcastically that it was because the matches were from Indonesia. Mau Hudo immediately replied to me, "We are fighting against the Indonesian government not against materials." I was impressed with that answer.

We talked with Mau Hudo from 10 at night until two in the morning. We discussed the guerrillas' strategy, how to develop and expand our activities in the underground movement, improve our network, educate people politically, and fight for the right of self-determination and independence. Everyone has to fight for this principle; independence is the final goal for every FRETILIN member and almost every East Timorese.

Mau Hudo put a lot of hope in young people. He urged us to hold demonstrations in Dili and other cities whenever foreign dignitaries or journalists were visiting, and he encouraged people to write letters to people outside of East Timor, as well as to send information to the resistance. He encouraged people to support the resistance army with material aid, and he urged us to continue our efforts to bring together more groups in the underground movement.

At the end of the meeting, Mau Hudo proposed the creation of a FRETILIN executive committee of the underground movement in the towns, specifically in Dili, based on the second national conference of the National Council of Maubere Resistance (CNRM) that took place in Aitana on May 28, 1990. The CNRM is a nonpartisan umbrella organization that incorporates all the factions of the resistance in the struggle for liberation within East Timor. In September 1989, Xanana had left FRETILIN, separated FALINTIL from FRETILIN, and founded the CNRM. Xanana made the decision with the consent of FRETILIN members within East Timor. As a result, FALINTIL no longer was under the control of FRETILIN, but under the direction of the CNRM led by Xanana Gusmão. The CNRM did not replace FRETILIN. FRETILIN became part of the CNRM, as did the UDT within East Timor.[1] This action helped create greater unity in the resistance because there were many in FALINTIL and in the underground who were not FRETILIN members. By creating the nonpartisan CNRM, Xanana eliminated the impression that the resistance was fighting only for the interest of one political party.

Given the state of war we existed in, it was impossible to have any sort of public consultation about the reorganization. But I know, through my personal contacts, that the vast majority of the population accepted and agreed with the changes. There were increasing numbers of young people who had never been part of any political party, such as FRETILIN, and who grew up during the war. If people didn't want to be part of FRETILIN, they should be free to make that choice. We had to put the national interest over the interest of a political party. We have to be open to everyone's ideas, and the CNRM provided the necessary space. That's why people accepted the CNRM as the legitimate organization incorporating all of the groups or organizations or political parties in the struggle for the liberation of East Timor.

After the CNRM was founded, Xanana sent a message to the underground movement explaining the changes. We then circulated the message throughout the entire territory. Everyone knew that Xanana had left FRETILIN and founded the CNRM. While there were some people who questioned Xanana's action, many people were excited to see such political changes. Some people even compared Xanana's changes with Gorbachev's *perestroika*.

Given these changes, a FRETILIN executive committee didn't really make sense at that point in time. So I decided unilaterally to make this new executive committee part of the CNRM in a direct sense, rather than part of FRETILIN. I convinced the other Orgão Oito leaders to support my idea. Because there were more and more UDT and APODETI members and their children involved in the underground, it would have been very divisive within the underground if we had made the executive committee part of FRETILIN; by making it directly part of the CNRM, the executive committee would be seen as nonpartisan. We set up the executive committee to monitor, coordinate, and supervise activities in the underground movement. Before the executive committee was founded, there were already many groups active in the underground movement, including Orgão Oito, especially in Dili, Baucau, and Lospalos. We wanted to make links be-

tween the underground groups, to try to make a more solid organization, and to take concrete actions, such as demonstrations, in the
towns. Demonstrations were the main objective of the committee.

One night in July 1990, several leaders of various underground
groups throughout the country gathered in Dili to form the Executive
Committee of the CNRM in the Clandestine Front and to elect its
leadership. We met at Externato de São José at midnight. We positioned people far from the building as guards. Because of security
concerns, the longest we could meet for was one hour. We didn't
want to spend a lot of time discussing problems without any solu-
tions. In the struggle, we have to think about situations concretely
and to determine our strategies and tactics quickly. Theory is good,
but sometimes it's overemphasized. People who exaggerate the importance of theory generally end up doing nothing.

About 10 people were present at the meeting. Those who couldn't
come sent their votes on pieces of paper, mentioning who they
wanted to choose as the secretary and two vice secretaries. The vote
was limited to those in charge of the groups, the *responsázeis*. The
group elected me as the secretary of the executive committee and
Donaciano Gomes and José Manuel as vice secretaries. It was a complete surprise, especially since I was only 27. Many of the other people there had more experience than I did in the jungle and during the
whole process of the struggle. I think I was elected because I gained
people's trust during my previous activities with the resistance, and I
was able to communicate with people from the English-speaking
world. I already had links with Amnesty International, José Ramos
Horta and the diplomatic front, FALINTIL and FRETILIN leaders in
the mountains, and clandestine organizations in Jakarta such as
RENETIL. The executive committee put a big responsibility on my
shoulders as the leader of the underground movement, not just for
Dili but for the whole country. But there was no way for me to refuse
the position.

After the election we informed David Alex of the results of the
election and asked him to report it to Xanana Gusmão and other resistance leaders. At this time José Manuel, Donaciano, and I began to
think about who would be responsible for the various tasks. We also

began thinking about some of the concrete actions we wanted to undertake, such as continuing with peaceful demonstrations, supporting the armed resistance, and sending information to organizations such as the United Nations, Amnesty International, TAPOL, and the CDPM[2] through the clandestine organizations for East Timorese students in Indonesia, RENETIL, and FECLETIL.[3]

All underground groups now operated under the supervision of the executive committee. The executive committee thus supervised all the Orgão Oito groups, as well as all the others that existed independently from it. The executive committee coordinated political activities after getting instructions from Xanana Gusmão. We also coordinated the underground activities with Mau Hudo, Mau Hunu, David Alex, and other commanders, but always with the knowledge of Xanana.

There were many tasks for the underground movement that the secretary and vice secretaries couldn't undertake, so we distributed tasks among the members and the heads of the various groups. Members of the executive committee were given special tasks, such as dealing with propaganda, medical care, channels of contact in and out of East Timor, women's organizations, military affairs, economic affairs, and transportation. I was in charge of dealing with foreign visitors to East Timor, as well as sending information abroad to places such as Australia and Portugal through Fernando de Araujo, the head of RENETIL in Jakarta. Some of the RENETIL members were also part of the executive committee at that time.

The executive committee didn't waste any time in organizing. On September 4, 1990, there was a mass for the 50th anniversary of the Dili diocese after which we held a big pro-independence demonstration. Before organizing the demonstration, we consulted with David Alex. We were not able to get responses from Xanana and Mau Hudo because the Indonesian army had a major operation in the jungle at that time.

The mass took place in Licidere, the neighborhood in Dili where Bishop Belo lives. Whoever goes to Dili will see a park with a big statue of the Virgin Mary near the bishop's residence. That's where the mass took place and where we usually celebrate holy days and other important days related to the Catholic Church. Because the anniversary was such an important day, all the priests from the mountains went to Dili to celebrate with Bishop Belo. The Papal Nuncio in Jakarta, Archbishop Canaline, was the special guest. More than 5,000 people gathered for the celebration. After the mass, the demonstrators went up to the altar and shouted out to Archbishop Canaline about holding a referendum in East Timor and chanted many pro-independence and anti-Indonesia slogans. The environment at that demonstration was not one of fear and panic, as it was during the Pope's visit. It was incredible; it seemed as if everyone was participating. People unfurled banners and even the FRETILIN flag. Most people were very courageous and stayed until the demonstration ended. Many soldiers and almost all the commanders from the police and the military were there, but they didn't dare do anything because of the presence of church dignitaries. I was there in an official capacity as the head of the Catholic scouts. Various underground groups in Dili organized the demonstration under the leadership of the executive committee. The demonstration didn't have any impact internationally because there was no foreign media coverage, but it had a very positive impact within East Timor. People from all over the country were present. So when people went back to their homes, they were confident that the struggle in the underground movement in the towns was growing.

I didn't openly participate in the demonstration because I was working on another plan at that time—the visit to East Timor of the Australian lawyer and journalist Robert Domm. The main purpose of his visit was to meet with Xanana Gusmão and the guerrilla fighters. At that time Australia was supposed to send a television crew to East Timor and Robert Domm was going to be one of the members. The team suspended its visit because of rumors of the killing of two journalists in Ainaro, but the news was not true. Instead of the team, they sent only Robert Domm.

Robert Domm's visit was the result of the cooperation between the executive committee and RENETIL, especially Fernando de Araujo and Domingos Sarmento. Domingos was the person in RENETIL who had direct contact with Robert Domm and José Ramos Horta, whom Xanana had appointed as the special representative of the CNRM outside of East Timor. The CNRM had three wings: FALIN-TIL, with Xanana as commander in chief; the diplomatic front, led by Ramos Horta; and the clandestine front, which I led as the secretary of the executive committee. Xanana was the head of the CNRM overall.

After Domingos heard from Ramos Horta, he told me to set up the meeting with Xanana Gusmão. I wrote to Xanana informing him about the plan and asked him if he wanted to meet. The response from Xanana was positive, so I began to coordinate the logistics of the trip with other members of the executive committee. Xanana instructed his contacts in Ainaro to prepare as well. While preparing the trip, I was in frequent contact with Domingos Sarmento and Fernando de Araujo. From Surabaya, Domingos contacted José Ramos Horta in Australia.

The trip was very risky. It was going to be difficult to take Robert Domm to Ainaro where Xanana was hiding. Robert Domm was a courageous man. He flew to Surabaya and joined up with Domingos Sarmento. From Surabaya, the two of them flew to Denpasar, Bali, and from Denpasar to Dili, East Timor. Robert entered Dili as a tourist, which was legal by that time. When he left Australia for Indonesia, I began to organize the people who would accompany him to meet Xanana. I was able to find good and very courageous people in Dili. There were 10 people, including myself, Domingos Sarmento, and others whose names I cannot mention, involved in the preparation of the meeting.

At the time of Robert's visit, I was working at the diocese of Dili, the administrative center of the Catholic Church, so when he and Domingos Sarmento arrived in Dili, Domingos came to my office and said, "*Companheiro*, brother, we have arrived from Jakarta." That was the first time I met Domingos Sarmento, but he already knew how to make contact with me. I asked him to be patient because we needed time to prepare.

Domingos came to my office alone, but he returned the next day with Robert Domm. Robert seemed very anxious; he wanted to go right away to meet with Xanana. I told him that we would go soon but that we still had to make preparations. I told him to give me two days. The next day I borrowed a motorcycle from one of my colleagues and went to Ainaro. Mau Mean (his *nom de guerre*), a friend who was part of the underground, accompanied me; he was a former guerrilla fighter who worked as a civilian intelligence agent in Dili for Kopassandha, an elite unit of the Indonesian army. Mau Mean went with me as my bodyguard, just in case there were any problems along the way, because he had a card identifying himself as intelligence.

Unfortunately, three or four miles before we arrived in Ainaro, we got a flat tire, so we had to push the motorcycle. Fortunately, we soon saw a truck traveling from Aileu to Ainaro. We stopped the truck and paid 4,500 *rupiah* to the driver to carry us and the motorcycle to Ainaro. When we got to the town we went to the local Kopassandha headquarters. They had a little place to fix the flat tire; it was the only such place in town. When we asked for help with our flat tire, an Indonesian said, "No problem. We are here to help," and fixed the flat.

"Where are you coming from?" he asked us.

"From Dili," I told him. "My grandfather died last night and we have come to tell our family here to go to Dili today or tomorrow to attend his funeral."

"Oh, I'm so sorry," he offered. He didn't know our real purpose. After he repaired the tire, we went to see our contact.

Our contact in Ainaro, Mariano, another former FALINTIL fighter, was also working as an intelligence agent for Kopassandha. Mariano told us that everything was set up for Robert Domm's arrival. After that, we returned to Dili.

In the morning, Domingos came to me to find out the news. I told him that I wanted to meet with Robert Domm in the afternoon in my office at the diocese of Dili. "We are leaving tomorrow," I told Robert when I saw him. "It's far away and you have to wear green and black clothes. You have to bring all your clothes and whatever materials you have with you. Someone will pick you up in front of the New Resende Hotel." In this way the Resende would think that he had gone somewhere, like Baucau, for sightseeing. I then gave Robert the license number and a description of the cab that would pick him up.

At five in the morning, my friend Mateus Pereira went to the hotel with a taxi and another member of the underground. Robert Domm followed our instructions. He was waiting for the taxi in front of the hotel when Mateus arrived. He pretended to flag down the taxi. Root, one of my colleagues, was hiding in the taxi, crouched down in the front seat on the passenger's side; it appeared to be just Mateus alone. He stopped the taxi as we had planned and opened the door by himself. Root continued to hide. Robert sat in the backseat. After 10 or 15 minutes, Root sat up in the front seat. Robert Domm, perhaps because he had forgotten the plan, was frightened and thought perhaps that he was in the wrong taxi.

Robert didn't talk to them because the taxi driver and the other person didn't speak English. He just kept silent. They took him right away up to the mountain of Marabia, not far from Dili. Domingos and I and two other friends drove separately in another car. When we arrived in Marabia, Mateus stopped the taxi in front of us, and Robert Domm and Root moved into our car. Robert became confident and more relaxed once he saw us. We arrived in Remexio at about seven in the morning. We stopped to receive proper blessings from our ancestors. One of my comrades, Leo, made a cross on each of our foreheads with saliva mixed with traditional medicine. Leo was older than the rest of us. He was sort of a healer and someone who was able to receive power from the spirits of our ancestors. Everyone, including Robert Domm, received a sign of the cross on his forehead. Leo said that it would protect us from bullets and make us invisible. I think Robert Domm was bewildered, wondering what my friend was doing. As for me, I was willing to try anything that might help us. After that, we continued our trip to Aileu. On the way, we stopped every now and then. If we hurried, we would have reached Ainaro too early and we wanted to be on time.

Our driver was Chinese Timorese. He had been working for the resistance for a long time, especially in our group. At that time, he was about 32 years old. There are a few ethnic Chinese who work for the resistance. The Chinese in Indonesia are seen by many Indonesians in a negative light. The Indonesian army doesn't like them very much in East Timor either. The Indonesians killed many Chinese Ti-

morese during the invasion of East Timor,[4] so the Chinese are sometimes very careful about working with the resistance. Those who
work with the resistance are really determined to struggle for the
cause of East Timor.

There were military checkpoints along the road as we drove. In
Aileu, we passed a police checkpoint. Luckily, most of the police were
participating in a flag ceremony. For some reason, the two remaining
police officials just waved us on. If the police had stopped us, our
plan was to say that Robert Domm was going to Suai as a tourist and
that we were taking him. But if the Indonesian army didn't believe us
and tried to arrest us, we planned to take violent action against them.
Under such circumstances, we knew that we would not survive at the
hands of the Indonesian soldiers. If the Indonesians did not kill us
right away, they would have tortured us to death.

When we entered the district of Ainaro, there were a few people
who already knew that Robert Domm was coming. As we passed
along one of the streets, there were some young boys playing who
told us to go ahead. When we arrived in a place close to a town, we
stopped for a while and asked some local people for water to drink.
We also brought some bananas for Robert Domm. It was 4:30 in the
afternoon and everyone was hungry and thirsty.

Before we reached to the point where we were to leave the car, we
saw Mariano along the side of the road. As we had planned, we
stopped and Mariano got into the car; he was wearing an Indonesian
uniform. Mariano's involvement in setting up the meeting was very
important because without him we wouldn't have known the situation of the Indonesian army in Ainaro. He was also the person who
had connections to Xanana Gusmão and local guerrilla fighters.

When Mariano got into the car, Robert Domm seemed afraid and
immediately asked me who he was. I told him that he was our comrade, and not to worry. We continued with the trip until we reached
the place on the outskirts of Ainaro where we had to stop. Everyone
took off. Domingos, Robert Domm, Root, and I got out of the car and
immediately ran. It was only about 50 yards from the road to the jungle.

There were seven of us, including Robert Domm, who came from Dili. Three of us accompanied Robert Domm to meet Xanana and the guerrilla fighters in the jungle, and the other three went back to Ainaro and waited for us to return the next day.

We didn't know Xanana's exact whereabouts. All of us just followed the instructions of our friends from Ainaro. There were about 10 houses near the place where we were dropped off. When we arrived the people came out of their houses to find out what was going on, but they never said anything. They probably were a bit shocked by the sight of a big, white person. Another guide joined us and immediately led us into the jungle. After we walked about 100 yards, we met the guerrilla fighters. They were waiting for us. They saluted us in military style. Robert Domm seemed very impressed with those guerrilla fighters. "These are guerilla fighters?" he asked.

"Yes, they are our guerrilla fighters," I replied. "They are going to accompany us to Xanana's shelter." He was happy. There were about nine guerrilla fighters led by Commander Alex. We went down a mountain until we reached a riverbank. From the riverbank we had to climb a steep mountain to Xanana's camp. Robert Domm was very tired and had a lot of trouble walking up the mountain. The guerrillas had to keep pushing him, practically carrying him up the mountain. He almost couldn't walk. After an hour, Robert Domm was almost out of strength. Just when it seemed that he had no more energy, we reached Xanana's camp. The camp was in a very good location. It was well covered by the dense forest, trees, and bamboo. The location, known as Bunaria, was practically a mountain cliff and was very difficult to climb.

Xanana came out from his tent and greeted us. When Robert Domm saw Xanana Gusmão appear with his green beret and Portuguese camouflage uniform, he immediately recovered his energy and with happiness shouted at Xanana, "Hello, Mr. President."

"No, I'm not the president," Xanana responded in English. "I'm the commander of FALINTIL. Welcome."

Xanana and I shook hands and embraced each other. He seemed quite happy to see everyone. Xanana had insisted that I come. When I got his invitation, I was a little afraid of taking the risk of meeting him. "Don't be afraid," he wrote. "You have to count on me." And that's why I gained the confidence to go with Robert Domm.

Xanana's camp was established just for the meeting. There were around three huts there. Over the years, Xanana had moved from the eastern part of the country, from Lospalos to Baucau, Viqueque, and Same. But I think he had spent a few years in the general area of Ainaro when we met. There were probably more than 50 guerrilla fighters in the immediate vicinity. If there had not been significant support from the local population, FALINTIL could not have been so strong in the area. We gave Robert Domm time to talk to Xanana. After some friendly conversation, he started to interview Xanana. Robert took notes of their conversation and recorded it as well. The interview went from about six at night until one in the morning. After the interview, we all had a very good dinner. The guerrilla fighters served us as if we were in the city. We had bread, rice, meat, and noodles. The food was delicious.

After dinner Robert Domm went to sleep. While he was sleeping, Xanana, Domingos Sarmento, Root, and I continued to talk. We discussed a number of issues, such as the military situation, politics, education, and a new CNRM peace initiative. Xanana seemed to be happy with our work in the towns. Xanana's concern at that time was not only politics but also the military struggle. He really wanted to better arm the FALINTIL guerrilla fighters. We discussed how to get ammunition and weapons from corrupt Indonesian military officials. We also talked about our communications with the resistance and solidarity and human rights groups abroad, and our future strategy.

At around three in the morning, we went to sleep. There were no beds; we slept on the ground. I could only sleep for five or 10 minutes; I was worried that something might happen. During the three years that I lived in the jungle with my family, we usually didn't sleep too much. We used to say that when you sleep, one ear has to be a sentinel. At four in the morning, I could hear the sound of a radio; Xanana was listening to the BBC in Portuguese. Xanana followed the world news through the BBC and many other outlets. At six, Robert Domm was still asleep so I woke him up. When I woke him, he said that he thought he was sleeping in Australia. After we took a bath in a nearby stream, we had a breakfast of bread, coffee, and milk, and Robert continued with the interview. After lunch, Robert Domm gave Xanana some Australian dollars as a present. In return, Xanana gave him a piece of carved sandalwood that had a bullet inside. But Robert couldn't bring the bullet to Australia. I think he just left the gift with Domingos or someone. After that, we took some pictures with the guerrillas, and of Xanana with Robert Domm. Those of us from the underground who accompanied Robert didn't appear in any of the pictures except with our backs facing the camera. I was afraid that if the Indonesians found the pictures I would get in trouble.

We left Xanana's camp to go back to Dili at one in the afternoon. It was so sad to be going back to the city where we had an easier and more comfortable life than they had in the jungle. Xanana instructed nine guerrilla fighters to accompany us. It took about one hour to go down to the river. Again, Robert Domm had a terrible time. He couldn't walk up the steep incline on the other side of the river and people had to help him. I also had difficulties because I was not used to climbing through the mountains.

When we reached our destination, Alex, one of the FALINTIL commanders, gave me a pack of dry deer meat to take to Dili. When we separated, we embraced each other. "Brother," he said to me, "please work hard and continue to fight. We will also continue to fight, but we want to see our families soon." And everyone began crying, including me. We separated. Who could know when we would meet each other again? The car was waiting for us where we got out the day before. We got into the car and continued our trip to Dili.

We later found out that a little after we left that small village, the Indonesian army arrived and asked the local population if our white car was the same one that had appeared the day before. The people told the soldiers that they didn't know, that the car was probably from the International Committee of the Red Cross because there was a red cross on the car door, but that was not true. Luckily, the soldiers did not follow us, probably because they thought we were from the Red Cross. We arrived in Dili around 10 p.m. We dropped Robert off near his hotel; he walked the rest of the way.[5]

The next morning, Robert Domm had to leave for Australia. I went to the airport to help him and Domingos, who was returning to Surabaya with Robert. At the airport there was a problem with Domingos; for some reason, he hadn't booked his return ticket. Soon, Robert Domm arrived. I had already told him to pretend that he didn't know me or Domingos. Domingos noticed that Robert had forgotten to cover the cuts on his arms made by thorns from the trees. Domingos just went close to him and whispered, "Please cover your arms." Robert unrolled his sleeves and covered them.

Domingos was panicked because there were no more seats available on the plane. But I had a friend who worked at the airport and asked him to help me. "My friend has an exam in Surabaya tomorrow; he has to leave today," I said to him. "Can you help him?" Luckily, he could. I didn't have to pretend that I was not with Domingos. Because we are both East Timorese, it wasn't dangerous for us to be seen with each other; neither one of us had ever been arrested at that point in time.

My friend at the airport finally issued a ticket to Domingos; it was one p.m. At 1:30 Domingos and Robert Domm went on the same plane, but they didn't talk to each other until they arrived in Bali. The next day, Robert Domm flew to Australia. After almost 15 years of war, Robert Domm was the first foreigner who was able to come to East Timor and meet with Xanana and the guerrillas.

8

Arrest and Torture

For the first few weeks after Robert Domm left Dili nothing happened. About two or three weeks later, Robert published articles about his meeting with Xanana in East Timor. The BBC, the Australian Broadcast Corporation, and many other radio outlets and newspapers ran the story. Indonesia was very upset. The news was like a bomb for Jakarta. Indonesia denied the information: they said that the media had just made up the story, that Robert Domm had not met Xanana, that it was impossible because they had soldiers everywhere, and that someone had just made up the photos. People within East Timor who listened to the radio and the news also began to comment on the meeting.

Ironically, there were certain East Timorese who had not been involved at all in the planning and organizing of Robert Domm's trip who started to talk to me about it. When the news began to spread all over East Timor, I began to consult people, just to try to see their reaction to the news. One friend of mine who knew nothing about my role in the underground said, "Have you heard the news recently? An Australian guy met with Xanana Gusmão. I didn't know about it! I just heard about it on the radio." I tried to pretend not to be interested, but my friend tried to show off. He said, "You know, we are not like you who just stay at home, eating, drinking, and sleeping,

and doing nothing else." He added, "I am going to tell you something, but you can't say anything to anybody else. We took Robert
Domm to meet with Xanana."

"Oh my God, how did you do that?" I said. "Was it easy for you to
get there?"

"My friend, it was tough," he replied. "Before we got to Xanana
we had to pass through five checkpoints."

"When did you meet?" I asked him.

"I can't tell you about this," he told me. "It's not for me to say. This
is just between me and you. Don't tell anyone else."

After several other people said similar things, inventing stories
that they arranged Robert Domm's visit, it became clear that many
people were claiming credit. I thought this was good. If many people
were claiming credit, this could only confuse Indonesian intelligence,
and I would more likely be safe. But I always recommended to the
people telling these stories that, for their own safety, they should not
tell anyone else.

In any case, I was prepared in the event that they found out who
took Robert Domm into the jungle. Just a few weeks after Robert left
Dili, the Indonesian army surrounded the camp where we had met
Xanana in Bunaria. The Indonesian army was able to capture many
things, including documents of our meeting and tapes of Robert
Domm's interview with Xanana. These were copies of the same tapes
that Robert took to Australia, so the Indonesians had my voice on
tape.

After the Indonesians raided Xanana's camp, one of my colleagues
from Ainaro came to Dili and told me about the situation. As a result
of this operation, a number of FALINTIL fighters who we met during
our meeting were killed, including Commander Alex, the man who
gave me the deer meat. His killing was very dramatic. He had many
important documents from the resistance in his backpack—lists of
names and so on—because he was responsible for the links to the underground in the villages and towns. He didn't die instantly when the
Indonesians shot him. Reportedly, in the last minutes of his life, he
took out the documents and burned them. Fortunately, Xanana was
able to escape from the encirclement with the help of the local popu-

lation and go into hiding in the suburbs of Ainaro.

The Indonesians did not discover Xanana's camp because of Robert Domm's visit. Xanana had a meeting with a group of young people from the underground, including a young woman, on August 20, the anniversary of the founding of FALINTIL, before Robert's visit. They had a very big party in the jungle, in a different place from where we had met but in the same general area. The young people took some pictures of the meeting. Because of the irresponsibility of some of the young men, the Indonesians saw the photos. The young men came to Dili and tried to develop the pictures. Somehow the Indonesians got hold of the photos from the photography store and arrested those who had gone to meet with Xanana; they were from an underground organization called FITUN. So the Indonesian army already had a good idea where Xanana was before we took Robert Domm to Xanana's place. The problem for Indonesia was timing. We knew that the Indonesians already had plans to capture Xanana, but we also knew that they needed more time to plan the operation to capture him. We took advantage of this small window of opportunity to bring about Robert Domm's visit.

Xanana didn't leave Ainaro. He was confident that his contacts would let him know if an attack was imminent and he wanted to stay for the Robert Domm meeting. I thought that Xanana was planning to leave soon after the interview, but for some reason he stayed for a few more weeks. It was probably a strategic mistake.

I don't know how many Indonesian soldiers were involved in the operation, but there were a lot. They even brought Try Sutrisno, the head of ABRI, the Indonesian military, to witness the operation. The Indonesians cut down every tree in the area so that they could see Xanana's huts and shelter very clearly. The Indonesians surrounded the whole area and called on Xanana to surrender, but he had already escaped. He had gone to a nearby village and hid in someone's house.

When I heard that the Indonesians had captured some of the documents from our meeting, I began to tell people that I probably would be arrested in the near future. Even though only my *nom de guerre*, Terus, was on the documents, I was afraid that a friend of mine who had escaped from Dili after the demonstration at the Pope's mass had been captured and that he might inform on me. His name was Zeca. He was persecuted so he decided to go to join the guerrillas. I was really surprised to see Zeca when we arrived at Xanana's camp, and he knew me well. So I was afraid of him because he knew my real name.

The Indonesians didn't find out who took Robert Domm to the jungle until they surrounded Xanana's camp. Then they found out that Domingos Sarmento and I were responsible. That's because they captured Zeca. The Indonesians tortured him. I'm not certain that Zeca told the Indonesians about my role, but one of the Indonesian commanders—Captain Edy Suprianto, the one who later interrogated me when I was arrested in Dili—gave me that impression. "We didn't know you," the commander told me. "You're a sneaky guy. But one of your friends gave us information that you were the one who took Robert Domm into the jungle."

When I found out about the raid, I called Fernando de Araujo, head of RENETIL (the National Resistance of East Timorese Students) in Indonesia. He was in Bali. I told him to prepare for the possibility that something would happen me. "If the military arrests me, tell Amnesty International about my situation." I also informed the International Committee of the Red Cross that the Indonesians were looking for me and that I might be arrested.

"We are going to give you some money to leave," some of my friends from the underground said to me. "It's better for you to escape to Bali or Java. You can hide there."

"No," I told them. "I'm responsible. I have to stay here." I was the leader of the underground movement. I couldn't leave the burden of the responsibility to other people. I was ready at that time to confront the Indonesian soldiers if they arrested me. I was also confident that international pressure would help me. So I stayed in Dili and continued to work in the underground movement with other executive committee members.

Also, Xanana was in a difficult predicament at that time. I received a message from him that he was in a terrible situation. While Xanana was in one room underneath the house where he was hiding, the Indonesian soldiers had a party in the same house. He said that he had no cigarettes and no food. He asked for money to buy some necessities. In response I sent Xanana some money and cigarettes.

But then I had to get ready for a meeting with Mau Hudo that was scheduled for January 25, 1991. I was really happy about the prospect of spending my birthday with Mau Hudo in the jungle. He had killed a deer as a present, and he came with a lot of meat and waited for me in Viqueque. Unfortunately, I wasn't able to meet with him. One hour before my departure to Viqueque, Indonesian police officers and military intelligence agents arrested me in Dili.

The Indonesians didn't arrest me right after they surrounded Xanana's camp. I think they took their time investigating the captured documents and tried to find more evidence. Indonesian agents followed me from October until the day they captured me. They told me that they had been following me. "You went to Externato. You went to Cristal. You went to the diocese. You went to Becora." They mentioned all my movements. I didn't know they were following me. They knew everywhere I had been and at what time. They had records of my activities and my movements. I was afraid that they would uncover many other people, but they didn't. I learned that they didn't discover any of my network linkages with other people in the underground.

My arrest took place on January 25, 1991, at nine in the morning. I was going to my office at the Diocese of Dili. I had a stack of newspapers from Australia and Portugal that Fernando de Araújo had sent me from Bali and I needed to make copies for Mau Hodu. I also had to pick up an identification card for my guide because he didn't have one. To get an identification card, I had to go to the office of the district administrator. Because we had people who worked there, they could provide an ID quickly. As I was going to pick up the ID, I didn't pay any attention to the street. The whole time I was thinking about the executive committee's meeting the previous night and my upcoming meeting with Mau Hodu. I already had points from the meeting that I wanted to discuss with him, including the upcoming visit to East Timor of the Australian ambassador to Indonesia.

The Indonesians had planned to arrest me for a traffic violation. They already knew that I had a motorcycle but no license. They thought that that was the best excuse to arrest me. But before they did this, a friend of mine happened to take a taxi to the center of town. The taxi driver was a policeman who might have been intelligence. The policeman trusted my friend and said, "Don't go out by motorcycle or car today if you don't have a driver's license because we will have a traffic stop. We will check everyone." Usually the police do this once a month or when something has happened.

"Why are you having this checkpoint now?" my friend asked. The taxi driver said the purpose was to arrest a teacher named Constâncio. My friend got out of the taxi and immediately went to my house to warn me, but by the time he arrived, it was too late. I was gone.

At nine, on the way to the diocese office, in front of the old municipal market, I suddenly found myself surrounded by police. I had all the newspaper clippings and the notes from the executive committee meeting the previous evening in my backpack. I immediately realized that I was in trouble. I knew that the Indonesians were already looking for me because we had people that were working for them. I knew that if I stopped, they would take me in because I didn't have a license, that they would take my documents, and that I would be in serious trouble. So I tried to escape with the motorbike. I went through the line and just took off. I went forward, but then I realized that I couldn't escape because they had blocked off the street. I turned around a little bit. There were two policemen. One hit me on my head, I fell down, and they grabbed me. They hit my head and my body. They called me Terus. They already knew my *nom de guerre*.

"Terus, where are you going?" they asked me. They began to beat me really hard, right there on the street in front of people. Immediately blood came out of my nose and mouth like someone had turned on a faucet. My head hurt incredibly. I felt like I was going to die. They kicked me in the stomach with their boots very hard, like someone kicking a ball, and in my back and my head. I couldn't move, and I was crying. They just kept beating me.

A lot of people were there. Everyone was scared, of course. People couldn't say anything. They put handcuffs on me, with my hands behind my back. They didn't put me in a truck, because I was right in front of the police station. They just walked me to the police station and beat and kicked me all the way there, in my stomach and my head. They were hitting me in the stomach karate style. One of the police, a guy named Martinho Alau who's East Timorese, approached me. (Later, he was responsible for killing many people during the Santa Cruz massacre.[1])

"If I had caught you," he said to me, "I would have broken your head immediately. You wouldn't have survived." And then many others came to me and said while laughing, "Look at this traitor." I just kept silent.

The police took me into a room. There were a lot of intelligence people there, men and women. They were there just to watch me. The police took off my clothes, so I only had underwear on, and they started to beat me again really hard, hitting my face and body, and kicking my legs and stomach. They ordered me to put my hands against the wall over my head. People outside the room shouted, "Look at that traitor! We'll teach him tonight. We'll teach him tonight!"

After that, they took me to an interrogation room. When I entered the room, there was a Balinese police captain named Edy and two others. The room was small, maybe 12 feet by 24 feet. I sat on a chair. They had maps and a schema of the organization of the underground. It showed Xanana on top, and then Xanana's links with Bishop Belo, Father Cunha, and Father Leão, and then Father Leão's links to me and then the links I had to many other groups. I don't know where they got the information, but some of it was true. I had contact with José Ramos Horta and others abroad, through journalists and through Fernando de Araújo in Bali, as the chart showed.

The police official interrogated me about the chart and tried to force me to say the schema was true. "Do you know Bishop Belo, Father Leão, and Father Cunha?" he asked me.

"I know Bishop Belo as the head of the Catholic Church," I replied. "I know Father Leão and Father Cunha because they were my priests and my teachers."

"Do you know that they are working with FRETILIN?" he asked.

"I don't know," I answered. "And I don't have to know. That is their business."

"You know, you traitor!" he yelled and he hit me in the face really hard. The interrogation continued, accompanied by torture. They asked the questions in Indonesian, so I had to respond in Indonesian as well. "We've known your name for a long time," one of them bragged. And they were laughing at me. "Where is Xanana Gusmão?" they asked. "How does the resistance work? Who took Robert Domm to meet Xanana?"

I knew that the Indonesians had captured many documents implicating me as the head of the underground three months earlier when they raided Xanana's camp; they already knew my *nom de guerre*, Terus, and they had arrested me with incriminating information in my backpack, so I couldn't deny that I was the secretary of the executive committee. They already had their proof, but I wanted to make sure that they obtained as little information from me as possible. Their objective was to destroy the entire underground; they wanted to know the identities of all my contacts. I thought that if I admitted to being the secretary of the executive committee and took responsibility for the activities of the underground, the Indonesians would concentrate on me, rather than on others whom they suspected of underground activity.

"You don't have to accuse me of having contacts with this one or that one," I told them. "Now you've got the right person. I am the secretary of the executive committee. I am responsible for everything."

They continued to hit me and I continued to refuse to give them the information they wanted about my contact with others. With each question, I would get two or three punches in the face. When someone punches you so much and so hard, it feels as if your face is broken. People hit me on my back and on my sides with their hands and then kicked me. "If you don't tell the truth, you will be responsible for your own life," they threatened.

I was crying, but they were beating me so hard that my body became like wood. They beat me like someone beats a cow. They beat me so many times I couldn't feel it. But as time passed I felt the effects very much; my body felt like it was broken. When they first started beating me very hard, I kind of lost consciousness. When they stopped beating me for a few minutes, I touched my head and my jaw to see if they were broken; I couldn't believe that they were not.

It's unbelievable how strong your body is. And it was not small people who beat me, but people who were strong and who beat me with all their energy. I prayed to God, and God helped me at that time. Without God, I would probably be dead.

I continued to ask my torturers why they had captured me, insisting that they present their evidence. "Where is your proof?" I demanded. "Prove that I'm Terus. You say that you already know that my name is Terus, but how? You have to present your proof that led to my capture."

They never showed anything to me. "We have proof," they told me. "We just want you to be clear, to be honest with us. You have to tell us everything. We already have information about your activities. You cannot lie to us now."

I had already told them that I was head of the executive committee because they already knew this. But I wanted them to show me their evidence, to prove that I was the secretary, to prove that my name was Terus. I wanted to see exactly what they had before I said anything, but they didn't want to show me the documents at the police station. As long as they didn't show me any proof, however, I was not going to betray any information.

Around 11 in the morning, the Indonesians allowed me to meet with Gabriela, my girlfriend, who had come to the police station to see if I was OK. I don't know why they allowed her to see me, probably because of Gabriela's persistence.

I first met Gabriela in 1988 when I was teaching English at Cristal, but I could not approach her while she was still a student there, so I waited until late 1989, after she stopped attending the school. Fortunately, Gabriela had feelings for me just as I had for her. Soon thereafter we became boyfriend and girlfriend with our parents' blessings.

Like my family, Gabriela's family had fled to the mountains when Indonesia invaded in 1975; she was only four years old and was living in Baucau at the time. They fled south toward Matebian mountain near Baguia. The Indonesians bombed and napalmed the area for a few months as part of the encirclement campaign and killed thousands of people. Somehow Gabriela and her family all survived the Matebian encirclement, but the Indonesians captured them in the mountains in 1979 and forced them to settle in the area of Baucau. Gabriela and her family moved to Dili at the beginning of the 1980s, but she had no involvement in the underground until she became my girlfriend. She knew very little about the resistance, but she did know a few people who were involved.

I never told Gabriela that I was involved in the underground because I didn't want to put her in danger. The less she knew about, I thought, the safer she would be. It became obvious to her that I was involved in the resistance, however, when I asked her to sew a FALINTIL flag and to make a cake for the 15th anniversary of FALINTIL in 1990 to send to Xanana in Ainaro. But even though she knew that I worked with the underground, she had no idea that I was the head of the clandestine front. And Gabriela never asked me anything about my work. I later found out that it was because she wanted me to be open with her, to tell her on my own.

At the time of my arrest, I was living in Gabriela's parents' house. I had moved there with her parents' permission in late 1990. I had a separate room from Gabriela because we were not yet married. I wanted to move because I feared that Indonesian intelligence was watching my house in Santa Cruz; I explained this to Gabriela's parents. Some intelligence agents had come to my house and asked my uncle and my neighbors questions about me. The military suspected my house because military intelligence had arrested one of my friends, Nuno Corvelo, at the house in mid-1989 because of his involvement in the underground; the Indonesians found out that he was showing people a video from Australia about José Ramos Horta's life. And their suspicions of me increased following the demonstration at Tacitolo.

When Gabriela came to the police station the morning of my arrest on January 25, 1991, the Indonesians were very angry. They made her wait for almost an hour before they allowed her to see me. The Indonesians asked Gabriela if I had any documents, photos, or flags from the resistance at her house. She told them that she knew nothing about my political involvement and that she had never seen any material from the underground at the house. "How does your girlfriend already know that you are here?" the Indonesians demanded of me.

"Because you arrested me in public on the street and everyone knows me," I replied.

Gabriela was very upset when she saw me; I was already in bad shape. She barely recognized me. She was crying because my face and body were already swollen. "Please don't cry," I told her. "Just go home and pray for me." They allowed Gabriela to bring me food, but my mouth was so swollen that I couldn't eat. The police allowed us to talk for only about five minutes, but there were three officers watching us while we were talking. We spoke in Tetum, in low voices. I immediately asked Gabriela whether she had hidden all the documents that I had at her house. I had many documents there, as well as a video camera that I was supposed to send to the jungle. During the interrogation, they asked me, "Do you have any more documents at your home?" In spite of the fact that I didn't know if my things were still there or not, I said, "I don't have any more documents. If you don't believe me, please go to my house and check." But I had a lot of documents, including letters from Xanana. If they had gone to Gabriela's parents' house or my parents' house within one or two hours of my arrest, they would have found many documents and Gabriela's parents and my parents would have been in serious trouble. As soon as Gabriela left the station, she returned home and brought all my materials to one of my friends in the underground.

It was a bit dangerous for Gabriela to come to the police station and inquire about me. But the Catholic Church and Bishop Belo were aware of my situation. The International Committee of the Red Cross was also informed about my arrest. Underground members in Dili had immediately contacted Fernando de Araujo in Bali, and he alerted many international organizations. The police knew that news of my detention was getting out because they had already received phone calls inquiring about me.

When Gabriela told me that friends of mine had already called Fernando, I felt stronger. After five minutes Gabriela had to leave and they took me back into the interrogation room and continued with the questioning.

Because I was arrested on a Friday, the various international organizations couldn't act immediately. So it wasn't until Monday that the media got the message from someone, and my name was broadcast on the BBC and the ABC. Because of the broadcasts, people knew about my arrest internationally. The Indonesians probably felt that they couldn't kill me at that time because of the attention.

After Gabriela left, the police continued to interrogate me. "Do you have contact with Xanana Gusmão?" they asked.

"No, I don't," I said. "I don't have contact with anyone until you show me proof otherwise."

"You are the man who took Robert Domm to meet with Xanana," they stated.

"No, it wasn't me," I responded.

They wanted to know my background: my name and my birthday, and those of my father and my mother.

"When were you born?" they asked.

"I was born in East Timor on January 25, 1963," I answered.

The police said, "Oh! It is your birthday today? How old are you?"

"I am 28," I answered.

"Tell your girlfriend to bring you presents," they said.

"Thank you very much," I responded. "I don't need a present from my girlfriend because I already have one from you. You gave me a present."

"What present?" they asked.

"Look at me," I said. "The blood that is running out of my nose and my eyes, this is your present. And I will not never forget this present as long as I live."

They became nervous and they hit me really hard. "You are politics!" they screamed. When they call you "politics" they mean that you are someone that is against them. "We don't have to make you any promises about East Timor. After we have given you a job and money and everything, you still don't like Indonesia?" They said this to me because I was a government employee. I didn't answer. I kept silent.

"Would you like to be president here in East Timor?" they asked.

"No, I am not fighting for personal ambition," I answered. "I am fighting for the liberation of East Timor."

"You don't like Indonesia?" they asked in disbelief.

"No, of course, I don't like Indonesia," I stated. "That's why I'm fighting against you." And they became agitated again and they kicked me even harder. It was as if somebody wanted to eat me alive.

"Do you know where Xanana is?" they kept questioning.

"I don't know," I asserted.

"We are sure that you know," they said. "You are the leader of the underground movement."

"But since this morning when you arrested me, things have changed," I responded. "From nine until now I don't know what has happened with the resistance movement. I don't know anything about Xanana. I don't know what happened to any of my friends. I don't know where they are because I was arrested."

"But no one knows that you were arrested," they stated. "They think that you were detained because you don't have a license."

"You arrested me on the street and you beat me in front of everyone," I responded. "Everyone knows me. Any time you people arrest a member of the underground, immediately the members change the structure of the organization and its mechanisms."

"You are lying," they accused me.

"No. It is true," I replied. "Now I'm here. Don't ask me about Xanana. You know that I am a leader. Why don't we just start negotiating?" Xanana and I had already talked about negotiations. Xanana had already proposed that negotiations about East Timor take place between the resistance and the Indonesian military. The proposal was serious, but I knew that they wouldn't agree to negotiate with me. "I am here. I'm the leader," I said. "I really want to negotiate with you. Please treat me as a human being."

"Human being! What? You are a traitor!" they yelled. And then suddenly two men—the commander from army intelligence, Edy Suprianto, and one other person—came into the room.

"Oh, Terus, you are here," said Edy Suprianto. "We have heard a lot about you. We have been looking for you so long, but now it's okay." Edy tried to be more persuasive, but the other guy, who was also a commander, yelled at me like a lion that was about to swallow a rabbit. "If you don't tell us the truth, I will drop you in the sea," he threatened. I was wondering, "Who's going to kill me, this guy or

Edy Suprianto?"

"I'm here. Why don't we just talk?" I said. "Why do you beat me?"

"Who beat you?" Edy Suprianto asked.

"The police have been beating me from the time I was arrested until now," I responded. "Look at me. It's not good to treat me like that."

"Oh, we won't beat you anymore," Suprianto promised. "I will tell them not to beat you." But he was a liar. As soon as he and his accomplice left, the police began again with the interrogation and the torture. Someone outside the room said, "I will teach him at midnight." When I heard this, I thought I would soon be killed. Usually Indonesian intelligence tortures people in their cells at midnight.

They hit me from nine in the morning when they first arrested me until one the next morning. I almost lost consciousness a few times. At one a.m., there was a telephone call from the head of military intelligence, Gatot Purwanto, Edy Suprianto's boss. He told them to move me from the police station to Colmera, a military intelligence jail. About half an hour later, they put me in a truck. I was in a lot of pain. I was afraid that they were taking me somewhere to kill me. They put two police behind me in the truck and two in front of me.

"Where are you taking me?" I asked. They didn't answer.

"Are you going to kill me?" I asked.

"No, we are not going to kill you right now," they stated. But then one of them turned to me and said, "Traitor, if I had arrested you, if I had captured you, I would have shot you right away." And then we arrived in Colmera, a neighborhood in Dili where there was a prison for political prisoners. Because the truck was completely closed I couldn't see anything. As soon as they pulled me out of the vehicle, I immediately recognized the place. They put me in a room and resumed the interrogation.

Edy Suprianto and three Indonesian soldiers were in the room. Two of the soldiers were East Timorese. For the first two hours, they psychologically tortured me; they didn't hit me, but they made strong threats to kill me. They even put a gun on the table. The psychological torture was intense. They interrogated me until four in the morning, and then they let me go to take a shower. After my shower they put me in handcuffs. Then we continued with the interrogation. They interrogated me for three days, 24 hours a day.

On the second day of my arrest, Gabriela and my eldest sister, Celestina, went to the police station to look for me. When they arrived at the station, they asked the police to let them meet with me. But I had been moved from the police station to the military headquarters.

"We don't know where he is," the police told them. "He moved and we don't know where he is." The police didn't want to tell them where was I at that time. One of the police officials told Gabriela, "We were supposed to kill Constâncio last night, but he moved." After half an hour, Gabriela got angry and began to threaten the police by saying that if they didn't tell her where I was, she would immediately call the International Committee of the Red Cross. When she threatened them, they called Edy, the Balinese officer who had interrogated and beaten me at the police station. He came to Gabriela and explained that I had been moved to SGI, the Indonesian military intelligence headquarters.[2] Then Gabriela asked them how to contact me. "We don't know how to contact Constâncio," the officers said. And then she asked for a phone number. "We don't have a telephone number either," they said. But later on, they gave her a telephone number and she called me at SGI. I spoke to her for only a few minutes.

At the beginning of the interrogation at Colmera, the Indonesians said the same thing as they did at the police station. "We know that you are the leader of the underground movement," they said. "We know you have a very close relationship with Xanana Gusmão. We know that you know everything about the underground movement. Please tell us everything. If you don't, you will be responsible for your own life."

Every time they asked me a question, the Indonesians would add a threat. "We know everything about you," they told me, "so just be honest. If you are not, you will suffer." As they were saying this, they would point a pistol at my head. "We are nice people, but we have colleagues who are not so nice, who use razor blades and electric shocks during interrogation. It's your choice." Sometimes the Indonesians would order me to smoke a cigarette and to take a few moments to think.

At one point, a group of East Timorese civilian intelligence agents who worked with Edy came into the room where I was being interrogated and yelled, "We would like to dance with Mr. Constâncio!" That meant that they wanted to beat me. Fortunately, Edy Suprianto did not allow them to. They never beat me at SGI, but others were not so lucky. I could hear the loud screams of another political prisoner in a nearby room.

"What you need to do is prove why you arrested me," I told the Indonesians. "I don't know who Xanana is. I don't have any linkages with Xanana, any linkages with the Church, any linkages with anyone. I don't know what the underground movement is. What you are saying is fiction as long as you don't present any documentation. As long as you don't provide any proof, I won't tell you anything."

On the first two days, they didn't show me any documents. On the third day, though, they showed me my documents. Imagine, they brought out all my documents and letters and put them on the table—letters that I had sent to Xanana over a period of almost one year. When I looked at those letters and documents, I began crying. I was crying at the sight of my letters. They laughed at me.

"We have copies of everything you've sent to Xanana," they bragged. But it wasn't true. They had the original documents captured from Xanana's camp. And I already knew that. "You sent letters to Xanana and we have copies. The people who worked for you are our people." They thought that I didn't know that the letters were captured.

After I saw the documents, I had to change my strategy. I tried to praise them in sarcastic way. "I really admire your work," I said. They seemed very proud of themselves when I said, "You have done a great job."

"We know that we've done a great job, so why don't you just tell us everything?" they replied. "That's why we asked you to tell the truth."

"Can I see the letters?" I asked them. I wanted to see them so I would know how much they knew and thus what I should say in terms of my work with Xanana and the underground. I quickly looked at my letters just to remember.

As I was looking at the papers, Edy Suprianto said, "Stop looking at the papers; that's enough for you." But by then, I had already recalled some important parts of what I had written.

"Okay," I said, "you have proven that it was fair to arrest me." I said that to make them a little bit happy. "Now I will provide you with information." I told them what I had written to Xanana, but only what they already had in the letters. They never realized what I was doing. Probably, they had some difficultly translating my letters from Portuguese to Indonesian. When I talked about the letters to Xanana, they acted as if I was telling them something new.

"Yes, that's what we need from you," they said. "Why didn't you tell us this before so we didn't have to torture you?"

I never told them about Robert Domm because it was a big embarrassment to the Indonesian military. In the end, they said to me, "Look, Terus, there are some things that are not clear to us. You are still hiding something." That thing was Robert Domm.

But I answered, "That's all I have. I have no more information for you."

"No, we know that you have it, but that you just don't want to tell us," they responded. "Why don't you tell us now?"

"No, I don't have anything else," I replied.

They began to try to intimidate me by saying, "Remember your name, Terus. *Terus* means to suffer. If you don't tell us, just remember your name."

Psychological threats are more powerful than physical torture in certain situations. I said, "Yes, I understand my name means suffering, but I don't have anything else to say." They insisted, and I insisted as well.

The military intelligence didn't want to hurt me anymore. Sometimes, in the case of people like me, they think they can get more information to destroy the network as a whole if they use persuasive methods. But many people are tortured terribly, by electric shock and razor blades. They pull out people's fingernails and toenails; they cut their ears off and slice different parts of their bodies. In my case, because I was a high-profile member of the resistance, they were a little afraid of the international pressure: people soon began to talk about me on international radio, and Amnesty International and the Red Cross began to pressure Indonesia to release me.

The psychological torture was serious. I was really scared. What they were threatening to do would have affected not only me but my whole family. "If you don't tell the truth, you will be responsible for your life and for the life of everyone in your family," they told me. "It's not difficult for us to kill anyone. We are here to do that. We just obey the orders. When the higher levels say kill, we will kill you. We are not here to amuse you. We're here to follow what our boss tells us to do. If they tell us to kill you, no problem. So be careful with what you say."

As they began to threaten me more and more, I tended to be careful. I didn't care about whether they killed me or not. "I'm here in your hands," I told them. "Whatever you want to do with me, do it. If you want to torture me and kill me, do it if that's what you want to do." I didn't worry about death, about being killed, until one of the Indonesian soldiers came to my room when I was sleeping and said, "Traitor, do you know those people who were killed in Manatuto? It was me who did it. If you don't tell the truth, I will take you out from this house and cut your head off like I did to those people in Manatuto."

"That's up to you," I said. "I'm here and I'm not going to hide from you. You can open the window or door for me. I won't leave this house. I'm here." I just said that, but I was really very frightened.

As they continued to torture me psychologically, I tried to focus on how to deal with the problem. I tried to study their behavior, to see what they needed from me, what they wanted from me. I always kept in mind that I was important for them, that they needed me. I always thought about that. In the end, I knew that they would ask me for something.

The last thing they showed me during my interrogation was a video camera. They said, "Look, this is Xanana's video camera. And he got it from you."

"Xanana must have received it from another person," I stated. "I don't know who gave it to him." Then he showed me a tape recorder and played it for me.

"Now listen to your voice. Is that your voice or not?" he asked. They played the tape of my translating Robert Domm's interview.

"Oh my God, what am I going to do now?" I thought.

After I listened to the tapes, I said, "This is the last crucial thing I'm going to tell you. It's a big embarrassment to the Indonesian military; that's why I didn't want to tell you. But now I'm going to tell you. I'm ready for whatever you want to do with me." And I started telling them about Robert Domm and that I took him to meet Xanana.

Edy Suprianto embraced me. "That's what we need to know from you. Why didn't you tell us this yesterday instead of making us spend so much time trying to find out this information?"

They asked me for names, but I just told them lies. I didn't mention Domingos Sarmento. I told them that Robert Domm had come to Dili and asked me to meet with Xanana. "And because I already had a contact with Xanana," I told them, "I contacted a friend and he drove us to Xanana's camp in Ainaro. I contacted your man, Mariano. Do you know him? He's your man. He worked for you. He's the double agent we used. He's already gone into hiding in East Timor. We went to Xanana's camp together." By the time of my interrogation, Mariano, the double agent who had worked with us, had already gone into hiding. I didn't mention anyone else because they didn't know who was in the group. They asked me about other people, but I just mentioned people who had left East Timor in the last four months or were in hiding. I didn't say Donaciano's name because he had left for Portugal before Robert Domm arrived in Dili.

They then put me in a tiny room. There was no bed, no blankets, and no toilet. I had to sleep on the floor. It was very cold. I just had a pair of pants and a shirt. Because I was exhausted, I fell asleep immediately. In my dreams I saw many images, images of people's legs and hands and of someone smiling at me. These images made me think that many people had been killed in the room. The spirits of the dead probably wanted to show me what had happened to others who had struggled for East Timor. I believe in the existence of spirits. Maybe they were trying to show me that it was a dangerous place.

The next morning when I woke up, Edy asked me, "Where did you sleep?"

"I slept here on the floor," I replied.

"Oh my God!" he exclaimed. "Why didn't you tell me? We had a bed for you." He tried to be nicer to me and gave me a small military bed to sleep on. He even invited me to have lunch with him. "We are going to meet with Gatot Purwanto, the commander of military intelligence, tomorrow," he said. It was the fourth day of my capture. During lunch Edy Suprianto pretended to be my friend. He put me at the same level as him. He ordered his soldiers to bring food and drinks for us and had them wait on us. We talked only about serious matters. He kept asking me about Xanana Gusmão. They were very eager to capture him. "Do you know where Xanana is? If you tell us where he is, we will give you money, whatever you want. We can give you everything you need." He acted very kind to me. We had spicy Indonesian rice and chicken.

That afternoon, Edy had two of his intelligence agents bring me to Gabriela's house so I could change my clothes, which were covered with blood. My face and many parts of my body were still very swollen from the beatings, and my eyes, as well as parts of my face, were black. While the agents were waiting for me in the living room, I had Gabriela take some pictures of me. I still have one of them. After changing, I had to return to SGI in Colmera.

After having breakfast the next day, Captain Edy took me to meet with Colonel Gatot Purwanto in the Farol section of Dili. "Commander Gatot will be happy to meet you," he said. "He already knows about you. So when you meet him don't be afraid to tell him whatever you know." But I already had my own plan.

While in the prison I found out that there were 30 other East Timorese who had already been there for a long time before I arrived. They were arrested for participating in a demonstration at a Catholic high school, Santus Paulus, in September 1990, and they had been kept in prison since that time without a trial. They were not in the same house as I was, but in a separate building in the same compound. The prisoners included Francisco Dias, Aleon, Talofo, and José António Galucho. I was actually able to meet with some of them after my interrogation. I met with them when Edy Suprianto and his cohorts took their afternoon nap. I quickly left my room, talked to them, and returned immediately. I could leave my room; I was not locked in. Even though it was impossible to escape from the SGI compound because of the intense security around it, inside the compound I could move around somewhat, perhaps because the Indonesians trusted me a little after I had told them what they wanted to hear.

The night before I met Gatot I thought to myself that if I stayed in the prison, I wouldn't be able to do anything else for the underground and my country. An important consideration was that Xanana Gusmão had already sent me instructions for the visit of an upcoming Portuguese parliamentary delegation. I hadn't yet delivered the instructions to the other underground leaders because I was afraid that it would be dangerous for the underground movement if we started preparing too far in advance. I knew that if I didn't get out of the prison, I wouldn't be able to deliver the instructions to the underground. What would happen when the Portuguese parliamentary delegation arrived? I realized that the Indonesians needed me and that they would probably ask me to work for them. I tried to think about what I would do if they said to me that they would release me on the condition that I would work for them as an agent.

Gatot's office was in an old Portuguese house near the lighthouse on the Dili waterfront. As I stepped into the room Gatot greeted me in Tetum. *"Pak Terus, diak ka lae?"* (Mr. Terus, how are you?)

"I'm fine. Thank you," I replied. I didn't know that Gatot spoke Tetum.

"Well, I have been looking for you for a long time, but now you are here," he said. "So, tell me, why do you do all these things against the Indonesian government?"

I tried to give a diplomatic answer. "I have done many things against the Indonesian government and I want to apologize. If you don't accept my apology, I am already in your hands. You can do whatever you can do to me. I am ready to accept it. I will consider your punishment of me as a punishment that comes from a father to a son. I consider the Indonesian government to be like my father. As a father you have to think how to give punishment as a form of advice in order to improve your child's behavior. I am here to receive that advice." I don't know if he believed me or not.

"Well, as you have already recognized your fault, I will let you go home, with the condition that you present yourself to us regularly and provide information to us," Gatot responded. "We are planning to release you in a few days with the condition that you work for us. Of course you've done a lot of terrible things against the government. You have to work for us now; you have to denounce all those terrible things that you have done. But remember, don't tell people that you were arrested for political reasons, but because you didn't have your driver's license and the proper motorcycle document."

"I promise, commander," I answered. "I won't tell anybody. I really want to work and cooperate with you." They were happy. "But even if you release me from jail, it will not be easy. It will take time for me to get things done. It could be one month or one day, one week, one year, or ten years. It will be difficult for me to help you because I have been arrested. People won't believe me if I go back and try to work as before. The structure of the underground movement has changed since I was arrested."

"But as I already said, you must not say that you were arrested because you are a political activist, because of political reasons. You were arrested because you didn't have your license. That's what you have to tell people," he responded.

"The problem, Mr. Gatot, is that your people beat me in front of so many people on the street," I told him. "You arrested me in public, not at my house. So many people saw your people beat me, so they won't believe that I was arrested because of my license."

"But no, you have to tell them that you were arrested because you didn't have a license," he insisted. "Don't tell people that you were arrested because you are secretary of the executive committee, because you have been involved in a lot of political activities. Don't tell people that. If you do, you will be useless to us."

Their main goal was to arrest Xanana Gusmão.

"OK, I'll try," I promised. "But I need time to build confidence with people in order to reach Xanana Gusmão because I don't know what has happened to those people I used to be in touch with, such as my courier to Xanana. They've changed everything now, and they won't believe me anymore, so I need time."

"OK, we can give you more time if you want," he replied. "We understand that it takes time."

But then I added another condition: the release of the 30 people who were held in that prison. "Commander Gatot, I appreciate your decision," I said. "But I think it will be difficult for people to believe that I was arrested merely because I didn't have my driver's license. If that were the case, why would you keep me here for almost a week? Another big mistake was to put me in the same jail where the others are imprisoned. I think it would be helpful if you release the other prisoners before you release me. If you don't release the others I would rather stay here. If you don't, people won't believe in me. How can you expect people to trust me if I was arrested just a few days ago and immediately you release me. People will say that I am working for intelligence. People won't believe me anymore."

Gatot was convinced by my argument. "I think you are right," Gatot said to me. The next day the Indonesians released the 30 people.

A couple of days later, after seven days in prison, the Indonesians released me as well. The date was February 1, 1991. They took me to Gabriela's parents' house. The military told Gabriela's family that nothing had happened to me, and just left me there. My family and Gabriela's parents were really happy that I was alive. My brothers came there, and also some of my friends. They all were very happy that I was back home. My parents weren't really upset or angry with me. I was already 28 years old so I was responsible for what I did. But they worried a lot about my situation. I was independent from them, so that's what they told the Indonesian military whenever they were questioned. "He's already 28 years old. He's independent from us. He's responsible for his own actions." I told my parents that whatever the situation, if there were ever a political problem with me, they should tell the Indonesians that they didn't know anything about my activities, which was the truth. But despite my release, I wasn't happy at all, because my life was on a very dangerous path. I was beginning to play an extremely risky game and I was conscious of that.

Cónstâncio da C. Pinto
Dili, 25-1-1991 (nm)

Em 25 de Janeiro de 1991, a tro
pa Indonésia capturou um professor
da Escola de Externato de S. José,
de nome Constâncio C. Pinto, 27 a-
nos, solteiro, quando regressou
da escola. Constâncio veio a ser
capturado por ser desconfiado como
activista da Frente Clandestina.
Depois de 5 dias de interrogató
rios e torturas, libertaram-lhe,
mas até agora esse encontra-se a

**Constâncio's arrest and torture announced in an underground newspaper.
(Photo by Gabriela da Cruz Pinto.)**

Constâncio (center) with other members of the Executive Committee of the CNRM in the Clandestine Front, José Manuel Fernandes (left) and Donaciano Gomes (right) in August 1990. (Photo by Amy Goodman.)

Constâncio, Tilson, Tima, and Gabriela in Rhode Island, August 1996. (Photo by Matthew Jardine.)

Constâncio with 1996 Nobel Peace Prize Winner José António Ramos Horta
at a demonstration in New York City in 1995.
(Photo by Charlie Scheiner.)

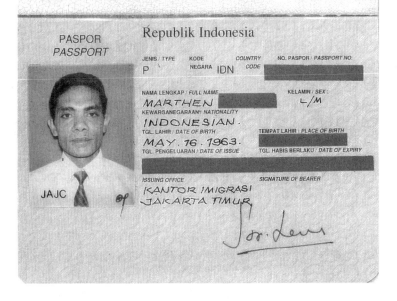

PASPOR
PASSPORT

Republik Indonesia

JENIS / TYPE   KODE   COUNTRY   NO. PASPOR / PASSPORT NO.
P   NEGARA IDN   CODE

NAMA LENGKAP / FULL NAME   KELAMIN / SEX:
MARTHEN   L / M
KEWARGANEGARAAN / NATIONALITY
INDONESIAN.
TGL. LAHIR / DATE OF BIRTH   TEMPAT LAHIR / PLACE OF BIRTH
MAY. 16. 1963.
TGL. PENGELUARAN / DATE OF ISSUE   TGL. HABIS BERLAKU / DATE OF EXPIRY

ISSUING OFFICE   SIGNATURE OF BEARER
KANTOR IMIGRASI
JAKARTA TIMUR

JAJC

**Constâncio's fake Indonesian passport.
The passport number and other identifying information have
been blocked out.**

Domingos Segurado right before the Santa Cruz Massacre on November 12, 1991 in Dili, East Timor. (Photo by Steve Cox.)

Amy Goodman and Allan Nairn after the Santa Cruz Massacre,
November 12, 1991, before their escape from East Timor.
(Photo by Russell Anderson.)

Robert Domm and Xanana Gusmão during their secret meeting in East Timor in September 1990. (Photo by FALINTIL.)

Col. Gatot Purwanto with Indonesian military map of East Timor. (Photo by Allan Nairn.)

Commander David Alex. (Photo by FALINTIL.)

9

Working as a Double Agent

After my release from prison in February 1991, I asked Edy Suprianto to give me two weeks to rest. I immediately went back to work as secretary of the Executive Committee of the CNRM in the Clandestine Front. I used the two weeks to reestablish my links with people I worked with in the underground, especially members of the executive committee. I was in a difficult position because I had to report every night to SGI headquarters in Colmera, specifically to Captain Edy Suprianto. At the same time, the Indonesians would often watch where I went, but there were always windows of opportunity when intelligence was not watching. By using trusted *estafetas*, I was able to communicate with members of the underground. I never met with anyone from the underground during the day, but sometimes I was able to sneak out at night to meet with people.

One of my first tasks was to disseminate the instructions from Xanana about the Portuguese delegation to the leaders of the various underground groups. Xanana had also sent us letters telling us that he wanted to come down to Dili, so I immediately had to help arrange accommodations for him. This was the first time that Xanana had tried to come to Dili since 1975.

Xanana was in a really bad situation after the Ainaro attack. By coming to Dili, he hoped to fool the Indonesian army, which for the past 15 years had always looked for him in the jungle.

In his letter, Xanana sent us a plan, detailing how to build a shelter for him in Dili. It would be underground with some compartments where he could sleep and work. He sent us a detailed drawing; I was surprised by his architectural skills. But we were not able to build the shelter because the materials would have cost too much; building it would have also required a lot of work, and drawn attention to us. But Xanana still decided to come. A few days later, two friends of mine drove to Ainaro, picked him up, and brought him to Dili. The trip was risky for the people who drove him. Xanana wore civilian clothes and he shaved his beard, so he looked different than the Xanana people knew. The driver, Jilman Tilman, was accompanied by Augusto Pereira, a man of great bravery; he worked as an Indonesian policeman. It was because of Augusto that Xanana was able to reach Dili without incident. The army never stopped the car because Augusto was in the car in his police uniform. No one suspected him. In any case, if the Indonesians had stopped the car, they probably wouldn't have recognized Xanana Gusmão.

As soon as Xanana arrived in mid-February 1991, he sent an *estafeta* to me. Xanana knew that I had been arrested, but he still trusted me. When I was arrested, I knew exactly where Xanana was hiding. The fact that the Indonesians did not arrest Xanana or anyone else from the underground after my arrest was proof that I was still trustworthy. As a result, Xanana continued to write letters to me after my arrest and asked me to help him come to Dili. When Xanana first arrived in Dili, I explained to him that the Indonesians had forced me to work with them and that they had released me with the condition that I had to report to them regularly. I explained that my strategy was to do something helpful for East Timor; if I had stayed in jail forever, I wouldn't have been able to do anything for the resistance. Xanana agreed.

As usual, I consulted Xanana about our plans and activities. But now it was easy for me because I didn't have to spend a week or two waiting for a response. I could get letters to and from him very quickly.

The house Xanana first stayed in was in a densely populated

neighborhood in Dili, Lahane; it was the house of the mother of
Aliança Araujo, Augusto Pereira's wife. The house was only about
100 feet away from a military post. When Xanana first arrived, the
house was very modest. The roof was made of zinc and *palapa* (palm
leaves). The walls were made of branches. But after a little time, they
rebuilt the house with a roof entirely of zinc and concrete walls to improve Xanana's security. Xanana had no armed bodyguards; his security depended on the secrecy and trust within the group that worked
with him, including the young children in the house where he was
hiding.

People in the neighborhood knew nothing about Xanana's presence. They only found out when Xanana was captured in November
1992. When the Indonesians captured Xanana, he was in his room,
which had been built below Aliança's mother's house.

Xanana didn't walk around the house where he was hiding during
the day. He would usually leave his room only at night to play with
the kids or to exercise. He would walk around the house early in the
morning, when everyone was sleeping, and late at night, but always
behind closed doors. Sometimes Xanana would be driven to a destination in Dili for a meeting. Mateus, the taxi driver who was shot to
death at the Santa Cruz Cemetery on November 12, 1991, was one of
Xanana's drivers. The other was Henrique Belmiro. The Indonesians
arrested Henrique in 1992 and sentenced him to nine years in prison. I
sometimes rode with Xanana in the same taxi, but not very often.
Sometimes when he needed to meet a foreign visitor, for example, he
would go to the downtown area. There were some Japanese, Australian, and Portuguese journalists, posing as tourists, who were able to
meet with Xanana.

Other people also had contacts with Xanana. I limited my contact
with him because of all the attention I received from Indonesian intelligence. I would only meet with him if it was necessary. The most important thing for us was to know what the Indonesian military was
doing. As long as they continued asking me about Xanana, we knew
that he could stay in Dili. It meant that they didn't know where
Xanana was. As long as I worked with the Indonesian military, I
could still find out things for Xanana. We contacted each other mostly

through letters. Sometimes I used Gabriela as the *estafeta* between us. Not many people knew that Xanana was in Dili. When Xanana first arrived in Dili, only a few people knew about his presence. But later on the number of people who knew increased somewhat because Xanana wanted to meet with many people, especially the leaders of the underground organizations.

From February through May 1991, Xanana and I worked together closely in Dili. Xanana's stay in Dili at that time was very successful. He even got an Indonesian identity card with a fake name. It was the first time he had ever used an Indonesian ID. Xanana was able to make contact with many people in the resistance. He met with guerrilla fighters from Ermera and Baucau to Lospalos and Viqueque. He hadn't seen these people and areas for four or five years, since the time he had moved from the eastern part of the country to the center of the territory, near Same. From Dili, it was easy for Xanana to travel to places in East Timor and to communicate with people abroad by letter or by phone.

Aside from working with Xanana and members of the underground, I was working very closely with Indonesian intelligence. I began to report to Edy Suprianto two weeks after my release. He asked me the same questions as during my arrest. The Indonesians were very preoccupied with Xanana. Whenever I saw them, they asked me about him. "Where is Xanana? Have you already linked up with Xanana? How about the underground movement? Did you meet with other leaders?"

"No, I'm sorry," I always said. "It's still difficult. Since people don't believe me anymore, I have to rebuild my credibility. My friends are all still afraid of me. They talk to me, but only about parties and women, never about anything political. I haven't seen any of my channels to Xanana. They used to come to my house, but I don't know where they live or even what their names are. They would just come, give me a letter, and that was it. That's why it's difficult for me to give anyone's name to you or to find them. I have to wait until they come to my house."

I realized that Suprianto and Gatot, his boss, would want to see progress, but it was difficult for them to pressure me right away. I was just trying to stall them until the Portuguese arrived. I was expecting that the Portuguese parliamentary delegation would soon arrive and help to resolve the East Timor situation. Once the Portuguese delegation arrived, we in the underground thought that the delegation would stay until arriving at some sort of agreement with the Indonesians that would end the occupation; we planned to do everything in our power to make sure that the Portuguese remained in East Timor until the people's demand for peace and freedom was fulfilled.

A few times, however, the situation between Suprianto and me became a little bit tense because they were not happy with my lack of progress. On such occasions, I would ask Suprianto and his cohorts to take me in their car to drive around the city. I would tell them that I wanted to see if I could point out people associated with the resistance to them, but this was not my real intention. My real goal was to show myself to the public. I would open the car window so people could see me with Indonesian intelligence while we were driving around the city. The Indonesians always tried to close the windows because they didn't want people to know that I was working with them. But I always tried to be seen.

I never identified people who were working for the resistance; but I sometimes pointed at people who I knew were working for Indonesia as spies. Sometimes Captain Edy and his assistants would point out to me groups of young people who were sitting on the edge of a bridge, at school, or outside a church. "Mr. Pinto," they would say, "that group of young people is working in the underground movement. We are just waiting for the right time to arrest them. We are watching them. We will arrest them when they make a wrong move." They were foolish to tell me that such and such a group was working in the underground. When they did, I was able to warn people, "Don't sit on the bridge over there because the Indonesian military will suspect you and arrest you." I rode around with the Indonesians to find out what they wanted and to discover exactly what they knew.

After two months, at the end of March, I went to Same; I wanted to leave Dili for a week to visit some relatives. "I have to go to Same," I told Suprianto. "I probably can establish linkages with people in Same that could connect with Xanana."

They let me go there, but a strange thing happened. I left Dili with Gabriela and another friend at eight in the morning. While I was on the way to Same, one of the Indonesian military's intelligence assets informed Suprianto that I was talking to Bishop Belo in Licidere at 10 that same morning. Of course it wasn't true, but they kept the information.

After a week, I came back from Same and went to Suprianto. He was really angry with me. "Mr. Pinto," he said, "you have to tell the truth. Where were you at 10 in the morning on the day you left?" I told him that I was on the way to Same. "No, you are liar," he replied. "You have to tell the truth. You're lying."

"How could I lie?" I answered. "I'm telling the truth."

"Weren't you in Licidere talking to Bishop Belo? What did you talk about?" he demanded.

I was very angry. I said, "We will see who is telling the truth. Who told you this? I want to know."

"An East Timorese," he replied. "But I don't want to tell you who." Fortunately one of my friends was working at the bus terminal at the time I went to Same. Everyone who goes to Same has to list their name. They had kept the list and I still had my ticket receipt. I went to the bus terminal immediately and I got a copy of the list with my name and the number of the bus. I put these together with the ticket and handed it all to Edy Suprianto.

"Who is telling the truth now?" I asked him. "Is it me or the person who provided you with the information?"

It was a big embarrassment to him. "You just listen to everyone without paying attention to the quality of the information," I continued. "You didn't bother to see whether the information is true or not. It's because of mistakes like this that the East Timorese don't like you. You spend a lot of money to pay illiterates and liars who not only give distorted information to you, but also damage your image in the international community. You don't trust me, the one who is loyal to you as your agent, but you trust people who lie."

He couldn't say anything to me. The funny thing was that the informant's lying made Edy Suprianto trust me even more.

I asked Suprianto if I could reduce my visits to his office. "I won't come to see you every afternoon any longer because I am afraid that people might see me and this could do damage to my work. So I will come to you at eight at night three times a week," I said to him. Edy agreed.

A frightening thing happened to me in early April 1991 soon after that meeting with Edy. I met with Xanana one night in Dili. Afterward I returned to Gabriela's house. Then, around midnight, someone knocked on my door. I was already frightened. I thought, "Oh my God. They probably know where Xanana is. They probably followed me."

"Who's there?" I asked.

"It's me," someone said. "I'm from SGI." I had just arrived home five minutes before. It was frightening. When I opened the door, the person said, "Good evening. Commander Edy Suprianto sent me to tell you that tomorrow morning at nine o'clock you will meet with the Panglima." *Panglima* is an Indonesian word that means high commander. He was referring to Rudy Warouw, the top military commander in East Timor.

"My God, why?" I wondered to myself. "I have never spoken to Rudy Warouw. Why is he so interested in me?"

"Yes, OK," I said.

In the morning, I was scared about going to the meeting. I was afraid that Indonesian intelligence already knew about Xanana's presence in Dili and my meeting with him. I brought Gabriela with me to meet with Edy Suprianto. I was thinking that if anything happened to me, Gabriela could come back home and tell people about my situation. I wasn't at all worried that the Indonesians would arrest Gabriela. They already knew that she was my girlfriend. If they had suspected her of anything, they would have already arrested her. The Indonesians were only interested in me.

We arrived at Colmera at 7:30 in the morning. Usually when I arrived at headquarters, Captain Edy would immediately greet me. This time, however, the environment was different. We sat there in the hall waiting for Edy Suprianto for almost one hour. I was very suspicious. I was afraid that Suprianto was angry with me or that he knew about my meeting with Xanana the previous night. I tried to calm down by smoking some cigarettes. As I waited with Gabriela, I tried to formulate my argument in case Edy accused me of anything. What was I going to say if he said he knew that I met with Xanana the previous night? I could only say that it was a lie. I decided that I would have to say that I knew nothing about Xanana, that it would be impossible for Xanana to come down to Dili if there were soldiers all over the territory supported by a vast intelligence apparatus.

After almost one hour, Edy Suprianto came to us. "*Pak Pinto*" (Mr. Pinto), he said, "*selamat pagi*" (good morning). Edy sounded fine. It seemed that he knew nothing about Xanana. I calmed down. "Why haven't we heard from you?" he asked. "We need information."

"Of course," I answered. "But things are still going tough. We need time, that's all."

"Well," he said, "today we are going to meet with the high commander, Mr. Warouw. Now you are going to have the honor of meeting with the highest-ranking person in the military in East Timor." I was struck by how the Indonesian soldiers respected their commanders, as if they were God. But I was not impressed. Warouw was my enemy.

Edy took Gabriela and me to Korem, a green building next to the Koni Athletic center in Kaikoli, Dili. At Korem, I ran into Chico Dias, an older man with whom I had been imprisoned. I had heard his screams when I was being interrogated at Colmera. He also was called to meet with Warouw. I think he was released as a result of my proposal to Gatot. Captain Edy took Chico to Warouw's office while I was waiting. After one hour, Chico Dias left. Then it was my turn. I went into his office; Gabriela waited outside. I was alone.

"Pak Pinto, I've heard a lot about you," Warouw said. The Indonesians always called me Pak Pinto because my last name was much easier for them to pronounce than my first name. The word *pintu* in Indonesian means "door." So it is easy for them to pronounce. "You are an intelligent man," he continued. "I really need you and want to talk to you about something very important for East Timor."

"I'm sorry. I'm not as smart as you think," I told him. "However, perhaps we could share some ideas about East Timor."

He didn't ask me at all about Xanana. He asked me about how to improve the human rights situation in East Timor.

"That is easy," I responded. "First, the army should withdraw from East Timor. Then, you have to fire all the intelligence agents you are now using in East Timor because you are using stupid, illiterate people who don't know how to behave in society. These people cause a lot of problems for you. They arrest, torture, and imprison people without reason. For these reasons, the international community always puts pressure on you."

Warouw seemed convinced by the second proposal.

"Yes, I was also thinking about reducing the intelligence presence," he stated.

"No," I replied. "Don't just reduce it; destroy it. Then you could reorganize it by using people who are responsible and more sophisticated. Also, the army should approach the population in a cooperative manner. The East Timorese are never afraid of being questioned; they will talk with anyone about the situation in East Timor, even about their personal situation. If the army suspects that someone is politically active in East Timor, why don't they just go to that person's house and ask them questions rather than arresting and torturing them? Because of the torture and general mistreatment of the East Timorese, the people still don't love Indonesia. If you beat someone, he will be your bitter enemy."

I was walking a fine line between trying to seem like a loyal Indonesian citizen and trying to help the resistance.

Warouw seemed persuaded. "Yes, that's a good idea," he said. But he didn't accept the first proposal, that the army should withdraw from East Timor. "That would be difficult," he said. "If we withdraw the army from East Timor, things will be chaotic; people will kill each other."

We talked for about an hour. As I left his office, he gave me 200,000 *rupiah*, which was worth about 100 U.S. dollars. "Mr. Pinto, this is for your expenses, to pay for your work," he told me.

Because I wanted to go to Jakarta to prepare secretly for the arrival of the Portuguese delegation to East Timor, I used the opportunity to

ask Rudy Warouw if I could travel to Jakarta. "Yes, you can go whenever you want," he told me.

I used Warouw's permission to pressure Gatot. The next day I said
to Gatot, "I already asked Bapak Panglima if I can go to Jakarta. He
said there's no problem." Gatot couldn't say no.

The visit of the Portuguese delegation to East Timor had been
agreed to by Indonesia and Portugal, after at least three or four years
of discussion. The purpose of the delegation was supposedly for the
Portuguese to see the reality of life in East Timor, to let them gather
firsthand information. Indonesia expected that all the development—
the roads, buildings, and other construction—would impress the Portuguese. From the perspective of the resistance, it was important
because we hoped that the Portuguese would see the reality of daily
life for the East Timorese people. They would meet with the people
and find out about human rights violations and the continuing aspirations of the East Timorese people for self-determination and independence. I first learned about the delegation in 1990 when I met with
Mau Hudo in the jungle. Xanana also told me about it in 1990 in a letter he wrote to the members of the underground movement.

The reason that I gave the Indonesians for wanting to go to Jakarta
was to establish contacts with people abroad, such as José Ramos
Horta. "I've lost my contacts with people abroad," I told them, "so I
need to establish contacts from Indonesia, especially through Fernando de Araujo. I'd also like to learn about the underground organization within Indonesia."

The Indonesians already knew Fernando de Araújo was working
in Bali as the leader of the underground within Indonesia. He had
sought asylum in the Japanese embassy in Jakarta, but he was unsuccessful. He agreed to leave the embassy and went back to school under the condition that the army would not arrest him. As part of the
agreement, the Japanese embassy promised Fernando that they
would monitor his security. The reason the Indonesians did not arrest
Fernando is probably because they had made a promise to the Japanese embassy to leave him alone and also because of pressure from
international organizations, such as Amnesty International, that kept
their eyes on Fernando.

My real purpose in going to Jakarta was to get the message back to Indonesian intelligence that people knew that I was working with them. Another purpose of my trip was to meet with Fernando, Domingos Sarmento, and others to coordinate the underground activities in Jakarta for the upcoming Portuguese parliamentary visit. (Domingos had fled to Jakarta soon after the Indonesians captured Xanana's camp and found out that Domingos had brought Robert Domm to East Timor; fortunately, Domingos narrowly escaped being arrested in Surabaya by the military and was able to go into hiding in Jakarta.) We were planning to hold a demonstration in Jakarta when the Portuguese arrived. Fernando and Domingos knew exactly what I was doing, of course. Xanana also knew about my strategy and agreed to it.

When Gabriela and I left for Jakarta in April, it became clear that my strategy of letting people know that I was working for the Indonesians was working. As soon as I left Dili, people in East Timor immediately called students in Bali and said, "Be careful of Constâncio. Gatot is paying him six million *rupiah* to go to Jakarta. He's a very dangerous intelligence agent."

So the news was that I was working for Indonesian intelligence; this became a big issue in Dili. Everyone was angry with me. The same information had spread around Jakarta when I was there. This is exactly what I wanted. As people began to talk about my situation, the Indonesians heard about it. They got mad. But they couldn't be angry with me because they allowed me to go to Jakarta.

While I was in Jakarta, Robert Domm sent someone from Australia to meet Domingos and me. Robert wanted to help Domingos, Gabriela, and me escape to Australia. But because of the Portuguese parliamentary delegation, we decided not to leave for Australia. We decided to go back to East Timor, while Domingos would stay in Jakarta.

Domingos and I did some secret lobbying in Jakarta at various embassies. Domingos had already had contact with a number of Western embassies and knew how to enter the embassies without attracting the attention of Indonesian intelligence. I introduced Domingos as a member of the CNRM in Jakarta in charge of lobbying in the Indonesian capital. We went to the embassies of Britain, Spain,

Australia, Japan, and a number of other countries. We didn't go to the U.S. Embassy because we were afraid that the CIA was working with Indonesian intelligence to track opponents of the Indonesian government, just as they had in 1965 when Suharto came to power in a bloody coup.

The standard practice for Western countries is to try to show that they are the pioneers of protecting human rights and self-determination. Often, however, this is more rhetoric than reality. When we met with the first secretary of the Australian Embassy, for example, he claimed that the human rights violations in East Timor were an important matter for Australian foreign policy. He never said, though, that the people of East Timor have the right to self-determination. Generally, however, the meetings were successful. It was part of our efforts to bring attention to the upcoming Portuguese visit to East Timor. Many of the embassies were very supportive of the visit. I also heard directly for the first time the perspectives of various Western countries on the self-determination struggle in East Timor and let them know about my own situation.

After returning to Dili, I tried to stay one week more at home, relaxing. Edy became angry because I didn't report to him. He sent someone to my house. "Why didn't you report to us?" the agent asked.

"Well, I have been tired," I replied. "But I have been planning to meet with commander Edy this week." The next day I went to Suprianto's office.

"Did you like Jakarta?" he asked.

"Yes, very much," I replied. "Everything was very interesting. It is a very nice city; I'd love to stay there."

"And how about the channels?" he inquired.

"I already set them up," I answered. "Fernando de Araújo will send me information, and I will pass it on to you." I had asked Fernando to send me newspaper articles and reports about human rights violations in East Timor published by Amnesty International, by TAPOL, the Indonesia Human Rights Campaign in London, and other human rights organizations. Fernando used to receive these publications regularly. He was supposed to send them to me through the post office, and I would pass them on to Suprianto. This was one of the arrangements we set up to satisfy Suprianto. He was happy.

"We really want such things," he said as he patted me on the back. "We want to get information from the outside." But the packages Fernando sent to me contained only newsletters and newspaper clippings that talked about human rights violations in East Timor.

After about three weeks, I received a packet of newspaper clippings from Fernando. I didn't want to open the envelope. I gave the whole envelope to Edy Suprianto and he was really happy. "Okay, now we begin to get information from the outside," he proclaimed. But he didn't know what was inside. In any case, he was happy, even if was only information about human rights violations. He read it and we kept doing the same thing. Fernando would send me newsletters and articles and I would give them to Edy Suprianto. It was not important material at all.

Nevertheless, the Indonesians came to rely on the documents that he was sending me as a way of monitoring Fernando's activities. Intelligence wanted to know about every channel in and out of East Timor and Indonesia, with the hope of eventually controlling the channels. Although the documents that Fernando sent weren't of great value to Edy Suprianto and his assistants, they probably were hoping that better things would come, that they would be able to learn a good deal in the future about the resistance and its links abroad. Edy's aim was to destroy the network of the underground movement and my contacts. He wanted to take over and control the relations between José Ramos Horta and the resistance.

Edy Suprianto was happy that I gave him letters from Fernando. He would give me money, sometimes 100,000 *rupiah*, even if I didn't want it. "This is just for you for coffee, beer, and cigarettes," he would tell me.

"I don't need this money," I would respond. But then he would just put it in my pocket. Of course, I gave some of this money to the resistance.

Edy expected to get more letters, but after a while they stopped. He kept asking me, "How about news from abroad?"

"Fernando did not send me anything lately," I would tell him. "He also is having trouble getting news from abroad." But Edy's main concern was always Xanana.

"Where is Xanana? You have to tell us," he would always demand.

"It's still difficult. Since I was arrested, those people who worked with me have disappeared," I would answer. "And I don't know where they live. Just wait until Xanana sends me someone."

I saw that Edy was unhappy with me even though I had established the link with Fernando because I was still telling him that I hadn't seen anyone who had contact with Xanana.

Soon after I returned from Jakarta, I suggested that we change the situation again. "I'm afraid that if I come to headquarters so many nights a week people from the underground might find out that I am working for you; the underground has its own intelligence network. Why don't we change our strategy? Why don't you guys come to my house a few times a week?" I proposed. "You can come to my house in the afternoon. Don't come in the evening. Come to my house at four or five in the afternoon."

My strategy was just to play with time, but then intelligence started coming to my house, and the result was terrifying. They came almost every day, and they constantly changed the time they would come. Sometimes they would come at midnight. Sometimes Edy's assistants would come and sometimes Edy himself would come and they would take me in their car and drive me around the city. Often they would do this very late at night. Other times, SGI would send someone to my house and have the person tell me to meet intelligence at a particular place and time.

One night Edy Suprianto and one of his friends took me to the Areia Branca, or white sand beach; the Indonesians call it Pasir Putih. It was midnight and they began to question me. The situation was tense: we were alone in the car and they had pistols. They said that they would kill me. "We will see who is the hero if you don't tell us the truth," Edy threatened.

"Mr. Pinto," they said, "you know Xanana very well; you know where he is. You have to tell us. Just tell us. Don't play games."

"I can't tell you anything," I answered. "I couldn't tell you where

Xanana is. I am not going to fabricate information for you. If I provide you with good information, I know that you're going to give me a good prize, more than what people gain from SDSB." (SDSB is the Indonesian lottery.) "If I know where Xanana is," I continued, "I will take you to him or maybe I will ask him to come to you and negotiate."

"No, don't tell him anything," Edy replied. "Just tell us where he is and then we will go see him. Then we will give you money, a car, a house, and, if you want, women. We have a lot of beautiful women in Java."

"If I find out where Xanana is, I will tell you immediately," I told them. "But I will need a lot of money. I will not be able to stay here in East Timor if we arrest Xanana."

"We can give you a home in Jakarta if you want to live in Jakarta," Edy told me. "You can meet with President Suharto."

I pretended to be impressed. I would tell the Indonesians whatever they wanted to hear while giving the impression that I was trying hard to help them uncover important information about the resistance. But I had to be careful; I was always worried that they would grow impatient with me and realize that I was playing games with them.

A few months after I returned from Jakarta, Suprianto showed me a tape cassette. "This is Xanana's message," he said. Xanana often sent his messages by tape. "You don't have connections with Xanana," he bragged, "but we do."

It was kind of stupid that he told me that. I said, "OK, you have connections to Xanana. Why don't I write a letter and I'll send it through you? I'd like to make contact with Xanana again. I lost my connections when I was arrested."

But Suprianto was lying. He was probably using the tape in the hope that I would tell him that I was in contact with Xanana. It didn't work.

After I returned to Dili from Jakarta, I continued working with Xanana. I spent most of my time writing letters and meeting with him occasionally, depending on when he needed me. By August, however, Xanana was in a very bad situation.

In July, Xanana had met with a Portuguese journalist, Mário Robalo, who was in Dili. I wasn't able to make the preparations for the meeting because I had to report regularly to Indonesian intelligence, and my movements and my house were closely monitored. So another group of people helped to prepare the meeting. It took place in the house of a nurse called Mateus Goveia. In the group, there was a young man named Cepeda. Xanana had given his camera to Cepeda to take pictures of the meeting.

Perhaps because of his personal ambitions, Cepeda decided to take one of the rolls of film to develop by himself. At the end of the meeting, Cepeda was supposed to give all of the rolls to Xanana. Cepeda, however, had replaced the last roll with a new one. In the morning, Cepeda stupidly gave the film to a developer who, according to our information, had very close connections with the Indonesian Red Berets intelligence. The person developed the pictures at Juwita Film, in Dili, which is owned by an Indonesian, and then sold one set of copies to the Indonesian military.

That afternoon someone from Indonesian intelligence came by my house. "Mr. Pinto, do you know that Xanana is in Dili?" he asked.

"I don't know anything about that," I said. "But how is that possible? It's impossible for Xanana to come down to Dili."

"We are certain that he is here. We have proof," he replied.

"Do you know where he is?" I asked.

"We know," he answered, "but that information is just for us; you don't have to know." But someone from the underground had informed me earlier that Xanana had already left the house where the meeting took place and had gone to a different area of Dili. The next day the Indonesian military went to the meeting house and arrested Mateus Goveia. But Xanana wasn't there. They came to me and told me that Xanana had escaped.

"I don't believe that Xanana is in Dili," I told them.

"No, he is here," they insisted, "but he has already moved to a new place. And the person who hosted Xanana has already been arrested."

I tried to learn more. "Who is that person?" I asked. I pretended not to know. "Where does he live?"

"We don't want to tell you," they answered. "That's just for us. We'll take care of it."

"I want to help you, but if you don't want to tell me, it's up to you," I told him. "Maybe I have better access to the East Timorese than you. You are Indonesian. I can talk to them and find out where Xanana is."

I was lucky that Cepeda did not tell intelligence everything. He could have told the Indonesian army that I was still working with Xanana and organizing in the underground.

I don't think Cepeda was working for the Indonesians. If he had been working for intelligence, the Indonesians would have arrested everyone the night when the meeting happened. I think he was an opportunist. He probably wanted to show off to people that he had met with Xanana Gusmão. Cepeda made a very bad judgment. The Indonesians arrested Cepeda and took him in for interrogation. I'm not sure whether he was tortured or not, because he had a close relative who was one of the high officials in battalion 744. In any case, Cepeda's actions caused great problems for Xanana.

For a whole month, from July to August, Dili was dense with soldiers looking for Xanana. He was hiding in a bakery in Dili the whole time. The Indonesian army was camped right by the bakery. After several weeks of looking for him, the military thought that maybe he had escaped from Dili and called off the search.

Xanana was probably angry with Cepeda, but he didn't really show it. Cepeda's stupidity made it difficult for Xanana to leave Dili. Because of Cepeda, Xanana had to stop his activities for almost six months. After that incident, he couldn't go to the mountains to visit the guerrillas because the Indonesians now had his picture and knew what he looked like. They suspected that he was in Dili, and they put checkpoints everywhere in the territory—all the way to Baucau and to the eastern and southern regions.

I wasn't in contact with Xanana while he was in hiding. I knew where he was and that he was safe, but I didn't want to jeopardize his situation.

10

Preparing for
the Portuguese Delegation

After my release from prison in February 1991, we began preparing for the arrival of the Portuguese parliamentary delegation. The delegation was originally supposed to arrive in Dili in late May 1991. It had taken two years for Indonesia and Portugal to reach agreement on the visit because Indonesia insisted that the delegation stop over in Jakarta. In the underground, we discussed whether it was best that Portugal accept the stopover or come to East Timor through another country, such as Australia. The Portuguese were really insistent that they wouldn't stop in Jakarta because they didn't want to give any recognition to Indonesia's occupation. Later on, Xanana and the other members of the resistance decided that it was best that the Portuguese parliamentary delegation agree to stop in Jakarta. For us, the most important thing was that the delegation come to East Timor. So Xanana sent a message to the members of the delegation telling them that we would like them to stop over in Jakarta, only for a few hours, to greet members of the Indonesian parliament and government and then continue to East Timor. Portugal agreed. But then, despite the agreement, there were a number of postponements of the delegation's arrival because of disagreements over details, especially the composition of the delegation. Finally, the delegation was scheduled to arrive on November 4, 1991.

The underground was well prepared. All over the territory we had discussed what we would do. Our plan was to have a big ceremony, something very formal, to greet the Portuguese delegation. We were going to gather a big audience to sing in an open area to welcome them and to create a situation of harmony between the East Timorese and the Indonesian army. We didn't want to provoke anything. We wanted to create an environment of joy and happiness.

For more than one year, the Portuguese parliamentary delegation visiting East Timor was in the daily prayers of all the East Timorese people. Our talk was full of hope and happiness. I myself was counting on the visit of the Portuguese to help alleviate the repression that we were experiencing. The East Timorese people put all their hopes in the Portuguese delegation to solve the East Timor problem quickly or at least to help find a way out of the conflict. The people were very confident because they knew that the Portuguese would not come to East Timor alone, but would be accompanied by United Nations officials, foreign journalists, and international dignitaries. We were planning to have thousands of civilians from Dili accompany them as well. As the parliamentary group visited each town throughout the territory, more people would join in. The plan was that everyone would join and stay with the Portuguese delegation in Dili day and night and urge them to hold talks with Indonesia and the East Timorese resistance. We actually had plans to set up a meeting between Xanana Gusmão, the Portuguese parliamentary delegation, and the Indonesian government.

We wanted to hold what Xanana had been proposing: negotiations without preconditions under UN auspices. Xanana actually came to Dili with the intention of meeting with the Portuguese delegation, but we didn't know exactly where in Dili the meeting would take place, or if it would be somewhere else altogether.

Under my leadership, the underground movement had prepared for the arrival of the Portuguese. People had prepared banners and planned peaceful demonstrations and parties. We disseminated information throughout the underground. We made preparations in Dili,

Baucau, and all other major towns, even in Oecussi. All these areas were ready to greet the Portuguese. We didn't prepare for the worst but for the best. We were hoping that our peaceful and amiable invitation to the Indonesian government would convince Suharto to instruct his soldiers to lay down their weapons and embrace the East Timorese people as their brothers and sisters, as they always said we were, and would set aside the past and sit around a table to discuss the problems affecting both sides. We have always said that FALINTIL would be happy to lay down their weapons whenever the Indonesian soldiers would do the same.

As the date of arrival of the Portuguese delegation approached, the situation in East Timor became very tense. The Indonesian provincial government and the military launched a campaign of political propaganda and intimidation throughout the territory. They threatened people every day. The number of Indonesian troops increased significantly. Many Indonesian immigrants returned to their hometowns because they were afraid that there might be trouble. The underground movement, on the other hand, organized the population in every town to greet the Portuguese.

The underground movement's preparations for the Portuguese delegation intensified at the beginning of May 1991 when Warouw, the commander of East Timor, reduced military activities. Warouw had implemented some of the ideas I proposed; after he met with me, he met with members of the provincial assembly in East Timor who put forth similar ideas. During May and June, for example, the military reduced the frequency of its house-to-house searches.

But soon the Indonesian army began to threaten people, returning to their old ways. They went from house to house, village to village, giving lectures and speeches, telling people that anyone caught attempting to organize a demonstration when the Portuguese parliamentary delegation arrived in Dili, or anyone who tried to make trouble for Indonesia, would be responsible for her or his life, as well as the lives of everyone else in their village. The Indonesian military said that they would kill anyone who participated in a demonstration and all the people of the village where that person lived. "If you talk to the Portuguese or demonstrate against Indonesia, that's against Indonesia. Whoever is thinking of doing this should be very careful. Whoever does this will be responsible for his life. We, the army, will kill them."

The threats were intense, taking place everywhere in Dili and in all the districts throughout the territory. The Indonesian military also went to state schools to talk to the students. The Indonesian commanders even had a meeting for every student in Dili during which they clearly explained their position on the Portuguese parliamentary delegation and what they would do if there was a demonstration. They were very open: "We will kill anyone who attempts to demonstrate against Indonesia." The Indonesians also tried to recruit people as part of a traditional, indigenous East Timorese army to perform some Timorese dances to greet the Portuguese parliamentary delegation. They even organized people to hold anti-Portugal demonstrations, but ironically they selected people who had been already trained by the underground movement, so we didn't feel threatened at all. We were confident that these people would turn publicly against Indonesia at the right time.

As part of their campaign of intimidation, the Indonesians dug mass graves in Tacitolo, Gleno, and Aileu as a warning to the people. We discovered these graves, but people did not believe that the Indonesians would take very extreme actions against the East Timorese because of the presence of the Portuguese and the representatives from international organizations such as the UN.

Indonesia's system of control was complicated and dangerous. I say complicated because the control is in the hands of the police and the army. There are also hundreds of people working for civilian intelligence; many of them come from West Timor. It is confusing because these agencies of repression play by their own rules. They all torture, imprison, and threaten people and rape women. The police who are supposed to protect the civilian population from crime are the ones who commit crime. The military does the same thing. There are infantry troops to fight the guerrillas, and there are territorial troops throughout the country as well.[1] The Indonesians claim that the territorial troops are there to help in the development of East Timor, that they are building roads and clinics and schools. But their real purpose is to monitor and control the civilian population in the towns. In each village, the Indonesians have a police official and a military official who work with the head of the district. And they have their own military and police intelligence networks throughout the country. And within the military, we have to distinguish between the territorial troops, the infantry, and Kopassus[2]—the Red Beret commandos, the elite soldiers. Each of them has its own intelligence apparatus.

The Indonesians also often created problems to test the population. They would send five or six intelligence agents to a village, for example, and have them fight against each other. One would say, "You are an Indonesian collaborator," and the other would say, "You are a spy," and so on. They did this to test the reaction of the population, to see who was going to support the one who was pro-Indonesian and who would support the one who was anti-Indonesian. If you supported the one that was anti-Indonesian, you would be in trouble. Military intelligence had all kinds of tricks and tactics.

During all this time, I kept approaching the Indonesian army to find out what my contacts knew about our preparations for the delegation. But it seemed that they didn't know that people were prepared to take actions when the Portuguese arrived.

At the same time that I was working for the arrival of the Portuguese, Gabriela and I were planning to get married. We had decided to marry and to give our names to the Church for marriage preparation after we returned from Jakarta in May 1991. Gabriela and I had been together for almost two years and our parents were encouraging us to get married. We also wanted to get married and have children before anything happened to me. I was playing a very dangerous game with the Indonesians and I feared that it was just a matter of time before they figured out what I was doing and arrested me again. In such a situation, they would have probably killed me.

I didn't want to have a big party; I wanted to try to limit it to our immediate families. But Gabriela's parents wanted to have one. "Gabriela is our oldest girl," they said, "and Constâncio is the oldest boy. Why don't we have a big party? This is the first wedding for our families." My parents agreed. I received a lot of help from my friends.

I also asked Colonel Gatot Purwanto and Edy Suprianto to help. They sent around 30 soldiers to set up a military tent for the party. It was in Kaikoli at Gabriela's house. The soldiers worked very hard. "Okay," they said, "we're working for Constâncio now. Constâncio's our man." My strategy in involving them was to strengthen the impression of people at the wedding that I worked with Indonesian intelligence so there would be additional news to the Indonesian military that my position as an Indonesian agent was exposed.

In addition to sending invitations to Purwanto and Suprianto, I sent one to Rudy Warouw and to other military commanders. Unfortunately, they were smart; the commanders didn't come. But they sent their intelligence people and a group of low-ranking Indonesian soldiers. They brought us an oven as a present. I thought that they were going to give me money, but they didn't.

The party was great. I didn't expect so many people to come; about 200 people attended, but most of my relatives didn't come because they were afraid of the Indonesians. My immediate family was there, of course.

The wedding took place on September 15, 1991 at the Balide Church. I was both happy and anxious at my wedding. I was very happy that Gabriela and I were finally getting married. But after we danced, after we ate everything and drank the wine and so on, I began worrying that the next day I had to go and present myself to Indonesian intelligence once again.

The morning after my wedding I received a phone call from Donaciano in Portugal to congratulate me. In September 1990, Donaciano left East Timor for Portugal with his parents through the International Committee of the Red Cross. There's an agreement between Portugal and Indonesia that Indonesia has to allow the International Committee of the Red Cross to help reunite East Timorese with family members abroad. Donaciano's departure was sad, especially for our group within the executive committee. But by having Donaciano in Portugal, our work abroad could be more effective than before. When Donaciano left Dili, hundreds of students went to Comoro Airport to say goodbye. I also went to wish him well. At that time Indonesian intelligence already suspected our group. When I hugged Donaciano to say goodbye, an Indonesian intelligence agent took our photograph. After that I became more careful doing my work in the underground.

After speaking with Donaciano on the phone, I reported to military intelligence. Gabriela and I brought a piece of our wedding cake to them. I also sent pieces of cake to all the commanders who I invited. I don't know if they ate it or not; they might have been afraid of poison in the cake, but I was kind. We thanked them for their present and for all their help. Xanana was there in Dili at the time; he also got a piece of cake. He sent me a very nice poem about my marriage to Gabriela. Unfortunately, I lost it when I went underground several weeks later.

I still remember one night a few weeks after the wedding when Colonel Gatot Purwanto asked my impression of what might possibly happen when the Portuguese arrived in East Timor. "Some sort of demonstration will probably happen because, as you know, there have been demonstrations before—during the Pope's visit and John Monjo's visit. This is not something new for us," I explained. I always talked in terms of "us," as Indonesians. I acted like a good Indonesian citizen. "Maybe something like that could happen when the Portuguese arrive," I continued. "From my point of view, if a demonstration happens, let it happen. I think it's important to tell the army to just watch. Don't take any action against a demonstration. Then Indonesia will have a reputation as a country where people are free, where freedom of speech exists." But Gatot didn't agree with my proposal.

"We have people who already support us," he answered. He mentioned Labut Melo and other East Timorese intelligence operatives who collaborated with them. "And we already have people who want to demonstrate against the Portuguese delegation," he said. "We will stop by any means necessary any demonstration that is against the Indonesian presence in East Timor."

A couple of weeks before the Portuguese delegation was due to arrive, Edy Suprianto asked whether I thought that the delegation was coming or not. I pretended to be pessimistic. "All this is simply a political maneuver on the part of the Portuguese," I said to him. "Politics can change at any time, just as someone changes his or her clothes every day. I don't think that it's certain that the Portuguese will come.

Portugal can easily decide at the last minute to postpone the meeting or cancel the meeting without any reason." Of course, I didn't know what was going to happen. We hoped that Portugal would come, but I didn't want to show that I was feeling optimistic.

As the date of the delegation's arrival approached, repression increased even more. In October, the Indonesians began arresting people they suspected of being involved in the underground movement. At that time, about 30 young men sought protection in the Motael Church in Dili because of Indonesian persecution. One day, the Indonesians shot at one of them when he was walking in the street in Colmera. They probably shot at him because he had been at the Motael Church. Fortunately, he wasn't hit by the bullet and successfully returned to the Motael.

After that, I went to the Motael Church and told the people there, "You have to be careful. One day the Indonesian army will kill some of you in public just to show the people that if you demonstrate, if you continue with your actions against Indonesia, you must pay a high price." I tried to save them; I advised them not to show their faces outside the Motael Church, to hide themselves, but many of them didn't listen. The upcoming visit of the Portuguese delegation gave them a false sense of courage. They would walk around in the courtyard of the church sometimes and taunt the intelligence agents watching the church. That's how the Indonesian army found out where they were hiding. This was a tactical error.

Indonesia's persecution of the young men followed their participation in a demonstration at Santus Paulus, one of the high schools in Dili, and the demonstration during the Pope's visit. The young men sought protection from the church. The church was the best place for the young people to go. A 50-year-old man, Afonso Rangel, also sought refuge there. The Indonesian military knew that all those people were hiding at the church. It was well known that they were there, but Indonesia decided to wait for the best time to surround the Motael and arrest them. Gatot himself told me this, as did Edy Suprianto. "There are some young kids who are now hiding in the Motael Church," he said. "We're trying to arrest them."

Suddenly, however, the situation changed. One week after I spoke to Suprianto, we heard strong rumors in Dili that Portugal had decided not to send the delegation to East Timor. In late October, the Portuguese ultimately canceled the visit because Indonesia refused to allow one of the journalists on the Portuguese list to accompany the delegation. When the news arrived in East Timor, it shocked and saddened everyone. We had prepared for almost one year for the visit. Almost everyone in East Timor was greatly demoralized by the decision.

The Portuguese cancellation was a victory for Indonesia. The Indonesians had opened the door to Portugal to come to East Timor, but the Portuguese let their pride get in the way. Indonesia was wrong to prohibit the journalist from coming to East Timor, but that was not a good reason to cancel the delegation; there are other good journalists. People were really angry with Portugal and upset with this decision; it made people afraid of what the Indonesians might do. I thought the Portuguese parliamentary delegation acted cowardly. We had spent all this time encouraging the delegates to come to East Timor. Xanana had sent them all the details about our preparations.[3]

The cancellation of the Portuguese delegation was really discouraging to the members of the resistance in East Timor. The news came to East Timor sporadically through the news and radio broadcasts and also from telephone calls from Portugal and Australia. People were really mad and disappointed. We feared that Indonesia would undertake mass killings because the military had already prepared to kill all the underground leaders and activists. The Indonesians had been very clear about their intentions to the East Timorese. The Indonesian army always said that if the Portuguese didn't come now, they would never come to East Timor, and that would mean that Portugal didn't care about East Timor. And they said that the political situation in East Timor could only become stable with the extermination of the underground leadership. The Indonesian army also began to leak the names of people it was going to arrest. Besides hearing public threats, we heard about Indonesia's intentions from members of the underground who worked with Indonesian intelligence.

Just as we feared, Indonesia immediately began to step up its terrifying actions after the Portuguese decided to cancel the delegation.

On October 28, 1991, at 1:30 in the morning, the Indonesians took advantage of the cancellation and surrounded the Motael Church where the 30 young men were in sanctuary. The Indonesians shot and killed my friend, Sebastião Gomes, and arrested 25 others.[4] Only a few people escaped. The young men tried to protect themselves but they couldn't because the military had weapons. An East Timorese named Afonso who was working for Indonesian intelligence also died during the attack on the Motael Church; he was stabbed by someone during the assault. The Indonesians destroyed things inside the church, including the *sacrário* where the host is kept. When the army assaulted the Motael, the church bell woke up many people, including myself. Afterward, a large crowd of people gathered outside the church. People were very angry and shouted at the Indonesian soldiers. The Indonesian military blocked the church and didn't allow anyone to enter. Fortunately, Bishop Belo went there early in the morning and helped to calm the situation. But we were afraid that Indonesia would continue its retaliation throughout the country. We were really worried that they might possibly arrest and kill everyone in the underground movement.

That afternoon, Sebastião's family took his body to their house to prepare his coffin. The next evening, on October 29, Bishop Belo celebrated mass at the Motael Church for Sebastião. A few thousand people gathered outside and inside the church for the mass. I wasn't there; I was trying to avoid such gatherings because I was afraid. The Indonesians had already arrested the young people at the Motael who had been working with me preparing banners and flags for the Portuguese visit. After the mass, people marched to the Santa Cruz Cemetery for the burial. It was a huge funeral procession led by Bishop Belo, complete with candlelight and many people spontaneously shouting out "Long Live Sebastião!" and "Long Live East Timor." Never since Indonesia's invasion had there been such a gathering. Sebastião's killing made people more angry and determined to carry out the struggle. For whatever reason, the military and the police did not interfere in the procession; they simply observed. I joined the crowd at the cemetery to pay my respects to Sebastião. I was not worried about my safety because it was dark and there were so many people gathered at the cemetery that Indonesian intelligence would not be able to see me.

Fortunately, foreign journalists covered Sebastião's killing. Journalists had already begun to arrive in East Timor in late October in anticipation of the visit by the Portuguese delegation. The foreign journalists included Max Stahl, Allan Nairn, and Amy Goodman. Max Stahl was a British television journalist. He and a camera crew from Yorkshire Television first came to East Timor in July 1991. They contacted me as soon as they arrived. They wanted to get information and some film footage of East Timor for a documentary, and they especially hoped to meet with Xanana. Xanana was already in Dili by that time. It was not possible for us to set up a meeting with Xanana, but we set up some interviews for them with people from the underground, including some of the young men who went into hiding at the Motael Church. You can see them in the documentary *Cold Blood*.[5] I organized some of the interviews myself, but other people did most of the work. I couldn't involve myself too much because of my activities with Indonesian intelligence.

At the time of Max's visit, I was playing a very dangerous game with Colonel Gatot Purwanto and his men. At first I refused to be interviewed by Max Stahl because I feared for my life if the Indonesians found out about the film. But after Max promised to black out my face in the documentary and just show my profile, I allowed him to interview me. The interview took place in a bathroom. I told Max about the political conditions in East Timor at that time and the preparations of the Indonesian military prior to the visit of the Portuguese parliamentary delegation. I told him how the Indonesian army was intimidating people, about the mass graves being dug in Tacitolo, and about persecutions, imprisonment, torture, and the mass mobilization of the military.

Max Stahl and his crew generally interviewed people who had been in prison, who had been tortured by the Indonesian military, or who had been in the jungle for many years. They also interviewed people from the Church; I can't mention their names for security reasons, with the exception of Father Domingos Soares, who is very brave and outspoken in the interview. Father Domingos is one of the

many courageous priests in East Timor. Max also filmed some or-
phanages in Baucau and Venilale.[6] Basically the film documents human rights violations and the desire of the people of East Timor for
self-determination. Max returned to East Timor by himself on the
morning of October 27. He immediately found me at the Motael
Church, where I updated him on the situation.

At eight on the night of Sebastião's burial, someone named
Honasan from Indonesian intelligence came to my house along with
an assistant. Honasan had threatened me a number of times before
Sebastião's killing. He used to come to my house looking for me; he
would sometimes say, "Mr. Pinto, if you don't want to tell us the
truth, we will see who will be the hero." Later, when I went into hiding, the same guy threatened to kill me.

Honasan and his colleague came to find out what I knew about
what had happened at the Motael. They asked me for information.
"Where is Xanana?" they asked. They didn't mention anything at first
about Sebastião or what had happened at the Motael, so I began asking them some questions. I tried to praise them to win their confidence. "You are a really good commando," I told Honasan. "You
were able to find those young men and their banners and kill Sebastião. I really admire the group that was able to infiltrate the Motael
Church." I asked them who went into the church.

Honasan was very proud of himself and he seemed to want to
show off. He immediately said, "It was me with my fellow soldiers. It
was a really successful operation." His description of how he attacked
the young people and killed Sebastião made me really angry. I became really angry and I couldn't hide my feelings. But I still tried to
pretend that I was working with them.

"Because of what you did it's difficult for us to work together," I
told him. "You're killing my people. I have told you many times that
the East Timorese always are ready to talk with anyone of us from the
Indonesian army, from the Indonesian government. They will discuss
things with you and they will accept whatever you suggest. Instead
of doing that, you are taking very extreme actions like killing
Sebastião Gomes. How can people trust you if you just continue to
kill the people even here in Dili?" I was really angry and I lost my

temper. "I don't have any information about Xanana," I yelled. "I was at the cemetery tonight and I saw that people were really angry with you. It's really difficult now for me to persuade and convince people to work with me. It's hard for me now to work with you. You have made a big mistake." As they already suspected me, they just laughed at me. It gave me the impression they had some sort of plan for me.

My fears turned out to be true. On November 1, Indonesian intelligence had a meeting about me in Villa Verde, a neighborhood in Dili. It was a meeting to discuss my arrest. The Indonesians had uncovered the game I was playing with them.

After they attacked the Motael on October 28, the Indonesians found the banners the young men were making in preparation for the arrival of the Portuguese delegation. I later found out that one of the young men arrested at the Motael, under intense torture, told the Indonesians that I was the one who gave the order to make the banners. The Indonesian military decided to rearrest me at five in the afternoon on November 2, 1991. They didn't know that one of the people at the meeting was part of the underground and knew me. I was very fortunate.

November 2 was the last meeting of the executive committee. It was in Dili at Francisco Branco's house. Afterward, as I was on my way home, I ran into a friend who was looking for me.

"Where are you going?" he asked. "I have been looking for you."

"I am going home," I answered.

"Don't go home," he warned. "They are going to arrest you at five o'clock. You have to go somewhere, and quickly."

I immediately decided to go into hiding. I never had the chance to say anything to my wife or my family before I went underground. I was very sad, and I was afraid. I felt almost as I did when I had to flee from the Indonesian soldiers into the jungle in 1975. I didn't know what was going to happen to me. I feared that I would never see Gabriela and my family again if the Indonesians caught me. I went into hiding without anyone knowing, but I was hopeful that it would be just temporary. Despite the cancellation, I still thought that there was a good chance that the Portuguese delegation would change its position and come to East Timor.

11

The Santa Cruz Massacre

I went underground on November 2, 1991. Two days later, I sent someone to my family to tell them that I had escaped. On the same day that I escaped, at the designated hour, Indonesian intelligence went to Gabriela's house and asked her where I was. Gabriela didn't know that I had already gone into hiding. "He went out this morning, and he hasn't come back," she told them. "Maybe you can come back later." They went back to the house later in the evening and asked for me again.

When I went underground, I immediately went to a friend's house in Dili for a couple of hours and then moved to another house of someone who worked with the underground resistance. Starting on that day, I went from house to house and slept in a different place every night. Friends in the underground helped find places for me to stay. From the various safe houses, I established contact with Xanana and other underground movement leaders through *estafetas*. A number of letters were sent to me asking what we should do in response to the cancellation of the Portuguese delegation. Some groups at that time were saying that if there were no instructions from the leadership, they would take the initiative in organizing demonstrations. I thought that it would be politically damaging if none of the underground leaders sent any instructions about a possible action.

I sent a letter to Xanana, who was still hiding in Dili, asking him if he thought we should go ahead with a demonstration. But before the members of the executive committee made any decision, we received news from Jakarta that the UN Special Rapporteur on Torture, Pieter Koojimans, was going to arrive in Dili on November 11, 1991. So we decided along with Xanana to take advantage of his visit and hold a peaceful demonstration. We didn't think that Indonesia would take any violent actions against the demonstrators in Koojimans' presence. In addition, we would be observing the fourteenth day since the killing of Sebastião Gomes. I sent a message to Xanana asking him whether he agreed that we should have a demonstration on November 12. Xanana soon responded and sent me instructions. "It's a good idea to have a demonstration," he said, "but be careful and be disciplined."

We had already planned to be fully peaceful and not to provoke anyone. None of the demonstrators were allowed to carry knives or anything that could be harmful. We told everyone not to attack or mistreat Indonesian police, soldiers, or government officials on the street. Our plan was to ask for a referendum in East Timor, and for dialogue between Indonesia and East Timorese leaders from the Church and the resistance, and to shout slogans such as "Long Live Xanana Gusmão" and "Long Live East Timor."

There were already journalists in Dili from a number of countries—from the United States, Great Britain, Australia, New Zealand, and other places. The U.S. journalists, Allan Nairn and Amy Goodman, who were working for *The New Yorker* magazine and Pacifica Radio, were there; they first came to East Timor in July and August 1990. At that time, the underground movement had restricted contact with foreigners who came to East Timor because we began to suspect some of the visitors. If someone wanted to meet with leaders from the resistance in East Timor, they had to make contact with resistance people on the outside. So before Allan and Amy came to East Timor, they had been in touch with people on the outside. That's how they learned my name. They knew where I was working, and came to the diocese in Dili to find me. When they arrived in 1990, we met and I helped them visit many places throughout the territory; I found taxi drivers for them, and organized meetings with prisoners, underground members, and other people who they could interview. Allan and Amy interviewed me, Donaciano Gomes, and José Manuel Fernandes one night at Externato. We were very scared, but nothing bad happened.

More than a year later, in late October 1991, Amy and Allan came back to Dili to cover the Portuguese parliamentary visit to East Timor. I heard from them a few days later, but I was already in hiding. They sent me a note saying, "We are here in town and we'd like to meet with you. We know that you are in a bad situation." I wasn't able to meet with them the first week, but then on November 11, at seven at night, the day before the demonstration was scheduled, we met at my hiding place. Amy and Allan interviewed me again and I took the opportunity to invite them to attend the demonstration the next day. I also asked them to invite the other journalists who were in Dili. When I said there would be a big demonstration, Allan and Amy were very excited and promised to be there. We had about a half-hour interview by candlelight. Amy took some pictures of me and then we separated. That was the last meeting we had in East Timor.

Very early in the morning on November 12, a huge crowd of people went to the memorial mass for Sebastião at the Motael Church. There was such a large crowd that many people had to listen to the service outside the church. Because I had gone into hiding, I could not go, but many participants told me what took place. After the mass, they marched to the Santa Cruz Cemetery to put flowers on Sebastião's grave. As the crowd marched through Dili, many of the marchers unfurled banners and shouted pro-independence slogans. Such a demonstration, such a large and open display of pro-independence sentiment, had not taken place in East Timor since Indonesia's invasion. By the time the procession reached the cemetery, there was a crowd of thousands of men, women, and children chanting slogans and waving flags and banners.

The UN Special Rapporteur on Torture was already in Dili. At the time of our demonstration he was having a meeting with Rudy Warouw, the Indonesian commander, at his office. Despite the UN visit, the Indonesian army had plans to take extreme actions against the demonstrators.[1] As the demonstrators began to march from the Motael Church, along the waterfront and past the governor's office, to the cemetery, some Indonesian soldiers, police, and intelligence agents tried to stop the marchers by throwing rocks at them and beating them. The demonstrators began to react. According to the Indonesian government, someone stabbed an Indonesian soldier. If this ever happened, it was almost certainly done by someone from the Indonesians' own civilian intelligence service, INTEL, because the demonstrators weren't allowed to carry any weapons.[2]

As a result of the altercation, the march was split into two: one group, which contained the vast majority of the demonstrators, continued to march about one mile to the cemetery, while the other group, the one that the army prevented from continuing, split up and took different routes but reached the cemetery about the same time as the others. As the demonstrators arrived at the cemetery, there were already Indonesian troops nearby. After the demonstrators arrived and had a brief ceremony in memory of Sebastião, a few army trucks came and started to unload troops. As the gathering was breaking up, soldiers began marching toward the crowd, and suddenly just opened fire without any warning. There was no provocation.

Allan Nairn and Amy Goodman saw the whole massacre; they are witnesses. They are people who can tell this story very vividly and clearly because they were at the front and were the first ones the soldiers saw.[3] The soldiers began to open fire on the defenseless demonstrators. People tried to flee; some people were shot down from the cemetery walls as they tried to escape over them. At least 271 people were killed and a few hundred more were wounded at the cemetery. Fortunately, some people were able to escape by jumping over the cemetery walls.

This massacre is a concrete example for the world of how the Indonesian military terrorizes the people of East Timor. Of course, such terror is not uncommon. The Indonesians are responsible for the deaths of about one-third of the East Timorese population. What made this massacre different was that journalists were present to document the crimes of the Indonesian military.

At the time of the march from the Motael, I was hiding in a house very close to the Santa Cruz Cemetery. I was with Juvencio Martins, a relative of mine who is now in prison, and Francisco Lelan, who passed away in 1992. We could hear the chants and shouts from the crowd as it approached. The noise was incredible. I knew that there must have been thousands of people. I didn't expect so many people, especially because the underground had let the public know about the demonstration only the day before. The size of the crowd, along with the shouts of "Viva Timor Leste" and "Viva Xanana Gusmão" made me really excited.

I decided to go join the demonstration in front of the cemetery and to film it even though I would be taking a real risk. I had a new video camera that I had received from some friends of the resistance in Japan that I had been planning to send to the guerrilla fighters in the mountains. I didn't want to miss what I thought was a very pivotal point in East Timorese history. The size of the demonstration made me think that something too big to miss—I didn't know what—was going to happen. I thought that the demonstration would grow and that Indonesia could do nothing to stop it. If Indonesia tried to stop it, I thought that there would have to be some sort of negotiation. Because of the size of the crowd and the presence of the foreign journalists at the cemetery and Pieter Koojimans, the UN Special Rapporteur on Torture, nearby, I didn't think that the Indonesian military would dare to use violent means to disperse the demonstrators.

As we walked out the door, the Indonesians opened fire. When we heard the shooting at the cemetery, we immediately turned back. Because the Indonesian army could have easily started searching every household, I quickly left the house and hid under a nearby bridge.

I was hiding close by the Santa Cruz Cemetery. From my hiding place, I could see trucks and ambulances going back and forth between the cemetery and the military hospital, carrying wounded people. Unfortunately, I didn't have a good camera; if I had, I could have documented the army carrying dead bodies in their trucks.

When the massacre first happened, I didn't think that anyone could have survived because the attack must have been well prepared by the Indonesian military. I was hoping to hear what had happened to the demonstrators from someone who escaped from the cemetery. I was really worried that everyone, including Allan Nairn and Amy Goodman, had been killed: bullets do not discriminate against anyone when someone randomly opens fire on a crowd. When I communicated through *estafeta* with friends from the underground after the massacre, the first question I asked them was how many people were killed and if they knew if any foreigners in the crowd had died. I was told that there was a white man who was killed at the cemetery and that some other foreigners had been wounded. I found out later that the foreigner who was killed was Kamal Bamadhaj, a New Zealand citizen; he was a human rights activist who was in East Timor to document the visit of the Portuguese delegation.[4] The wounded foreigners were Allan Nairn and Amy Goodman. Indonesian soldiers beat Allan with M-16 rifle butts and fractured his skull. They kicked Amy many times, and they almost killed both of them. Fortunately, they shouted that they were American citizens as they were being beaten. The soldiers probably stopped beating Amy and Allan because they realized that the two of them came from the same country that supplied many of their weapons. The Indonesians probably would have killed them if they had said they were Australians, just as they had killed a number of Australian journalists in East Timor in 1975.[5] After the beating, Allan and Amy escaped to Guam, but I didn't know where they had gone. I was worried, but I was confident that they had not been killed.

I wasn't worried about Gabriela because I didn't think she was at the cemetery. I had warned Gabriela not to go to the demonstration because she was seven months pregnant at that time. But a couple of days later, I found out that she had gone to the mass at the Motael Church and had joined the demonstration at the cemetery. When the Indonesians opened fire, she was near the front and was almost killed. She was right in front of the cemetery gate and was buried under a pile of bleeding bodies. Somehow she escaped. I don't know how she was spared, how she could climb over the cemetery wall, especially since she was very pregnant; it's high, but she climbed over it.

When the Indonesian army opened fire, I was worried about my sisters and brothers, some other friends I worked with, and all the people who participated in the demonstration. The killing of one affects us all. But I wasn't able to get information about my family at first. Two days later I sent someone to my house to check to see if anyone in my family had been arrested, killed, or wounded. Luckily, everyone in my family was fine. Then I found out that Gabriela had been there but had escaped.

Domingos Segurado, a wonderful friend, was not as fortunate. I spent one night with Domingos right before the Santa Cruz demonstration. The Indonesians killed him at the cemetery. Domingos was very courageous and determined. He had lived with his relatives in Dili. He didn't have any immediate family: the Indonesian army had already killed both his parents and all his brothers and sisters. I had met him at Externato de São José while he was teaching at the school; he was also my neighbor.[6] Many of the people who were killed at the cemetery helped me tremendously between the time I went underground and November 12.

Everyone knew a parent or sister or brother or friend who had been killed or disappeared by the Indonesian military at Santa Cruz. No one knew where their loved ones had been taken. On the night of the massacre, I moved from the house where I was hiding to another safe house. The underground had safe houses throughout the city. I saw candles everywhere, in every house, and people praying, hoping that maybe God could help bring their brothers, sisters, and parents back home.

The massacre was a complete surprise. We didn't expect this would happen. I was shocked. With the presence of Pieter Koojimans and foreign journalists, it was impossible for us to imagine that Indonesia would do anything so barbaric. The worst that we had expected was that the Indonesian army might arrest some of the demonstrators and take them to prison.

Immediately after the massacre, I wrote to Xanana and told him what had happened; I also wanted to know if we should take action. For the first time, I didn't know what we were going to do. Should we fight back against Indonesia? Or should we just inform the international community of what happened? I was indecisive. It was crazy. Everyone was trying to find out who was killed, who was wounded, and who was disappeared. I was also wondering about what was going to happen to me and how I was going to respond to the parents of those people who were killed if they came to me and asked if their son or daughter had been killed or disappeared. "You are the one who gave the order to demonstrate," they could have said, because I was the head of the executive committee and, therefore, was ultimately responsible for any of the underground's activities.

At one in the afternoon on November 12 one of my colleagues in the underground was able to contact José Ramos Horta in Lisbon and tell him what had happened. Ramos Horta sent a message to us that he was going to put the case before the United Nations Security Council. There were many people in East Timor who wanted to take some action against the Indonesian military. People were really angry. "We have to do something now!" many people said. They talked about asking FALINTIL to intervene or to organize an uprising in Dili. Others wanted to attack the Indonesian army headquarters in Dili with arrows and stones. This would have been really risky. Because Ramos Horta said that we were going to put the case to the UN Security Council, I said to people, "Be calm. Let's wait to see what's going to happen. Let's wait for the decision from the UN."

When Ramos Horta mentioned that the UN would take action against Indonesia because of the massacre, the news encouraged the people in East Timor. I used it to convince other leaders in the underground to wait. I also informed Xanana, and he agreed that we should wait to see what happened at the UN. We were hoping that the UN would send some peacekeeping force to East Timor because the situation had really deteriorated.

The following day many diplomats began to arrive in Dili to get firsthand information about the massacre. People calmed down while we were waiting for the UN to take action. The delegations met mostly with the Indonesia's governor in East Timor, Mário Carrascalão, Indonesian military officials, Bishop Belo, and other people from the Catholic Church. That was it. It wasn't possible for any civilians to make contact with the delegations or other foreigners who came to East Timor at that time because everyone was scared of being arrested if they talked to these people. The army was in a position of high alert, and had soldiers stationed all over the city. They walked up and down all the streets and drove all around Dili. They put checkpoints everywhere on the hills surrounding Dili and all over the countryside.[7]

The situation in Dili and throughout East Timor was very tense in the days following the massacre. Indonesian soldiers were arresting young people throughout the city. Many were brutally tortured. The Indonesians killed many of those wounded at the cemetery who they transported to the military hospital by crushing their skulls with rocks and injecting cold water into them instead of medicine.[8] On November 15, I received information that the military had taken 68 people arrested at the cemetery to the bank of the Be-Mos River a little more than one mile south of Dili and gunned them down. Such reports were common.

Despite the continuing terror, people throughout East Timor continued to hope that the international community, through the UN Security Council, would take action to help us. But as the days went by, it became obvious that the Security Council was not going to take any concrete action. We never heard about any decision from the UN. When nothing happened, people began to get discouraged. "What's going on?" people would ask. "We haven't heard anything. We lost our children and never heard anything from the United Nations."

Although the UN took no action, word of the massacre did spread. A few days after the massacre I was listening to a radio broadcast from the United States, the Voice of America. Suddenly I heard Allan Nairn's voice; he was being interviewed from a hospital in Guam. He was describing the massacre. When I heard this news report, I was thrilled. There was now someone who could tell the story of East Timor and of the massacre itself in the United States. This was very important.

We also heard about demonstrations and actions all over the world against Indonesia because of the massacre. There was even a demonstration in Jakarta by 100 East Timorese students a week after the massacre. I had sent a message to Fernando de Araujo asking him to organize a peaceful demonstration in Jakarta. Unfortunately, the Indonesians arrested Fernando, along with 80 others. Today, Fernando is still in prison because of his participation in the demonstration. The Indonesians sentenced him to nine years in prison for "subversion." I continue to write him letters.[9]

A few weeks after the massacre there was news of the *Lusitania Expresso*, a Portuguese peace boat full of young people planning to sail to Dili to pay their respects to those killed at the Santa Cruz Cemetery. The report about the peace mission gave new hope to the East Timorese. The Portuguese delegation could not come to East Timor, but at least the *Lusitania Expresso* could. So we decided to organize another demonstration. The parents of those who were killed at the cemetery took the initiative to organize the protest. Even though the parents were ready to organize the demonstration, I was asked by the leaders of the underground who survived the massacre to organize it; Xanana Gusmão and the National Council of Maubere Resistance gave the instructions through the executive committee, and made the final decisions. The parents couldn't initiate such an event on their own. Discipline is always important in whatever organization and in whatever conditions, war or peace. The parents asked my opinion about the demonstration and offered their proposals and then I transmitted their ideas to Xanana.

No one I met, including some parents of the victims of the November 12 massacre, expressed anger toward me over the deaths of their children. I met some of them and I said, "I'm so sorry. I apologize for those who were killed in the massacre."

"Don't apologize," they would reply. "They have died for our country, for our nation. We are ready to continue this struggle if needed."

If they had been angry with me, I wouldn't have been able to come here to the United States. They were the people who took care of me, who hid me from persecution. The parents saw that their sons and daughters died for their love of the people of East Timor. Their children are now the heroes, the martyrs of the country.

The resistance agreed to have a demonstration when the *Lusitania Expresso* arrived in Dili. We prepared banners, coffins, and flowers.

The coffins were supposed to represent people who were killed in the cemetery and whose bodies we had never seen. We also made crosses and T-shirts. Everyone was supposed to dress in black when the *Lusitania* arrived. Our intention was to occupy the ship and to accompany the people on the *Lusitania* when they went from the harbor to the Santa Cruz Cemetery to lay flowers on Sebastião Gomes' grave as a tribute to those who were killed on November 12, 1991.

The peace boat was big news in East Timor. The Indonesian government showed the *Lusitania* on TV and broadcast news of the ship when it began its preparations in Portugal, presenting the mission as an insult to Indonesian pride and a threat to national security.

The Indonesians began to distribute 30 soldiers in each *bairro*, an area even smaller than a village or *desa*, and also increased the number of civilian intelligence agents. At the same time, Indonesian immigrants began to leave Dili and go back to Jakarta and West Timor because they were afraid that something might happen when the *Lusitania* arrived. Suddenly Dili was empty of Indonesian immigrants. Even the Indonesian prostitutes seemed to have left. We saw only Indonesian soldiers in the streets.

East Timorese began to go to the waterfront and up to the mountains, watching to see if maybe the *Lusitania* would appear on the horizon and come to Dili. Some civil servants stopped going to their offices to work. At that time, the Indonesian government started to raise the salaries of every civil servant, and some of them refused the money!

I was supposed to leave Dili in January. Because of my situation—I was the most wanted man in East Timor after Xanana Gusmão at that time because of the Santa Cruz demonstration—Xanana and I decided that I had to escape abroad. But I decided not to leave until after the visit by the *Lusitania*.

"I think you need to stay here until the boat arrives," Xanana said to me. I wanted to stay and join the demonstration, even though Xanana wasn't that optimistic that the *Lusitania* would make it: the situation was not really favorable because the Indonesian military's security was so strong. There were seven Indonesian ships, all moving in and out of the waters off Dili for almost the whole month before the *Lusitania's* voyage. Indonesia spent a lot of money to prevent the peace boat from coming to Dili. For one month trucks and soldiers were moving around the city and ships and helicopters were patrolling the sea. Every day and every night the army was circulating from house to house. Xanana thought that, by whatever means, the Indonesians would block the *Lusitania* at sea. But Xanana always said, "In any case, we have to prepare. Maybe the Indonesians will let them into East Timor."

I thought that Indonesia would be afraid to sink the *Lusitania* after the November 12 massacre and the international outcry. It was carrying people from the United States, Canada, China, Europe, Indonesia, Korea, and all over the world. Inside the boat there were some important figures, including journalists and the former president of Portugal, Ramalho Eanes. Many East Timorese put their hope in international pressure because we thought that if anything happened to the people on the boat, the governments of the different countries would hold the Indonesian government accountable.

But the Indonesian navy prevented the *Lusitania* from entering East Timorese waters and forced it to go back to Australia when it finally arrived on March 11, 1992. Everyone was extremely discouraged when the Australian radio and the BBC broadcast the news. "What we are going to do now?" people wondered. People began to be scared. Many people had exposed themselves and were afraid that the Indonesians would kill them. There were many people crying because they spent so much time, almost four months, hoping that the *Lusitania* would bring peace to East Timor.

The resistance didn't think that the *Lusitania* would solve the problem of East Timor by itself. But, at the very least, we hoped that it would help bring more attention from the international community. In any case, the people on the *Lusitania* were braver than the Portuguese parliamentary delegation that had officially agreed to come to East Timor and then backed down. Even though it was turned back, the *Lusitania* made a lot of progress in terms of bringing East Timor to the world's attention.[10]

12

Life Underground

After the November 12 massacre, I didn't stop working. We were preparing for the *Lusitania Expresso*, but I also tried to find out who had been arrested, killed, wounded, and disappeared at Santa Cruz. Working together with other leaders in the underground, I found out that the Indonesians had arrested a number of members of the underground movement and even members of the executive committee. I thought that most members of the executive committee would be safe because we had prohibited them from participating directly in the demonstration. There were only two who joined the demonstration, to help organize it: Gregorio Saldanha, who was the main organizer, and Carlos Lemos, who tried to take some pictures that we hoped we could show to the international community. The other members of the executive committee, such as Francisco Miranda Branco, Juvencio Martins, Filomeno Pereira, Agusto Gama, and Jacinto Alves, tried to keep as low a profile as possible so we could continue to function as a group and to maintain contact with Xanana Gusmão. But the Indonesians arrested all of them. Someone close to a member of the executive committee who had been arrested and tortured the night before the November 12, 1991 demonstration named them. The Indonesians arrested Juvencio Martins right after we met in a safe house where I was hiding a few days after the massacre. I only learned about his ar-

rest a week later when he sent me a note smuggled out of prison. Juvencio warned me that the Indonesians were looking for me: "Every
time they interrogate one of us, they always ask about you, so be careful," he wrote.

During interrogations, Indonesian intelligence said to a number of
people arrested at Santa Cruz, "You don't know Constâncio. He's our
agent. He pretended to be working for you, but you didn't know that
he was our agent." The Indonesians were trying to confuse the resistance.

That's why there were accusations after the massacre saying that I
was a spy for Indonesian intelligence, even though I was organizing
the resistance. Even today, some people say that I'm an Indonesian
agent.

After all the arrests, there were no other leaders from the executive
committee with whom I could work. But there were some leaders
from other organizations who had not been arrested, so the underground was able to continue. I worked with several organizations
and tried to collect the list of those people who were killed, wounded,
and disappeared on November 12. In the end, 271 people were listed
as killed. We also compiled a list of those people who were wounded
and disappeared.

The real death toll was definitely more than 271 people. We realized at that time that if we gave out a list with too many people on it,
the international community wouldn't believe us. People would think
that we were exaggerating, especially because Indonesia stated that
the number of people killed was 19 and then, later, 50 people. We
only listed people for whom we had complete information, including
their full names, and dates and places of birth. But the true number of
dead is certainly a lot more than 271; we think that more than 600
people were killed at the cemetery and during its aftermath.

We started to collect the names beginning in December 1991 and
weren't able to finish the list until March 1992 because of great difficulty getting people to provide us with information. The relatives of
those killed at the cemetery didn't trust anyone. Sometimes when the
underground members would go to houses where we knew that the
family had lost someone in the massacre, the family would not admit

it. They thought that the Indonesians were sending someone to find out if that family was involved in the demonstration. So it took a long time to make them trust us. Sometimes we had to go over the information two or three times until people would confirm the names of their children who were killed at the cemetery. After this, we sent the names to Xanana. Xanana and I then worked together and calculated the figure of 271 and then sent the list of dead, wounded, and missing to Paz é Possivel, a solidarity group in Portugal.

During this time Xanana and I kept in contact with each other through written messages. There was always at least one *estafeta* who knew where we were. If Xanana learned something about my situation, he would send me a note telling me to move. I would do the same thing when I knew something about Xanana. If the Indonesian military was preparing to go to a particular place or a particular neighborhood, I would tell him about it.

While I was underground, most of my movement was at night. Sometimes I would walk from one place to another; other times I would take a taxi or go by motorbike. Often someone would drive me. I received a lot of support from the underground movement. I never stayed in one place for more than a short time. I stayed one night in one house, another night in another house. Sometimes I would stay for one week in a particular house. It depended on the situation. I also had friends who were working for the Indonesians who gave me information about when and where intelligence was looking for me. I was always informed of what was going on inside the Indonesian military regarding me and Xanana.

At one point I was hiding in the house of Leo Lima (his *nom de guerre*), a friend of mine. One day, he and his wife left me alone with their daughter. She was only about seven years old, but she knew that I was in hiding there. She was sitting near the front door waiting for her parents, but also to see if any strangers approached the house so she could warn me. That day, however, she was probably distracted; suddenly there was an Indonesian soldier with an M-16 rifle at the front door. The soldier greeted her and began to joke with her. He even gave her some candy. The soldier then showed her my photograph. "Do you know this man?" he asked.

"I am sorry," she answered. "I don't know him." I was in the house listening to their conversation and I feared it was the end of my life. Fortunately, the soldier did not persist and left. After 15 minutes or so she came to me and said, "Uncle, an Indonesian soldier came to our house. He gave me candy and showed me your picture, but I told him that I didn't know you and he left." I gave her a big hug.

When I moved around at night I walked on paths and trails, not on the streets, to hide from the Indonesian army as much as possible. My position was much worse than before I went into hiding. It was the same situation for my wife and my family. The Indonesians threatened them because of me. "If you don't tell us where he is," the military threatened Gabriela, "we will kill you and everyone in your family. Let us know where he is. You know where Constâncio is." They also went a number of times to my parents' house, searched all the rooms, and interrogated and threatened my family members. At other times they would go to my parents' house and make up stories about me. "We already know where Constâncio is," they would report. "Just tell him to come down; otherwise we will send troops there and then kill him." The Indonesian soldiers never hit my parents, but my parents suffered a lot psychologically.

Indonesian intelligence practically occupied Gabriela's house for a whole month. They sat in front of the house, playing cards, walking around the house, waiting for me. They didn't sleep inside the house but very nearby. They would ask Gabriela and her family many questions. Sometimes they would sarcastically refer to me as the *liurai* or the minister of foreign affairs. "Where is Minister Constâncio?" they would joke. "Where is the *liurai*? We are looking for him." They were very agitated. They searched Gabriela's house and they even tried to take our wedding pictures, but Gabriela wouldn't let them. Then the soldiers went to the office of the *bupati*, the head of the *desa*, because he had a recent picture of me. Intelligence took the picture and reproduced it, and then they began to circulate my picture all over the territory. The Indonesians printed my picture and news about me in newspapers, and broadcast stories about me on the radio and television. All of the intelligence agents had my picture. They would carry my picture as they walked around Dili, asking people if they had seen me. They looked for me on the street and at various checkpoints. They moved from house to house; I did too.

It was really dangerous and risky when I moved around. I was always afraid that the Indonesian military would catch me. But sometimes I was lucky. One evening as I was going to another safe house I passed right in front of one of their intelligence agents, Inocencio Freitas; for whatever reason, he didn't see me. I know him because he is married to my mother's cousin.

A few months after the Santa Cruz Massacre, Edy Suprianto went to my house and asked for Gabriela. "Where is Constâncio?" He gave about 200,000 *rupiah* to Gabriela and said, "This is Constâncio's salary. I've kept this money for almost three months. I have been looking for him since the November 12 incident. I miss him a lot and I would like to give him this money and a letter. I want to go back to Jakarta to study, and I would like to talk to him before I leave."

Gabriela wrote me a note telling me about Edy Suprianto's visit. Suprianto wanted to know whether I received the money and letter or not. He was waiting for a response from my wife. "Just keep the money," I wrote to Gabriela. "Don't spend it. If they come back, show them that you still have the money and the letter."

I don't know what the letter said. I didn't want Gabriela to send it to me because if they had asked for the letter and the letter wasn't there, Gabriela would have been in trouble. She kept the letter and the money until she eventually left Dili. She spent the money before she left. The letter's still in East Timor.

Through secretly delivered letters, I kept some contact with Gabriela. I told her to tell the Indonesians that I had been killed at the Santa Cruz Cemetery. "No, we didn't find Constâncio's body," they told her. "We checked everyone who was killed there. We didn't find his body, so Constâncio's still alive. You know where he is. It's better to tell him to surrender to us because if we find him, we will kill him."

I told Gabriela to pretend to be mad at me for my involvement in the underground to make the Indonesians stop with their intimidation, harassment, and threats. "Just kill him and bring his head to me," Gabriela would tell them. "I don't know what he's doing. I want nothing to do with politics." But they continued to bother her. Indonesian soldiers would come to her house every day. The soldiers harassed her until she left East Timor.

For safety reasons, Gabriela and I were not in contact with each other that often, sometimes only twice a month. But I would send people to walk by her house to make sure that everything was fine. If no soldiers were around, one of my colleagues would sneak into the house to deliver a note and talk with Gabriela. I was very careful about sending letters to Gabriela. I was always afraid that if the army found any letters from me at her house, she would be in serious trouble, so I tried to reduce my contact with Gabriela to as little as possible.

Similarly, I didn't have any contact with my family while I was underground. I wanted to avoid creating problems for them, so I avoided writing letters or visiting. My parents knew that I was underground through Gabriela, because she would sometimes go to my parents' house. She would move back and forth, staying with my parents for a week and then going back to her parents. In East Timor, people often do this to establish good relations with the parents of their husband or wife. Such behavior is normal, so it didn't bother the Indonesian military.

On January 30, 1992, Tilson, my son, was born. The Indonesian army thought that I would be anxious to see Tilson. I knew he was going to be born, but I couldn't go to see him. I just asked my friends to bring Gabriela to the hospital. At the hospital the doctors and nurses asked for Tilson's father. "He works in the mountains very far away," Gabriela told them. Three days after Gabriela gave birth to Tilson, they returned home. The army was there, waiting for me. They thought that sometime I would go there and visit my son, but I didn't. I knew that they were waiting for me.

I was very happy to hear that Tilson was born, but I was worried that no one would take care of him, that he would never see his father. I was also uncertain about my own life. I didn't know whether or not I was going to live or be killed by the Indonesian army. Gabriela and I wanted to have a child because we did not know how much longer I would live. If something were to have happened to me then, people could now look at Tilson and remember me and say, "That is Constâncio's son. That is Terus' son."

Before Tilson was born, I asked Xanana to be his godfather. Xanana suggested three names, but my choice was Tilson. *Til* means "Timor Leste," or East Timor in Portuguese, and *son* is from the English language. Thus, Tilson means the son of East Timor, the son of Timor Leste. Xanana accepted this. Then I put Victorio, one of Xanana's suggestions for the first name, as his middle name. So our son's name is Tilson Victorio da Cruz Pinto. Gabriela's surname is da Cruz, and also he went to the Santa Cruz Cemetery on November 12, 1991. And then his last name is Pinto. Xanana and I chose his name and I sent it to Gabriela and all of us agreed. Six months after Tilson was born, Gabriela sent me a picture of him being baptized at the Motael Church.

Living on the run was very difficult for me, but it gave me an opportunity to get to know Xanana Gusmão. Sometimes we would hide together in the same safe house. Xanana is a great human being. He loves people. He's really determined to fight for East Timor's cause without any personal ambitions whatsoever. He is not vengeful. Xanana also has a very good perspective on East Timor's future in terms of developing the country economically and politically after we reach independence. Independence is not the final goal, because the fight for a just society and world will continue after independence. The fight after independence will be even harder than the fight for the liberation of East Timor.

Sometimes Xanana can be very funny; he would always play jokes on people. He would often tell jokes during lunch or dinner and he always kept everyone laughing. He had a lot of interesting stories about the guerrillas and his childhood. One thing that I noticed about Xanana is that he loves children very much. He would always give special nicknames to babies who were born while he was in Dili. The names were always revolutionary ones, such as Maubere.[1]

Xanana works very hard. Usually we would work from after we had breakfast in the morning until noon, when we would have lunch. After a one-hour nap, we would continue to work for another three or four hours. After dinner, Xanana would work even more. Most of the work he did was writing letters to people abroad, to members of the underground, and to FALINTIL fighters all over the territory, coordinating and sending instructions to leaders of the resistance. He would always follow what was going on around the world by listening to international radio broadcasts such as the BBC, Australian radio, and Portuguese radio. Xanana would also do work around the house, such as washing the dishes and cooking for the family that was hiding him.

Xanana is a very brave person. He never gave any sign of being afraid. One day in February 1992 Xanana and I were hiding together. We were working on the list of people killed at Santa Cruz. Suddenly a military aide appeared at the door. He came to the house and told the residents that the Indonesian army was coming to search their house and that they should wait in the house until the soldiers arrived. At that time they were searching people's houses frequently.

Immediately after the RT left, the family put me and Xanana in a ditch underneath the house. We stayed there from nine in the morning until six in the evening. Fortunately, we had a small hole to breathe through, but that was it. The ditch was not that big, only big enough for two people to sit down. Xanana remained very calm, but I was terrified. I thought that it was a big mistake for us to hide together; if the Indonesians found one of us, they would arrest or kill us both. I stayed awake the whole time sitting in that hole. Xanana, on the other hand, was sleeping. As he slept, I was thinking about why he was forced to live such a life, sleeping in a cave when he used to live a decent life. He had a good job; he even lived in Australia for a while before the war; but now he suffers.

The soldiers never came to the house, but I was still anxious when we crawled out of the hole at 6 p.m. I wanted to leave the house as soon as possible because the soldiers could come at any time. "We have to leave here right away," I told Xanana. But he was very calm and made some coffee and washed his hands because we were very dirty. He even spent time stretching. It took about 10 minutes for him to get out of the house. I left there by taxi, and he left by motorbike; someone gave him a ride to another place. From that time until today

I have been separated from Xanana. We have not seen each other at all. We have been able to communicate only by letters.

Xanana was very protective of me. The next morning, he sent someone to the house where I was staying, asking if I had arrived safely. I did the same thing for him.

Xanana has never lost hope. He is always confident that one day freedom will come to East Timor. He's generally a very positive person. But he could get upset sometimes, especially during the November 12 massacre when the Indonesians killed hundreds of demonstrators. He didn't eat for a whole week afterward, thinking of all the civilians massacred by the Indonesian army.

Xanana and I never talked about whether he thought he would ever be arrested. It was funny. When I first escaped to Jakarta, he sent me a letter. "You are the first one to break out of the encirclement," Xanana wrote. "I don't know whether I'll get out or not." At that time, Xanana was the most wanted man in East Timor. Apart from that one letter, I had never heard Xanana talk about the possibility of the Indonesians capturing him. I was confident that the Indonesians would never find him.

Xanana told me that the many years of war had changed his mind about many issues. He seemed to love the country of East Timor, to love the people at least as much as his own family, his own wife, his own children. He never complained that he had not seen his children for many years. He never said that. He said that 16 years of struggle changes people's attitudes.

13

Escape Abroad

After the *Lusitania* returned to Australia, I decided to make final preparations to escape from East Timor. I began to ask people in the underground movement about the possibility of taking me away by car or maybe motorbike. But first I needed to get a false identification card, and I had to change my appearance to disguise myself. I had to figure out the right responses to give to the Indonesian army in case they stopped me at the military checkpoints. I was very concerned about being arrested because I was the second-most-wanted man in East Timor at that time after Xanana Gusmão. Indonesia had circulated my picture all over the country. Every Indonesian intelligence agent carried my photo.

The first checkpoint I would have to pass was in Tibar, west of Dili. It's a dangerous one. At Tibar, the army usually searches everyone going to the western part of East Timor or into Dili without exception. Given the difficulties, I was planning at first with a friend of mine to pretend to be jogging by the checkpoint. But Tibar is about six miles away from Dili, so the Indonesians would have been suspicious. We dropped this plan.

Another plan was to buy some fish and then sell them in the area of Tibar. But then I realized that the Indonesian army would ask us why we didn't sell the fish in Dili. Usually people sell fish in Dili, not in Tibar. Then I asked some priests whether I could go with them in their cars through the Tibar checkpoint and across the border into West Timor. But the Indonesians stopped even priests and checked their cars. It was too risky.

Then in late April, Alla, a good friend of mine from the underground, said that he was willing to accompany me all the way from Dili to Java. I tried three times to leave. The first time it wasn't successful because the army had an intense operation going on, searching people at the checkpoint more intensely than usual. The second time I was about to leave and the same thing happened. And then, the third time, I was able to leave Dili.

For me there were two options: going to the mountains or escaping. If I had stayed in Dili, I wouldn't have been able to do anything. I could have also gone to the jungle to work with the guerrilla fighters, but, along with Xanana, I decided that I could do more for the resistance outside East Timor. So I decided to escape. Xanana helped me with some money and advice. He told me to be careful with my body and spoken language when I met any Indonesians. I had to be calm. I had to pretend that I was someone else. I didn't tell anyone, not even Gabriela, that I was leaving. I told Gabriela only after I arrived in Java. I did not discuss it with Gabriela because at that time her situation was extremely dangerous. The Indonesians were interrogating and threatening her daily. I did not want to send her any letters that discussed my trip to Indonesia. I was afraid that the Indonesians might search her house. If they found my letter, they would have increased security on the roads to West Timor and it would have been impossible for me to escape.

It was a difficult decision to leave, but I had no other alternative. I was very sad to leave because I had not seen Tilson and I would miss Gabriela and my family. I knew that I wouldn't be able to go back to East Timor for a long time—until East Timor was free. I was afraid that I would never see my son and wife again, though I knew that as long as I stayed alive I would at least have a chance to see them one day. My sadness became deeper when everyone in the place where I was hiding began crying as I was leaving. I knew that I would miss everything—the whole country, all the people who worked with me, especially Xanana, and those who took care of me for many months. I still remember what Xanana wrote to me when I was in Jakarta: "Constâncio, please go ahead with your trip. When you arrive in the land of the sunset, don't forget the blood of FALINTIL."

Alla and I left Dili at five in the morning on May 16, 1992; two other friends from the underground who I cannot name went with us to make sure that we crossed into West Timor. We went in the direction of Kupang. At 5:30 we arrived at the checkpoint at Tibar. It was incredible: when we arrived at the checkpoint none of the soldiers were awake! Even though we stopped the car for about two minutes, none of the Indonesian soldiers woke up. No one came to check the car and ask for identification, so we kept on going. When we passed this first checkpoint, I was really happy. That was the one thing I was really afraid about. I believe that God, the souls of my ancestors, and the fallen heroes of East Timor kept the soldiers asleep to let me pass.

If the soldiers had stopped us, we had planned to tell them that we were going to Liquiça, the next town west of Dili. I had a false identity card with the name Sebastião that said that I was from Dili, and I had changed my appearance. I had a mustache and wore a hat. After Tibar, we passed through Liquiça and continued toward Batugadé, a town at the border with West Timor. When we arrived in Batugadé, it was one in the afternoon. There were two military police officers there. One was playing guitar and the other was sitting nearby. One of my friends collected our IDs and took them to the soldier and told them we were going to Suai. If you go to Suai from the western part of East Timor, you have to pass through Atambua, the border town in West Timor. Fortunately, there was no problem, so we left Batugadé and drove to Atambua where we stopped for a while to have lunch. I was really happy. After lunch, Alla and I got on a bus to Kupang while the other two went back to East Timor.

Alla was a good friend who helped me while I was underground. It's always good to travel with someone else. In case anything happened to me, there would be someone who could tell people that I was arrested; that's why we never sat together in the bus or boat during our trip. Also, it's good to have someone for advice and to work with. If one is weak, then the other one can help. I really appreciated

Alla's willingness to go with me even though he knew that if something happened to me, it could endanger his life. He was very courageous.

It was raining on the way to Kupang. Nevertheless, I had on my sunglasses. Alla and I pretended not to know each other. On the way to Kupang, the bus stopped right in front of a police station. Suddenly an Indonesian police officer boarded the bus and sat next to me. "Oh my God," I was thinking. "This guy will recognize me." I kept my sunglasses on and pretended to sleep. I tried to figure out what I could say if he asked me any questions. I was preparing to tell him that I was going to Kupang to visit a friend of mine who was in the army. Fortunately, we never exchanged conversation. The police officer got off before us.

When we arrived in Kupang, we went to a hotel. It was already nine at night. After we paid for the room, I changed my clothes and tried to be calm. I had a look outside and saw a sign hanging on the door right in the reception area that made me realize that the owner of the hotel was a policeman. I began to panic. Luckily, Alla was very brave. He helped calm me down. We stayed there overnight and left immediately the next morning. We walked all over Kupang looking for a way to continue our journey westward to the island of Java, but we were not successful finding any information about the boat to the next island, Flores. We were thinking about getting a plane, but it was dangerous because the security at the airport was tight. Ironically, while we were looking for the way to Flores, Alla remembered that he had family in Kupang. We asked a taxi driver if he knew Alla's relative, someone he hadn't seen since he was 10 years old. The taxi driver immediately said, "Oh yes, I know him." The taxi driver then drove us to Alla's uncle's house; we stayed there for two days until we left Kupang.

The uncle was married to a West Timorese woman. He didn't know anything about politics and understood very little about what had happened in East Timor. "What are you doing here?" he asked me.

"We are planning to go to Flores to see my sister there," I told him. "She is a nun in Flores, so we are looking for a boat." Of course, it was a lie.

When Alla introduced me to his uncle, he said, "This is Sebastião, my friend. He is studying at the seminary. He intends to be a priest." Alla's uncle and his family treated us very well.

After two days, we got tickets for a ferry to Flores. I was anxious because this was the last step to leave the island of Timor and I had heard that there was very tight security at the harbor in Kupang. But I had to go ahead.

We took the boat at one in the afternoon. Again, there were no problems. We arrived in Ende, Flores, the next morning at six. When we arrived, we didn't have any place to go. We just followed people and went from the harbor to the town and looked for a *losmen*, a low-budget guest house, to stay for another day before we looked for the way to the next island. When we arrived at the *losmen*, we checked in and the same thing happened to us as in Kupang. The *losmen* belonged to a policemen. We figured this out after we paid the bill and had been shown our room. I saw a policeman's picture on the wall. Fortunately, we found out from the policeman's wife that he was out of town. So we decided to stay and tried to get information about going to the next island, Sumbawa. When we found out that there were no seats on the airplane for the next day, we decided to take the bus from Ende to the town on the western end of the island, Labuhanbajo.

On the way to Labuhanbajo, the bus stopped to pick up other passengers. At one point two Indonesians wearing Muslim hats, sarongs, and no sandals got on. They both looked very fit and had very short haircuts. They looked like Indonesian military. One came and sat next to me and another one sat next to Alla. "My God," I thought, "they are following us." After about an hour passed, the guy who was sitting next to me began to ask me questions. "Where are you from?" he asked me.

"I'm from West Timor," I told him.

"Where are you going?"

"I'm going to Ruten," I answered. Ruten was the next town.

"So what are you doing here?" he asked.

"I'm just visiting." I tried to say as little as possible to him.

"Have you been here before?" he continued.

"No, this is my first time," I responded.

After that, he stopped asking me questions.

A few hours later, we arrived at a crossroads, and he asked me, "Do you know where that street's going?"

At that point I became really suspicious. I had already told him that this was my first time there. "I'm sorry," I said to him, "I told you that this is my first time going to Ruten." His questions were really frightening. I knew in my heart that this guy was working for intelligence. I thought that they were going to arrest me in Ruten. I tried to be calm. I called in Tetum to Alla who was sitting nearby. "They know who we are," I told him. "We are in trouble."

Alla was really strong. "Don't worry," he said.

I was holding *aqua*, bottled water, in my hand. You can buy *aqua* throughout Indonesia. They sell it everywhere. A little bit later the guy next to me asked, "What's that?"

"This is *aqua*," I told him.

"It's for drinking?" he persisted. It was a very stupid question.

"Yes, *aqua* is for drinking," I responded.

Because the bottle was still sealed, he asked me, "Oh, is it sealed like that?"

"Yes," I said, "I just bought it from the market, so it came from the factory sealed like this." Only intelligence would ask such stupid questions. I knew I had to do something.

"Your questions are like intelligence questions. Are you an intelligence agent?" I asked him.

He quickly became upset. "How do you know that?" he asked.

"Because I work for intelligence," I told him. "Do you know General Warouw or Colonel Gatot Purwanto?"

"No, I don't know them," he responded.

"They live in Jakarta," I told him, "and I work for them. I am one of their agents."

When I said that, the guy didn't want to ask me questions anymore. He was also stupid. He didn't ask me for any sort of identification. I only mentioned those generals. We started talking about something else. Thankfully, we were already close to Ruten and finally we arrived.

From Ruten, Alla and I caught another bus. It took us all day to arrive in Labuhanbajo. After three days there, we were supposed to take a little motorboat to Sumbawa, but someone lied to us and took our money. It costs 10,000 *rupiah* to get to Sumbawa, so we gave a guy 10,000 *rupiah* each. The morning he was supposed to pick us up at the hotel, he didn't show up. We had to wait another day to get a ferry.

I still remember that day because it was my wife's birthday, May 24. Suddenly in the middle of the trip between Flores and Sumbawa, they put on the karaoke machine and invited people to sing, especially if anyone was celebrating a birthday. A woman got up and sang "Happy Birthday" in English. A lot of people sang along. It made me cry because it reminded me of Gabriela. I had forgotten my wife's birthday. It was that invitation and the song that made me remember. As the woman was singing, I could hear the blast of the waves and feel the cool air of the Pacific Ocean. The music hit my heart, the waves reminded me of the sea near Dili, and the cool air made feel as if I were on the veranda of Gabriela's house in Kaikoli, Dili. All this made me very sad. I was thinking that at the same hour my wife was celebrating her birthday and embracing our son, Tilson. I was trying to imagine what our lives together would be like without the Indonesian occupation. I thought that I would never see my wife again and that I'd never have the chance to meet my son.

We left Labuhanbajo at nine in the morning, and we arrived in Sape on the island of Sumbawa at five the same day. Then we took the bus from Sape to the island of Lombok, and then from Lombok to Bali. It was a nonstop bus; the bus would drive right onto the ferry and then we would continue to the next island. It took a long time.

We arrived in Denpasar, the capital of Bali, the next evening, at 11:30. I decided to stay in Bali because a friend of mine lived there. But then, when we got out of the *bemo*—it's like a big taxi—I found that I had lost my little backpack with my one additional pair of pants, my one shirt, my diary, and my shortwave radio. As soon as I discovered this, we decided to immediately leave Denpasar and go to Jakarta. We were afraid that the *bemo* driver would bring my belongings to the police. Because I wrote my diary in a language that only I myself understand—in Tetum mixed with Portuguese—we were worried that it would draw attention or suspicion, and so, with the help of my friend in Bali, we caught the last bus to the island of Java. Another friend with the resistance in Bali courageously accompanied us.

We went to Banyuwangi on the eastern tip of Java. A ferry carried our bus from Bali. When the bus got off the ferry, the police were waiting there. As the bus drove off the ferry, I heard loud police sirens, and then I saw that the bus driver was following a police car. Soon the bus stopped and the doors opened. A number of policemen entered the bus. My heart was beating very fast. One officer asked whoever got on the bus in Denpasar to please stand up. It was sort of a stupid question because everyone who was in that bus had boarded in Denpasar. No one stood up. Then they asked for everyone's identification card. When they began to collect the IDs, I was scared. If I had shown them my identification card, they would have asked me what I was doing in Java. It was a few weeks before the general election in Indonesia and they would have wanted to know why I hadn't stayed in East Timor to participate in the elections. In Indonesia, you have to join the elections. I couldn't show them my ID, so I began to collect the IDs of those who were sitting near me, about six or seven people, as a ruse.

When the officer came to me, I handed the IDs over to him. He looked at them and didn't ask me any questions. He gave all the IDs back to me and left. I immediately returned them. Two minutes later, though, the police officer came back and asked me about my identity card.

"I already gave it to you," I told him. "You already saw it. I showed it to you just a few minutes ago." He asked me for my ID three times and I just told him the same thing. For whatever reason, the policeman stopped asking me. A few minutes later, the police apologized to everyone on the bus. "We are really sorry," they said. "We got information from Denpasar just a half hour ago that someone we were looking for was on the bus. We apologize for the inconvenience. Have a good trip."

I did not want to go to Jakarta directly because I needed to establish my contacts with people there. So we went to Malang, a city in
eastern Java. In Malang I bought Alla his plane ticket back to East Timor so he would not miss the upcoming general election. If he had
not been in East Timor, the Indonesians would have suspected him: if
someone does not participate in the election, the army immediately
labels the person a member of FRETILIN or GPK,[1] which means that
he or she will be arrested and put in jail.

I stayed in Malang for five days with a friend from the resistance
who was living there as a student. He accompanied me on the bus to
Jakarta, and we arrived on June 1. In Jakarta, a friend of mine, Salarkosi (his *nom de guerre*), met me with another friend whose house I
stayed at for almost one week. I wasn't happy with the situation,
though, because there were too many people who came in and out
visiting the owner of the house and Salarkosi. I trusted my contact,
but I was always suspicious of the people who came to the house.

After one week I linked up with Domingos Sarmento. I proposed
to Domingos that he find a more isolated place for me to hide. Fortunately, Domingos had a relationship with Pak Harto, who allowed
me to hide at his house in Jakarta for five months.

While in Jakarta, I continued to listen to the radio and to read
newspapers; I also watched television. I was basically trying to follow
outside political developments and to improve my English by reading books. I also tried to learn some Japanese greetings because I was
thinking about escaping to Japan.

One of the reasons I read the newspapers and watched television
was to find out about my own situation. One night I was watching
the evening news on Indonesian television. I was sitting next to an Indonesian man at Pak Harto's house. And suddenly there was a report
showing Try Sutrisno—he's now vice president of Indonesia, but at
that time he was high commander of the Indonesian army—telling
Suharto, the Indonesian president, about the number of people killed
at the November 12, 1991 massacre and about the people who were
missing. Sutrisno reported that the army had already found 32 missing people but that it was still looking for 66 people, including Constâncio Pinto, the "mastermind" of the November 12 demonstration.[2]

I was lucky because they didn't put my picture on the television screen. After the news, I asked the guy, "What do you think about that guy named Constâncio?"

"The Indonesian army will definitely kill him," he said.

"Yes, people like this guy should be killed by the Indonesian army," I told him. "He's a traitor."

After a few months, I asked Pak Harto for help getting a fake identity card and passport. Pak Harto began to approach someone who he knew could get an ID for me. The guy asked for 400,000 *rupiah*, approximately 200 U.S. dollars. He promised to process my ID within two weeks. After two weeks, I hadn't received anything. I was already scared. I was really afraid that the contact might be an intelligence agent. Immediately I asked him for my photos back. "If you don't have time or it is too difficult for you to get the ID, I just want you to give me back my photographs and pay me back the money whenever you have it," I told him. The guy had already spent the money. I didn't want to push him; I could have created problems if I pushed him. He never paid back the money.

Pak Harto then looked for another person to help me. This time the ID cost 600,000 *rupiah*. For me, the money didn't matter; the most important thing was my life. After two weeks we learned that my identity card was ready, so Pak Harto asked the same person to work on the passport. With the fake ID, I could have gone through the normal process to get a passport, but it takes a long time, sometimes a month, and it would have given the immigration office the opportunity to check my file and possibly recognize me. That's why I wanted to get it quickly so there would be no time for the authorities to check up on me.

A week later I met the contact at Pak Harto's house for the deal. He worked at the immigration office. I was afraid that the contact might be intelligence, but I had no choice. I told him that I was a businessman and needed a passport to go to Singapore in December 1992 for a vacation and then proceed to China for some business. Due to the slow bureaucracy at the immigration office, I decided to go to someone who could get me a passport in as short a time as possible. In return, I was willing to pay an amount equivalent to his salary. I told the person that it was not a business transaction but simply our helping each other. Finally, the guy said, "I think there will be no problem. For this work, I only ask you for two million *rupiah*." This is equivalent to $1,500; friends of the resistance abroad had sent me the money. "The money is not for me, but for friends who work at the immigration office," he explained.

"No problem at all," I told him. "It is your business, but don't give all the money to them. You must keep some for yourself. OK?"

The guy laughed. "To make the process easiest, I need you to go to the immigration office tomorrow morning at nine. We need you to fill out the application and to get your fingerprints, take photographs, and interview you. I will be waiting for you at the office."

I agreed to be at immigration the next morning. My heart was beating fast. Going to the immigration office was like surrendering myself to the Indonesians. But believing in God's inspiration and protection I decided to go without fear of capture. I couldn't sleep at all that night. I kept praying and planning strategies and arguments in case the Indonesians suspected my identity. This was the last big obstacle between me and escape. At midnight, I lit the candles in my room and prayed, asking for protection from God and from the spirits of those who were massacred at the Santa Cruz Cemetery.

In the morning I woke up, took a shower, and dressed like a businessman. I wore a long-sleeved shirt, with a blue necktie that I borrowed from Pak Harto, a pair of sunglasses, nice trousers, and a pair of leather shoes. Domingos and Pak Harto accompanied me to the immigration office. Domingos stayed outside of the office just to make sure that if something happened to me, he could immediately inform the media and human rights organizations. Domingos had very good connections with many diplomats in Jakarta, including some from the United States. Pak Harto and I went into the office. Our contact was already there. Immediately he took me to the counter to fill out the application forms. After I was finished, I returned them to the counter. Then I got my fingerprints and passport photos taken. I was then asked to wait for an interview. I kept smiling at the Indonesians working there.

As I was waiting, I asked our friend what sort of questions they usually asked in an interview. He told me that they ask about family background, education, and the reason you need the passport. I was afraid that they might ask me for something like a school certificate. At that time, I didn't have any papers except the fake ID. Suddenly, I remembered an accident that occurred in Jakarta months before the November 12, 1991 massacre, in which a whole *desa* was burnt down. It was a village called Bendungan Hiller. Fortunately, Domingos Sarmento had lived there before. I quickly went outside to Domingos and asked him the names of the *desa*, the head of the village, the street where he lived before, as well as the number of the house.

The first thing they asked me was where I was from. I told them that I was mixed blood, that my father was from Ambon, that my mother was from Java, and that I was born in Solo, Java, in 1963. At a very young age, my family moved to Kupang in West Timor because my parents were doing business there.

"I see," said the interviewer. "So do you have a school certificate?"

"Sorry," I replied. "I did have all of the papers, but they were destroyed in the fire in Bendungan Hiller so I don't have any official document to show you."

"Well, because you don't have them you need to make a sworn declaration," he told me. "You must say that all your documents were in this city, the number of the house, and the name of the street." I had no problem making the sworn declaration. The interview continued without any problems. After the interview I returned to my place, but Pak Harto stayed to make sure that everything was okay. I left half the money with him as an advance.

At one, Pak Harto returned home and said that the passport would be ready at five that afternoon. According to our agreement, the guy from the immigration department brought the passport to the house at five to receive the rest of the money. When he entered the house, the guy immediately looked for me. But I didn't show my face at first because I still suspected him. I tried to make sure that he came to Pak Harto's house alone and not with the Bakin, the Indonesian intelligence. After a few minutes, I came out. When he gave me the passport, I thanked him and then gave him the rest of the money. He looked very happy. As is the custom, I also gave him a beer and a pack of cigarettes. I also tried to give him some hope for future business.

Before he left, he asked me when I was leaving for Singapore. "Maybe in December," I told him. "I'm still busy."

"So what are you going to do there?" he asked.

"Aside from vacation, I will do some business—in ceramics," I explained. Ceramics are very expensive in Indonesia, and people like them very much.

"Could you bring one back for me?" he asked.

"I will bring you two pots when I return," I promised.

After I got a passport, I decided to leave Jakarta as soon as possible. First I had to book a ticket, but only one day in advance. Also I had to buy some clothes. I had to be well dressed, like a businessman. So Domingos and I went to a store and bought a pair of trousers, a long-sleeved shirt, a pair of shoes, and a suitcase. While Domingos and I went shopping, Pak Harto went to a travel agency to purchase a round-trip ticket to Hong Kong. Immigration requires you to have a round-trip ticket to prove that you will be able to return to the country if there is a problem. Later that night, my last night in Jakarta, I went shopping with Pak Harto to buy some other clothes.

Pak Harto and I were the last people who were let into the store. As we stepped in the door, the attendants were rushing to close the windows and were cleaning up the counters. There was music playing; it was the melodious voice of someone singing "Adios, Amigo." As we saw that they were about to close the store, we quickly grabbed some clothes and took them to the cashier. While the cashier was folding the clothes, the song "Adios, Amigo" became lower and lower. It was a remarkable coincidence. It was as if they were saying "Adios, Amigo" to me.

The next morning, October 23, 1992, Pak Harto and I took a taxi to Cengkaren International Airport. When we arrived, I went to the immigration desk and bought an exit visa. From there, Pak Harto took me to the immigration checkpoint. He was watching me to make sure that everything went all right. Finally I reached the counter and the immigration officer asked me for my passport. He looked at my passport and then looked at my face, while I was smiling at him.

"Are you going to Hong Kong?"

"Yes, I am."

"For how long?"

"Just for three days," I told him.

"What's the purpose of your visit?"

"Tourism," I said. After two minutes he stamped my passport. He handed it back to me and wished me a nice trip. As I left the counter, I looked at Pak Harto and waved, happy to be leaving Indonesia but sad to be leaving him.

I still felt unsafe while waiting to board. One minute for the enemy is too much time, I thought to myself. The enemy may arrest me even one minute before I departed. I tried to calm down by smoking a cigarette. I was really anxious. At 7:30 there was a boarding announcement. I grabbed my suitcase and immediately went to the boarding gate.

There were a lot of Indonesians on the airplane. Some were going to Singapore and some were going to Hong Kong. Even though I was already in the airplane, I was still really nervous. The Indonesian authorities could arrest me at the last minute. After half an hour or so, the plane began to move away from the gate. I began to cry—from happiness and sadness.

Only one hour later the plane landed in Singapore. I waited there for one hour and then continued with my travel to Hong Kong. I arrived in Hong Kong at five that afternoon. At the airport in Hong Kong, the immigration officials asked me how much money I had. Luckily, I had about 1,000 U.S. dollars in my pocket, money that was sent from solidarity groups abroad. You have to have money in your pocket; otherwise Hong Kong immigration will send you back.

I arrived on a weekend. I hadn't booked a hotel in advance. I was thinking that I would get a hotel from the airport, so I took a taxi to the downtown area. I asked the taxi driver to bring me to any hotel that he knew. He took me to a hotel that was very expensive. Unfortunately, there were no rooms. From there, I carried my suitcase and walked around Hong Kong looking for a hotel. I walked for hours. At every hotel, I received the same answer: the hotel is booked.

In the middle of such difficulties, God is always on your side. I felt very tired, so I stopped for a while and sat on the edge of a street and prayed. After praying, I continued to search for a hotel. I was afraid that I would have to sleep on the street. And if I slept on the street, the police would probably arrest me and take me to the Indonesian embassy, which would be the end of my life. For some reason, I didn't even think about going to the Portuguese consulate.

Just before midnight, I found a fancy hotel. When I asked the receptionist for a room, he looked at me and laughed. He probably thought a skinny person like me could not afford to stay at such a nice hotel, even for one night. He told me that the hotel was booked. Luckily, as I left the hotel, I saw an Indian guy who worked there as the porter. I approached him and greeted him. "Good evening. Could you help me please?" I asked him.

"What's wrong?" he asked.

"I can't find a hotel room anywhere."

"Are you Indian?" he asked me.

"Yes," I lied, "but I have lived in Indonesia for a long time."

"Well, let me call a friend of mine to see if he has a room for you." He called his friend and finally he got a room for me at the Emerald Hotel. "I got one for you—just for tonight—but it is very expensive."

"No problem, my friend," I told him. "I am lucky to meet you. Thank you very much." He called me a taxi and asked the driver to take me to the Emerald Hotel. It was such a relief. I finally felt as if I had escaped.

The next morning I had to check out of the hotel. From there I went to a motel in Kowloon, another part of Hong Kong. Once there I contacted José Guterres in Macau. Macau is a Portuguese territory very close to Hong Kong; I was really hoping to reach it as soon as possible. José is a good friend. We went to Externato together. He had been a political prisoner on Atauro Island. He later worked for the International Committee of the Red Cross in East Timor and was able to leave around 1988.

José sent another East Timorese, Alfredo Pires, to pick me up in Hong Kong. I was really happy when Alfredo came. He was very helpful. We took a boat to Macau; it only took one hour. I had a small problem in Macau harbor when I arrived because of my passport. I had no documentation that proved I was really Constâncio Pinto. The immigration officials—they were Chinese from Macau—didn't let me pass because I had an Indonesian passport and they kept on asking me where I was from. They spoke to me in English, so I responded to them in English. But then I began to speak Portuguese to them. When they found out that I spoke Portuguese better than they did, they said, "You're really Timorese. Please go ahead."

It was such a relief for me to be in Macau. I was in Portuguese territory and nothing else could happen to me. I knew that I wouldn't be in danger anymore. For the first time in many years, I felt free.

14

Reflections on the Struggle

With the help of East Timorese friends and the Portuguese government, I was able to fly to Lisbon a couple of weeks after I had arrived in Macau. Because Macau is a Portuguese territory and the East Timorese are legally Portuguese citizens, East Timorese refugees are entitled to receive such assistance. I arrived in Lisbon on November 11, 1992. I wanted to be there for the anniversary of the Santa Cruz Massacre. When I arrived at the airport, José Ramos Horta was there waiting for me with reporters and camera crews from the main television networks in Portugal. A number of newspaper and radio journalists and about 20 members of the East Timorese community came to greet me as well. I was really happy to see all those people. There were many old friends of mine who had been in Lisbon for two or three years. Unfortunately, I did not have time to greet all of them. I didn't accept any interviews at the airport because Ramos Horta had already set up an interview at RTP, Portuguese central television, for later in the evening. Horta immediately put me in a car and we went to his apartment. Then we went to the television station so they could interview me. In the middle of the interview, they showed an excerpt from the film *Cold Blood*, which shows people fleeing from the Indonesian soldiers firing on the crowd at the demonstration at the Santa Cruz Cemetery in 1991. This was the first time I had seen the actual video footage. I was shocked.

The East Timorese community in Lisbon had a mass to commemorate the anniversary of the Santa Cruz Massacre on November 12 that I attended. Many people came. I introduced myself. "I'm Constâncio Pinto," I told people. "I just arrived yesterday from Macau."

When I introduced myself to an old East Timorese priest, he responded, "East Timor is a lost cause; we cannot win the struggle." I was really angry.

"No, that will never be true. We will win one day," I promised. "Two hundred thousand people have lost their lives because of Indonesia's war. Now we are the new generation. We were born during the war and we are still fighting."

My first few days in Lisbon were very busy. A number of newspapers, local radio stations, and international radio outlets interviewed me. I also attended a number of events in Lisbon and met with the Portuguese president, Mario Soares.

On November 20, however, I received terrible news. I had an appointment with Susana Diogo, one of the people who dealt with East Timorese matters in the Portuguese foreign ministry at the time. When I arrived at the ministry, she seemed very upset. She had just learned that the Indonesian army had captured Xanana Gusmão in Dili.

At first I thought that it was impossible because Xanana was no longer in Dili. While I was in Jakarta, I had heard that Xanana had left Dili to return to the jungle. I immediately tried to phone a friend of mine in Bali and ask for information, but I couldn't get through. Later on, I called Dili and they confirmed that Xanana had been captured.

At first we thought the Indonesians captured Xanana through Henrique Belmiro, a taxi driver who often drove Xanana; the Indonesians had arrested him a week earlier. But actually he wasn't the one who exposed Xanana. The Indonesians tortured Henrique badly, but he never betrayed Xanana. People say that there was someone within the resistance who betrayed Xanana, but it is not clear what happened. Xanana is the only one who can tell the story. Maybe he can tell us one day when he is out of prison and free.

When my contact in Dili confirmed Xanana's arrest, I was really shocked and depressed. I began to think that the situation in East Timor would only get worse. Xanana had reorganized the resistance after the Indonesians almost destroyed it; people put a lot of hope in him. I was afraid that his capture would completely demoralize the people in East Timor and the resistance. I cried.

Almost everyone was upset and demoralized. Who could replace Xanana? But then I tried to imagine the situation when the Indonesians killed Nicolau Lobato, the president of FRETILIN, after the arrest of Xavier do Amaral, on December 31, 1978. Everyone thought it was the end of the struggle because Lobato was the heart of the resistance; but the resistance continued and grew even stronger.

A few days after Xanana's capture, Ramos Horta announced that Xanana was no longer the head of the CNRM. We did this to invalidate any statement he made while he was under arrest because we were afraid that the Indonesians would torture him, drug him, or otherwise coerce him into making false statements.

Beginning in December 1992, I started traveling as a representative of the CNRM, speaking in a number of countries and campaigning for Xanana's freedom, asking people to call on their governments to support Xanana and to write letters to the Indonesian government to make sure that they treated Xanana well in prison. I went to Spain in December and in January I went to the Netherlands for a conference. In the Netherlands, I was able to meet with Dutch foreign ministry officials to discuss Xanana's situation. And then in April I traveled to the United States and Canada for a two-month speaking tour with some other East Timorese refugees. Xanana was always on our agenda.

I was very happy to see the growing solidarity movement in the United States and Canada. The East Timor Action Network/U.S. was founded in the aftermath of the November 12, 1991 massacre and has grown rapidly. In Canada, the East Timor Alert Network had grown significantly since Santa Cruz. These two groups organized the speaking tour as part of their efforts to raise consciousness about the Indonesian occupation of my country and their own countries' criminal relations with the Suharto regime. Both groups were heavily lobbying their governments to change their foreign policies toward Indonesia and East Timor.

During the tour, I spoke in more than 20 cities in the United States and Canada. I spoke to students at universities and high schools, community groups, and political activists. While the growing interest in East Timor encouraged me, I was very surprised to see how little most people in the United States and Canada knew about the East Timor issue.

I was very concerned about Gabriela when I was in the United States. In April 1993, Indonesia announced that the army had arrested me in Dili. I was in New York at the time. Of course, the Indonesians were lying. One of the Indonesian officials had reported to the *Far Eastern Economic Review* and many other newspapers that the military had already captured me.[1] The situation became even worse when I met with Al Gore, the U.S. vice president, in Washington, D.C. The Indonesians denied that the meeting had happened and claimed that I was still in East Timor. I immediately tried to call Dili to check on Gabriela. For the first time, soldiers took her away for interrogation. She had to leave Tilson with her parents. Almost every day Indonesian soldiers would take her away to be interrogated. They interrogated and intimidated her probably because I was speaking here in the United States. Someone with Indonesian intelligence was most likely providing information to Jakarta, telling them that I was criticizing Indonesia and trying to persuade U.S. citizens to support the struggle in East Timor. The Indonesians harassed Gabriela to intimidate me, to make me stop my struggle and end the speaking tour.

I began working to get Gabriela and Tilson out of East Timor as soon as I arrived in Portugal. I informed the Portuguese foreign minister about the situation, and when I came to the United States I worked with Allan Nairn to get in touch with some U.S. senators and representatives. Senator Claiborne Pell of Rhode Island even made a public statement in the Senate about the situation of Gabriela and Tilson and spoke to the Indonesian foreign minister, Ali Alatas, about the matter in April 1993.[2] Alatas lied to Senator Pell about Gabriela. "She's OK," Alatas told him. "If Gabriela wants to leave East Timor, at any time, we will let her go." But the Indonesians didn't allow Gabriela to leave East Timor until one year later.

I was also in contact with Caroline Croft from the State Department and Alexandra Ariaga, an aide of Representative Tom Lantos of

California. They both worked very hard to get Gabriela out of East Timor. Her case was also on the agenda of the United Nations Secretary General.

I had a chance to talk with Gabriela by phone on her birthday, May 24, from New York. She was very brave. "Whatever happens to me, I will face it," she said. It had been almost a year and a half since the last time I spoke to her. In East Timor, almost every telephone call is taped. So I had to limit my phone conversation with her; it would have been dangerous otherwise.

It was so sad. Gabriela explained to me how the Indonesian army would take her away and interrogate her. They tried to force her to tell them that I was still in East Timor. "Constâncio has already returned to East Timor with a woman," they also told her. "He's working here in Dili." And sometimes they would say to her, "We won't let you go to Portugal unless you tell us where Constâncio is."

I tried to give Gabriela hope that I was working to get her and Tilson out of East Timor. "Be strong," I told her. I encouraged her to be closer to the Church, to the bishop, and to other priests there because the Church is the only organization that could look out for her.

The Indonesians didn't beat Gabriela, but they tortured her psychologically. They threatened to kill her and her family. Gabriela also told me that the soldiers wanted to take Tilson. They said to her, "Okay, we couldn't find his father. Let's just take the child." They even interrogated her father at his office every day because of me. That's why her father quit working at the *desa* office. He's now doing work in construction.

The Indonesian soldiers also tried to convince Gabriela to marry one of them. "Why do you wait for Constâncio?" they would ask. "Constâncio's now in Lisbon. He has a nice woman there. Constâncio is an ugly man, but we are good looking. Why don't you marry one of us? Forget Constâncio." They played all sorts of games with her. Indonesia was probably afraid to do anything more to Gabriela because, ironically, the United States Embassy in Jakarta was keeping an eye on her. Two U.S. diplomats from the embassy in Jakarta went to Dili and met with her. They told Gabriela that they were working to get her out of East Timor. So Gabriela had some level of security because of the U.S. Embassy and the International Committee of the Red Cross.

When I came to the United States from Portugal, I already had decided to try to find a U.S. university where I could study and work for East Timor. No East Timorese had lived in the country since Horta left for Australia in the early 1980s, so there was no East Timorese in the United States who could work and speak publicly on behalf of our struggle. The United States is one of the key countries that we have to change if East Timor is to become independent. And to change government policy here, we need to educate the American public.

Allan Nairn had a friend, David Targan, who was a dean at Brown University. So when I went to Providence, Rhode Island, to speak about East Timor at Brown, I met with one of the members of the admissions committee and David Targan. After that meeting, I decided to apply to Brown. Before the end of the speaking tour and my return to Lisbon, I found out that Brown had accepted me. So I was very happy when I went back to Portugal.

In June 1993, I went to Vienna for the UN World Conference on Human Rights. Thousands of organizations and advocacy groups attended. It was very confusing. It seemed that whoever made the most noise during the conference in Vienna found support or influenced people. I was very excited to see all this. Even though we had a small delegation from the CNRM, we were able to talk to many people and to meet with representatives of solidarity movements, human rights groups, and the media. I had the opportunity to speak to a crowd of thousands of people at a rally organized by Amnesty International.

I even joined Amnesty on a trip from Vienna to Zagreb, Croatia, in the former Yugoslavia to visit a Bosnian refugee camp. My visit was the first time that an East Timorese spoke in Zagreb about East Timor. No one there knew about East Timor, though in many ways it sounded as though their experiences were similar to ours. People said things to me like, "My parents were killed, and my brothers and my sister were raped by soldiers." But, in some ways, the Bosnian refugees were in much better condition than the East Timorese because the UN supported them with housing and food. The Bosnians have similar problems as we have in East Timor, but they have received a lot more attention from the UN and the international community.

The United Nations is a very complicated institution. The most striking thing about it is that the countries that are judging human rights issues are countries that have committed gross human rights violations. Indonesia, China, and the United States, for example, are all members of the UN Human Rights Commission. All of them are countries that have oppressed people and committed numerous human rights violations, yet they are there to judge others. The UN is still important, however. We continue to put our hope in the UN to solve the East Timor problem; we don't see any solution for East Timor through military means; the Indonesian military is too big and powerful for the East Timorese. Just as the UN has helped to address some other problems in the world, such as the conflict in Namibia, it can help to solve East Timor's problems through diplomatic means, but only if the member states of the UN, especially the powerful countries that control the Security Council such as the United States, France, and the United Kingdom, respect and support East Timor's right to self-determination as called for by the UN. But it is doubtful that this will happen unless there is strong pressure on the governments by people in those countries.

The invasion of East Timor is very similar to the invasion of Kuwait, except that the case of East Timor is in many ways much worse. When the United States, through the UN, took the initiative to get Iraq out of Kuwait, it gave a lot of hope to the East Timorese people. Everyone hoped that, after Kuwait, the United States and its allies would move to other problems, such as East Timor. But, after solving the Kuwait problem, the United States government never said a single word about East Timor. The reasons behind this are U.S. economic interests: Kuwait produces a lot of oil and the United States profits from it.

In East Timor's case, however, we don't want the United States to invade; we need the United States to involve itself actively in the diplomatic process to resolve the issue. The United States can support the UN Secretary General and negotiations between Indonesia, Portugal, and East Timorese leaders. The most important thing, however, is to end U.S. economic and military aid to Indonesia. And if the U.S. cuts off aid to Indonesia, it is likely that many other Western countries will do the same.[3] Any aid to Indonesia helps its occupation of East Timor. Foreign aid to Indonesia doesn't benefit the Timorese people or the Indonesian people. It benefits only a small group of Indonesian officials, Suharto's family, and his generals. The resistance doesn't expect the powerful capitalist countries like the United States and the United Kingdom to change their policies toward Indonesia and East Timor overnight; but change can happen if there is strong grassroots pressure within those countries. The pressure can take many forms, including letter-writing campaigns to public officials, demonstrations, civil disobedience, and consumer boycotts of corporations that help support Suharto and his occupation of East Timor. By joining one of the many solidarity movements for East Timor around the world, individuals can play a very positive role in East Timor's future.[4]

The growing political unrest within Indonesia could also force Western countries to end their complicity with the Suharto regime; the increasing instability threatens Western economic interests in the region. I have no doubt that we will see a very different Indonesia in the next century. If Western capitalist countries do not alter their policies toward Indonesia and East Timor, the coming changes within Indonesia will force them to change.

After Vienna, I went back to Portugal and then to Japan because there was a summit meeting there of the Group of Seven (G-7), the major capitalist countries. When I met with Vice President Al Gore when I was in the U.S., he promised that President Clinton would raise the East Timor issue with Suharto in Japan. Suharto was in Tokyo because he was the chair at the time of the Non-Aligned Movement and supposedly wanted to represent the interests of developing countries to the G-7, but the G-7 members wouldn't allow Suharto to participate in their meeting; the U.S. and Japan, however, were willing to meet with Suharto separately. After the summit, Clinton told reporters that he had talked with Suharto about East Timor for about 10 minutes.

During this time, I followed Xanana's trial very closely. I still remember one day when Xanana declared that he was an Indonesian citizen and was in favor of the integration of East Timor into Indonesia. Ramos Horta was really angry. He called me from Australia. "Why did Xanana say that? What do you think about this?" he asked me. I also became angry. "If Xanana said that," I told him, "he is not Xanana anymore." But we didn't know exactly what Xanana was doing. Xanana was just trying to build the confidence of the Indonesians. If he said what they wanted him to say, he knew that Indonesia would allow foreign journalists to interview him and follow his trial. And that's what Indonesia did. Indonesia expected that Xanana would say the same things he said during his trial when he spoke to UN and other international observers and members of the international media. But at the end of the trial, Xanana spoke out against the Indonesian occupation in the presence of foreign journalists and international observers. As the process went on, we saw that Xanana was changing his message, and we began to understand that his earlier statements were tactical.

Xanana continues to be at the heart of the whole resistance in East Timor. His arrest and imprisonment has not meant the end of the struggle. The struggle in East Timor depends on the decision of the Timorese people to continue to fight. Of course, the resistance suffered a lot because of the capture of Xanana, the person who drew up the strategy of our struggle. The Indonesians thought that the arrest of Xanana would demoralize the whole resistance and bring about an end to the struggle. The Indonesians were really happy; they considered Xanana's capture a victory for Indonesia. But, contrary to what they thought, the struggle continues, even the armed struggle.

When I came to the United States to study at Brown in September 1993, Ramos Horta immediately appointed me as the representative of the CNRM to the United States and the UN. This was later recognized by Xanana. But my first year at Brown was difficult. It was really difficult for me to adjust to my new life. Everything was different. I felt lonely and isolated. There were no other East Timorese in the United States at the time, and I had difficulty adapting to U.S. culture. Most students at Brown always seemed to be busy, so busy they didn't even have time to talk.

What struck me most was going to school with people who were mostly between 18 and 22 years old. Fortunately, I lived in a dormitory for graduate students, so I lived with students closer to my own age.

Academically, Brown was very challenging for me. Each semester I had to take four classes. I thought it would be like high school and that it would be pretty easy. But it was very difficult, especially because my English was so poor. Many of the students had accents that sounded very strange to me. In East Timor, I used to listen often to the BBC on shortwave radio, so I was used to the British accent. Sometimes I used to listen also to the Voice of America, but the radio journalists always spoke slowly and clearly, so I was able to understand. At Brown, however, I couldn't even participate in discussions during my first year; I felt comfortable only saying a few words. I could not follow what my classmates were saying. They spoke too fast and used terms that I had never heard before. I often had the same problems with my professors during lectures. And there was a lot of reading! I couldn't read so fast. My writing was also terrible: sometimes it would take me three days to write a four-page paper. But step by step, my speaking, comprehension, and writing skills improved. I received a lot of help at the Brown writing center.

At the same time, I began to receive invitations to speak about East Timor from places like New York, San Francisco, and Cambridge. For one of the engagements I was asked to appear with Noam Chomsky, the world-famous linguist and outspoken critic of U.S. foreign policy and the corporate media.

Although Brown gave me a scholarship to pay for my room, board, and tuition, I didn't have a lot of money for most of my first year. Once during a school break, when the cafeteria was closed, I had to survive for three days on only three dollars. I would have liked to have worked at Brown, but then I wouldn't have been able to do any work for East Timor. It is very hard being in exile. I'm determined to work for my country, but the CNRM doesn't have any money.

During my first year at Brown I was frequently in touch with the International Committee of the Red Cross in Geneva regarding Gabriela's case. On May 5, at one in the morning, the Red Cross called me from Geneva. "Your wife and son will arrive in Portugal on May 7," the Red Cross told me. It was very sudden. I already knew that they would leave the country soon, but not exactly when. When the Red Cross called me, Gabriela and Tilson had already left East Timor and were on their way to Jakarta. There was not time for me to call them and let them know that I would meet them in Portugal. Fortunately, I had only one more paper to write before the end of the semester. I left the same day at five in the afternoon. I arrived in Lisbon on May 6, and Gabriela and Tilson arrived on May 7.

The Red Cross helped Gabriela and Tilson to get out of East Timor. The Red Cross organized the whole trip and gave Gabriela a travel document but only gave her 24 hours' notice before her departure. So she didn't have time to say goodbye to everyone in her family. Gabriela and Tilson flew to Jakarta, then to Zurich, Switzerland, and then to Portugal.

On May 7, I went to the airport in Lisbon. There were some East Timorese families there, and then some journalists and television crews came. I don't know who called them, but they were there. I was really excited to see Gabriela and Tilson when they came out of the waiting room from the airplane. I tried to embrace and kiss them, but Tilson hit me in the face. The television man filmed this and it appeared on television the same day.

The Portuguese social security department took us from the airport to one of their apartment buildings in Queluz, a suburb of Lisbon. On the way to Queluz in the car, I tried to play with Tilson, but he didn't want to play with me. He was crying, saying, "Who is this man?" as if I were a stranger. He didn't like me. I kept trying to play with him and to act like his father, even though he didn't want me to. "Where is your father?" Gabriela would ask him.

"My father is dead," Tilson would respond.

"This is your father," Gabriela would tell him.

"No, this is not my father," Tilson would insist. "My father died."

Gradually, Tilson began to be nicer to me, but it was very difficult. I began to buy things for him such as toys, chocolates, shoes, and clothes. Little by little he became accustomed to me. I would take him to the park, we would walk around Lisbon and meet people, and we would go to the train together. After about three weeks he began to call me father, *Papa.*

A number of East Timorese lived in the building in Queluz. We lived in an apartment with two rooms: one room for us, and one for another family. We lived in the room for three months. Living conditions in Queluz were really terrible. We had a tiny space to live in and we had to share the kitchen and bathroom. The Portuguese government provided us with the apartment; it paid for the rent and utilities and provided Tilson and Gabriela with social welfare as refugees— about $200 a month. So during those three months, we barely scraped by. Fortunately, we didn't have to pay for health insurance because health care in Portugal is offered by the government.

The move to Lisbon was very difficult for Gabriela. Her first reaction was to want to return to East Timor. She missed her family in East Timor, and she thought a lot about her friends. She was lonely. Fortunately, the presence of other East Timorese in Lisbon helped her to adjust to the new life.

It was not difficult for Gabriela and I to get used to one another again. We were happy because we were finally together. But sometimes Gabriela felt sad. She had spent most of her time with her parents, not me. This was the first time we lived together as parents. By that time, I felt like a father. I felt myself going through a real change. When I was away at Brown University, I felt like a young, single man, running from one place to another, socializing and having fun and so on. Although I was really concerned about Gabriela and Tilson, I didn't feel like a father. But when I met Gabriela and Tilson in Lisbon, I immediately felt myself changing, shifting from being a young man to a father and a husband. Now I had a lot more responsibility.

Gabriela and I spent May to July together and then I had to leave for one week. I had to come back to the United States to testify at the UN Decolonization Committee. It was a difficult week for Gabriela. Lisbon was still strange to her and Tilson. When I returned from the U.S., I obtained Portuguese identity cards and passports for Gabriela and Tilson. We came to the United States in August 1994 and have been here ever since. Now we have a daughter as well. We named her Tima, for Timorese American. She was born in April 1996.

Since I was 11 years old, when I first became involved in the struggle for East Timor's liberation, I have always been hopeful. Sooner or later, East Timor has to be free and independent, because we are more willing than ever to continue the fight. The resistance in East Timor is more than 20 years old. It is still strong. Since 1975, the resistance has suffered a lot of setbacks, especially the killing of the leadership, many of the best guerrilla fighters, and of an enormous part of the population. The resistance was weakened in the late 1970s, but it survived. Now, after the massacre of November 12, 1991, we see that the resistance is more solid and more active than ever, even with the capture of Xanana. The resistance is in the hands of the new generation. All the young people who grew up during Indonesia's invasion and the more than 20 years of occupation, those who were born during the war, are now on the front lines of the struggle. It is now the struggle of the new generation and it will never end without an internationally acceptable solution. The East Timorese are ready to fight for another 20 years if necessary.

The existence of FALINTIL in the jungle is very important. In many places throughout the world, guerrilla warfare is a very important element of liberation movements. As long as FALINTIL fighters are still in the jungle, we still see the light of the resistance. We know that we will never defeat the Indonesian military on the ground, but we can cause many problems for Indonesia. As Konis Santana, the new leader of FALINTIL, says, we can increase the number of FALINTIL fighters at any time we want.[5]

In unexpected ways, the Indonesian military has helped the resistance. Every time Indonesian soldiers go into the jungle, they bring weapons. Every time FALINTIL has an operation, a guerrilla fighter will capture one or two weapons from the Indonesians. That's why the guerrilla fighters have been able to survive. We feel proud that we are able to use tools that were created by the colonizers to fight against them.

If Indonesia did not partially develop East Timor, we would have more difficulties in our struggle. For example, many East Timorese students go to university in Indonesia or East Timor, and many students graduate from high school. The Indonesians have educated many more East Timorese than the Portuguese ever did. And many of these East Timorese who have gone to Indonesian universities are now fighting against the Indonesian occupation. Because they have gone to university, they better understand the political situation. Another important area of development is telecommunications. Before telecommunications networks were established in East Timor, we had a difficult time sending letters to the outside and it was very difficult to make phone calls abroad. But today we can call Jakarta; we can call all over the world from East Timor. Indonesia has inadvertently helped the East Timorese resistance in this way.

Portuguese colonialism has also helped the resistance in certain ways, most importantly by establishing the Catholic Church in East Timor. The Church in East Timor was very conservative during the colonial period, but it has changed a lot during the Indonesian occupation. There has been a dramatic increase in the number of Catholics in East Timor. The war itself made people more solid and united. During the first few years of the war, some priests joined the guerrilla fighters in the jungle. They worked for the Church and prayed in the jungle. So they were very influential at that time. Because of that, the number of Catholics increased. And as the number increased, the resistance as a whole was strengthened.

The Church is helpful because the Church is the people. If there are no people, there is no church. And when the people suffer, the Church also suffers. The Church is the only East Timorese institution that is outspoken about the atrocities committed by the Indonesian army in East Timor. The East Timorese put their hope and trust in the Church. It's the only institution that we can complain to about our suffering. The Church has made the resistance even stronger. It gives inspiration to the East Timorese to continue to resist and to fight.

Before the invasion, the Catholic Church hierarchy was against independence and against FRETILIN. Then, when Indonesia began to massacre the East Timorese people, the Catholic Church had to take a position. The Catholic Church now is taking a position, not because it is supporting FRETILIN or supporting the UDT or whatever organization that exists in East Timor, but because it is supporting the East Timorese people, trying to protect the people from Indonesian atrocities. The Church now officially supports self-determination for the people of East Timor.

In terms of the diplomatic struggle, it's far more effective now than it was 15 years ago. We have a strong international solidarity movement fighting for the East Timorese. We now see more and more solidarity groups all over the world—in Europe and North America, in Africa, and in Southeast Asia. The problem of East Timor is also still alive within the United Nations, in the Decolonization Committee and in the office of the Secretary General, who is facilitating negotiations between Indonesia and Portugal about East Timor.

The goal of the resistance is a complete withdrawal of Indonesian troops from East Timor and, eventually, an internationally supervised referendum on self-determination. I'm confident that the pro-independence position would win if such a referendum were held. Indonesia says that the East Timorese have already chosen integration and don't need to have a referendum in East Timor because almost all the people support Indonesia. But if Indonesia is confident of the support of the people, why don't they accept a UN-organized referendum in East Timor? There are East Timorese in favor of integration, but they are a very small part of the East Timorese population. And many of those who at first supported integration have changed their minds and are now against Indonesia.[6] I would say that well over 90 percent of the East Timorese people support independence.

East Timorese independence is inevitable; as long as the Timorese people are determined to continue the struggle, I am certain that we will win. Our hope for self-determination lies on three, interrelated fronts: the intensification of resistance activities within East Timor; increased activity on the diplomatic front and by solidarity movements; and political and economic change within Indonesia. As we see now, East Timor is the concern of people not only in Western countries but also in Indonesia. That's something that never happened before. Before 1991, we never heard about Indonesians discussing East Timor; today, however, we see many Indonesians publicly protesting the occupation of East Timor and arguing that the government should give independence to East Timor. The Indonesian people are also fighting for the democratization of Indonesia itself. Political change in Indonesia is one of the key means to solve the East Timor problem. But as long as Suharto and the military rule the country, the problems in Indonesia will take a long time to resolve.

We are not fighting against the people of Indonesia. We are fighting against a regime that the Indonesian people are also fighting against: Suharto and his generals. The Indonesian soldiers who have been sent to East Timor over the last 20 years, who have committed so many atrocities, have been forced to go there. They are poor people, and they were trained by the military how to treat people in East Timor. We don't want any revenge in the future. We will be a good neighbor and we will build a positive relationship with the Indonesian people, as brothers and sisters, and we will have a normal life as long as the Indonesian government, the new government, respects the rights of the East Timorese people as a people separate from Indonesia.

I personally didn't have any Indonesian friends in East Timor. It was hard for me to trust Indonesians because so many of them were working for the government or the military. Since I've left East Timor, however, I've met many honest and friendly Indonesians, like George Aditjondro, a courageous Indonesian academic who has spoken out strongly in favor of East Timorese self-determination. Here in the United States, I have had the opportunity to meet with Indonesians, not only dissidents but also Indonesian students who were sent by the government to study at universities. Many of them are very sympathetic to the independence struggle in East Timor and are brave enough to criticize their government. Some Indonesians have gone to Geneva to the UN Human Rights Commission and made statements accusing Indonesia of violating human rights both in East Timor and in Indonesia.

I think it is time for us to build our relationships. In the resistance, we have always said that we all are fighting against the Suharto regime and not against the Indonesian people. We know that the Indonesian people also are suffering. There are even some Indonesians in East Timor who are sympathetic to our struggle. After the Santa Cruz Massacre, some Indonesian people tried to protect East Timorese youths who were escaping from the cemetery in Dili. As the struggle goes on, Indonesians are becoming more sympathetic to our cause.

The struggle for the freedom of East Timor continues. One day, we will win. I am sure.

Epilogue

In the aftermath of the Santa Cruz Massacre of November 12, 1991, United Nations-sponsored negotiations on East Timor between Portugal and Indonesia resumed in January 1992, spurred by Secretary General Boutros Boutros-Ghali. Nevertheless, they have achieved little because Indonesia refuses to discuss the political status of the former Portuguese colony, which it calls its "27th province," and Portugal, under international law still the "administering power" of its former colony, will accept nothing less than East Timorese self-determination. While encouraging, the negotiations are not likely to move the Suharto regime to withdraw from East Timor barring radical change within Indonesia or significant pressure from the United Nations' ruling powers, most notably the United States.[1]

The United Nations

The talks were mandated by the last UN General Assembly resolution on East Timor in 1982. The UN General Assembly and Security Council passed 10 resolutions in support of East Timorese self-determination in the period between 1975 and 1982. Since 1982, because neither Indonesia nor East Timor and its allies in the General Assembly have been confident of the outcome of a vote, and because negotiations have been taking place, the issue has not been brought again to a vote. Despite the strength of the resolutions that have deplored Indonesia's invasion, called on Jakarta to withdraw its troops, and called for the holding of an internationally supervised referendum on self-determination in East Timor, the United Nations has not been able to compel Indonesia to abide by the resolutions because of the indifference and complicity of its ruling powers.

The UN's paralysis on East Timor is inherent in its structure. The World War II victors ensured that the new global body would allow them to pursue their narrow national interests on the global stage without collective constraints. A number of countries in 1945 had supported the establishment of a world legislature and a world court with compulsory jurisdiction. A 1946 Roper poll, for example, showed that 63 percent of the U.S. public supported the creation of a democratically elected world congress with binding decisionmaking power. The key post-war powers, such as the United States, France, the United Kingdom, and the Soviet Union, however, ignored this post-nationalist sentiment and laid the basis for a UN oligarchy. As the Mexican delegate to the founding convention in San Francisco in 1945 noted, the UN Charter assured that "the mice would be disciplined, but the lions would be free."[2] But as the recent history of East Timor has shown, the mice with whom the lions are on good terms are also free.[3]

In the aftermath of Indonesia's December 1975 invasion of East Timor, the United States ensured that the UN Security Council, whose resolutions are binding on all member-states, did not take any meaningful steps against Indonesia. As U.S. Ambassador to the United Nations Daniel Patrick Moynihan bragged, "The Department of State desired that the United Nations prove utterly ineffective in whatever measures it undertook [on East Timor]. This task was given to me, and I carried it forward with no inconsiderable success."[4]

U.S. Support for Indonesia

Even though the Santa Cruz Massacre and its aftermath have resulted in increased attention to and criticism of Indonesia's occupation, the patterns of Western assistance to Jakarta have not changed. While the United States long remained Indonesia's most significant partner in the West, the United Kingdom is now Jakarta's principal military supporter and Japan is now its biggest provider of economic aid.[5] The reasons for such support are clear: Indonesia is the world's fourth-most-populous country; an area of great natural resources such as oil and natural gas; a major market for Western goods; and a hospitable area for multinational corporate activity.[6]

With the inauguration of President Bill Clinton, many human rights and peace activists thought that there was hope that U.S. policy toward Indonesia and East Timor would change for the better. As a presidential candidate, Clinton called U.S. policy toward East Timor "unconscionable." And while grassroots pressure has pushed his administration to ban the sale of small and light arms, riot control equipment, helicopter-mounted weaponry, and armored personnel carriers to Jakarta, Indonesia's economic and strategic importance has exposed the limits of Clinton's concern for human rights and international law. His administration has provided almost $400 million in economic assistance to Indonesia over the past four years and has also sold and licensed the sales of hundreds of millions of dollars in weaponry to Indonesia. The Clinton administration even side-stepped a September 1992 Congressional ban on International Military Education and Training (IMET) funds to Jakarta, allowing Indonesia to purchase the training. Now the administration has won Congressional approval for a revamped form of IMET (now called Expanded IMET) that restricts training to non-military matters. And joint U.S.-Indonesia military exercises continue.

Indonesia, which President Richard Nixon once referred to as "by far the greatest prize in the Southeast Asian area," is today one of the Clinton administration's "big emerging markets." The administration's aggressive pursuit of lucrative business opportunities in Indonesia has certainly paid off, resulting in 15 separate business deals totaling $40 billion over the next decade, including a $30 billion deal signed during the November 1994 Asia Pacific Economic Conference (APEC) meeting in Jakarta[7] for Exxon to exploit the country's natural gas reserves. As a senior Clinton administration official effused about

Suharto during the Indonesian ruler's visit to the White House in October 1995, "He's our kind of guy."[8]

Increasingly, such economic opportunities for multinational corporations are not limited to Indonesia proper, but can be found in Indonesian-occupied East Timor, specifically in the so-called Timor Gap. The Timor Gap, also known as the Kelp Prospect, is a continental shelf area between northern Australia and the island of Timor; that is thought to be one of the world's richest oil deposits.[9] In a December 1989 ceremony on a plane flying over the Timor Sea, Australian Foreign Minister Gareth Evans and his Indonesian counterpart, Ali Alatas, signed the Timor Gap Treaty, which detailed the final delimitation of the seabed. A number of major oil companies, such as British Petroleum and U.S.-based Marathon Petroleum, are already engaging in exploratory drilling.[10]

International Solidarity

Nonetheless, the international allies of the East Timorese resistance continue to grow. These are principally its friends in the international solidarity and human rights community and certain national governments such as those of Ireland, the former Portuguese colonies in Africa, and Portugal. After having largely deserted the East Timorese, Portugal has been playing an increasingly supportive role since the early 1980s, motivated by a combination of strong public sentiment and national embarrassment over its abandonment of its former colonial subjects.[11] Through these channels, the East Timorese resistance is increasingly challenging Jakarta's support abroad and even within Indonesia proper. And since the Santa Cruz Massacre, East Timor has become the focus of contentious debate in the legislative bodies of a number of countries, most significantly in the West in countries such as the United Kingdom, Canada, and the United States, where before 1991 the conflict barely received comment. While none of Indonesia's powerful Western allies publicly suggests that Indonesia withdraw from the territory, elite discourse is increasingly critical, as demonstrated by editorials in favor of East Timorese self-determination in establishment publications such as the *New York Times* and *The Econo-*

mist. Moreover, within Indonesia proper, support for East Timorese self-determination is growing, especially among those critical of President Suharto's three-decade dictatorial rule.

This became evident on December 7, 1995, the twentieth anniversary of Indonesia's invasion, when 36 Indonesian human rights and pro-democracy activists joined dozens of East Timorese in occupying the Russian and Dutch embassies in Jakarta to draw attention to the ongoing Indonesian occupation. Such actions within Indonesia only add to Jakarta's worries. These greater levels of criticism and scrutiny of Indonesia's occupation have helped create room for anti-occupation activity in both Indonesia and East Timor. Given the increased attention since the 1991 Santa Cruz Massacre, Jakarta has had to be more circumspect in dealing with demonstrations and protests in East Timor. This relative space for anti-regime activity serves only to enhance the contested nature of the occupation on the international level.

Indonesia's Resettlement Program

Despite these important cracks in Jakarta's international armor, Indonesia's military and administrative apparatus is still firmly entrenched in East Timor. A long-term threat to East Timorese self-determination is the increasing "Indonesianization" of the territory's population. Through its "transmigration" program, the Suharto government had resettled a total of 662 Indonesian families, or 2,808 persons, in East Timor in 1992 and 1993.[12] Under the guise of relieving population pressures in the relatively crowded islands such as Java and Bali, and filling "empty" land in places such as East Timor, the Indonesian government uses the migrants to create a pan-Indonesian identity and to serve the security needs of the military.[13]

Far more significant than the relatively small number of Indonesian transmigrants in East Timor are so-called voluntary or spontaneous migrants, who are not sponsored by the government but move within the framework of the law.[14] While there are no precise estimates, most observers place the number of voluntary transmigrants in the vicinity of 150,000 out of a total population of roughly 800,000.[15]

The heavy population influx is leading to increased competition for jobs, land, and commercial opportunities,[16] Jakarta facilitates the large-scale voluntary migration of Indonesians by giving them license to relocate and often providing them with the resources, such as land, necessary to establish themselves. The Indonesian government also draws people to East Timor through jobs opportunities in fields such as education and administration, thus furthering Indonesia's nation-state-building project. The heavy influx of Indonesian migrants, businesspeople, and capital has overwhelmed traditional East Timorese society, marginalizing the indigenous population economically.[17]

Military Repression

Since the mid-1980s, the military situation in East Timor remains stalemated, with the Indonesian armed forces controlling the main population centers and strategic locations and FALINTIL working in small units throughout the territory, with links to the resettlement villages and the underground network in major towns.[18] Even to the casual visitor, the presence of the Indonesian military throughout the territory is pervasive. While firm data is unavailable, probably upward of 20,000 Indonesian soldiers occupy the former Portuguese colony. Of growing concern is the Indonesian military's increasing emphasis on sytematically recruiting and training East Timorese youths to participate in armed and unarmed militias, apparently to exacerbate tensions and provoke conflict among the East Timorese.[19]

FALINTIL, now under the leadership of Nino Konis Santana, currently numbers about 600 to 800 full-time guerrilla fighters and approximately 1,500 "reserves." According to Santana, FALINTIL would grow quickly and significantly if it had enough weapons.[20] In addition to engaging in occasional skirmishes with ABRI, FALINTIL maintains links to a large and sophisticated clandestine front active throughout East Timor and in parts of Indonesia where there are East Timorese students and workers.

Over the past two years, the East Timorese opposition, seemingly outside the formal organization of the resistance, appears to be moving into open confrontation in the towns, with many of the major towns of East Timor, such as Dili, Baucau, Viqueque, and Ermera, experiencing sporadic riots, often spontaneous reactions to specific incidents. In conjunction with the Asia Pacific Economic Conference meeting and in the presence of visiting foreign journalists in Dili in November 1994, two weeks of intermittent rioting took place in which pro-independence youths clashed with police and attacked Indonesian homes and businesses. Several waves of rioting took place in late 1995 as well. In response, Indonesia has increased repression in the territory. While the Indonesian military has been careful to avoid another large-scale massacre, repression beyond the view of the international community continues and is intensifying. Even the U.S. State Department, in its 1996 report on East Timor, acknowledged, "Reports of extrajudicial killings, disappearances, and torture of those in custody by security forces increased" in 1995. As Armindo Maia, vice rector of the University of East Timor, recently remarked, "The situation in East Timor is one of terror, tension, and persecution."[21]

This growing repression has led to a series of embassy "invasions" in Jakarta by East Timorese youths in search of political asylum abroad.[22] Such actions have greatly embarrassed Jakarta and have served to publicize the East Timorese plight throughout the world. By initiating such actions, the East Timorese resistance has successfully called into question Indonesian sovereignty—political, moral, and legal—over the former Portuguese colony.

Prospects for Self-Determination

But there are limits to what the East Timorese people can do, given the overwhelming power of the Indonesian military and its Western supporters. As António Ramos Horta, a member of the underground, said to me during my visit to East Timor in 1992, shortly before he died, "Politically, we have already won. However, it is a question of force, something we do not have."[23] Friends of East Timor throughout the world, and even within Indonesia proper, can play an important role in challenging the forces underlying Jakarta's 20-year occupation.

The vast majority of the East Timorese strongly rejects the Indonesian presence in their country and still dreams of independence. Internationally, East Timor is a far more contested terrain today than it has been since the early years of the occupation. Within Indonesia, there is increasing awareness of and opposition to the Suharto government's conduct and presence in the former Portuguese colony. In the absence of a relatively strong resistance within East Timor and Western attention and pressure on Jakarta, however, the United Nations-sponsored negotiations, despite their largely symbolic character up until this point, would probably cease. While what happens within the territory is of primary significance, barring radical changes in the Indonesian political regime, the levels and nature of the involvement of the West could prove decisive. In this regard, the international community (often shorthand for the West, given the unequal power relations on the global scale) could potentially play a very positive role in helping to end one of the twentieth century's most tragic conflicts. But that is unlikely to happen without a significant increase in grassroots pressure in countries such as the United States, Japan, Australia, and the United Kingdom.

Apart from such international pressure or radical changes within Indonesia itself, it is doubtful that East Timorese self-determination will become a reality in the foreseeable future. Although there is a growing pro-democracy movement and political and workplace instability within Indonesia,[24] the challenges to the Suharto regime's grip on power are still a far cry, for example, from the movement that drove Ferdinand Marcos from power in the Philippines in 1986.[25] Barring such change, only Western, principally U.S., pressure—in the form of an end to military and non-humanitarian economic assistance, combined with strong diplomatic activity—can make Jakarta perceive a withdrawal from East Timor to be in its best interest. Anxious to maintain good relations with the United States, Indonesia would likely withdraw from East Timor in the face of such clear U.S. resolve. But without such a strong signal, Indonesia's occupation of East Timor will continue.

The South African and Central American solidarity movements demonstrated the power of ordinary citizens to limit the West's imperial destructiveness and to facilitate progressive change abroad. Thus far, human rights and peace activists and East Timor solidarity groups have played a key role in making East Timor an issue of public discussion and in bringing about the small but significant changes in the policies of a variety of Western countries. Since the 1991 Santa Cruz Massacre, the East Timorese solidarity movement has grown by leaps and bounds. There are groups in numerous cities in the United States, Canada, Japan, Australia, the United Kingdom, and New Zealand. In the Philippines, Malaysia, Thailand, and other countries in Asia, activism around East Timor is growing rapidly. Throughout Western Europe, active solidarity networks exist. Groups in Brazil and South Africa have also recently emerged. The October 11, 1996, announcement of Bishop Carlos Filipe Ximenes Belo and José Ramos Horta as the winners of the Nobel Peace Prize can only help to further this trend.

By legitimizing the struggle for self-determination of the East Timorese people, the Nobel committee has given a great boost to the people of East Timor and has sent shock waves through Jakarta's political establishment. The award is the culmination of growing worldwide support for East Timor's struggle for freedom and of increasing criticism of Indonesia's occupation. But while even Suharto's traditional allies, such as the U.S. State Department, have voiced their official congratulations to Bishop Belo and Ramos Horta, the Nobel Peace Prize, in and of itself, will change little for East Timor.

In its announcement of the award to Bishop Belo and Ramos Horta, the Norwegian Nobel Committee expressed its hope that the prize would "spur efforts to find a diplomatic solution to the conflict in East Timor based on the people's right to self-determination." Such a diplomatic solution will certainly require the active support of Western governments, given the dominating role that countries such as the United States, United Kingdom, France, and Japan play in international organizations.

But despite the increased attention and criticism of Jakarta's occupation over the last few years, the West continues to supply Jakarta with billions of dollars in economic assistance and military aid. Grassroots activists must challenge these funding sources. We must also pressure our national governments to *actively* support the United Nations negotiations on East Timor between Indonesia and Portugal, and to push for the participation of representatives of the East Timorese resistance and the Catholic Church, with the goal of holding a plebiscite on self-determination in the territory.

Ultimately what takes place within East Timor and Indonesia is of greater direct importance to the prospects of East Timorese self-determination than what transpires in the United States and the West. It is possible that Jakarta's ongoing efforts to "Indonesianize" East Timor will eventually succeed. But as the East Timorese resistance has demonstrated, the will of the East Timorese people for self-determination is extremely strong and will be difficult to dampen. As Xanana Gusmão stated in September 1990, "To resist is to win." Through resistance, East Timor survives. Those of us outside of East Timor must work to help the East Timorese not only to survive but to live. We must not only advocate for East Timor, but also challenge the global structures of socio-economic inequality that underlie the West's sacrifice of East Timor. We also must work for global political structures that, while allowing our world's great diversity to flourish, do not allow the powerful to flout international law and ignore human rights. Without such efforts, there is little hope for our common humanity.

— Matthew Jardine

East Timor Peace Plan

José António Ramos Horta
for the National Council of Maubere Resistance (CNRM)
November 1993

Phase One (one to two years)

Indonesia-Portugal talks under the auspices of the UN Secretary General, without initial East Timorese participation. Three such talks sessions have been held to date, with modest results so far. A communiqué issued in New York after the last round of talks by the Foreign Ministers of both countries on 17 September 1993 gives reason for optimism, provided its points are actually implemented by Indonesia.

Subsequent talks, in which East Timorese need to be invited to participate, should aim to achieve:

• An immediate end to all armed activities in East Timor.

- Immediate and unconditional release of all East Timorese political prisoners.

- Significant reduction of the large numbers of Indonesian military personnel currently in the territory.

- Removal from East Timor of all heavy weapons, long range artillery pieces and armed transport equipment.

- Expansion of the presence and activities of the International Committee of the Red Cross (ICRC) into every district of East Timor and in strict observance of the Geneva Conventions.

- Significant reduction of Indonesian civil servants in the territory.

- A comprehensive population census to be undertaken by competent UN bodies.

- Access to the territory by UN Specialized Agencies such as FAO, UNDP, UNICEF, WHO and others, for the purpose of carrying out, within their respective fields of competence, a comprehensive program of restoration and protection of the environment, voluntary resettlement of displaced persons, district development projects, women and children care and public health and immunization programs.

- Restoration of all basic human rights in the territory, including freedom of political activities and assembly.

- Removal of any restrictions on the use and teaching of Portuguese and Tetum languages.

- Setting up of an independent Human Rights Commission in Dili.

- Appointment of a Resident Representative of the UN Secretary General in East Timor, responsible for the implementation of all UN activities in the territory and for reporting on the implementation of the accords.

At the end of Phase One, the following results should be achievable:

- Normalization of Portugal - Indonesia relations.

- Legal existence of East Timorese political parties.

- Establishment of a resident European Community Legation in Dili, representing Portugal in East Timor.

- Setting up of a Portuguese Cultural Institute in the territory.

Phase Two (five years)

This is a transition stage of autonomy in which East Timorese would govern themselves democratically through their own local institutions. This would require:

- Election of a local Assembly with a five-year mandate, according to universally accepted democratic norms under UN supervision and technical assistance. Only East Timorese duly identified as such may vote and be elected.

- Election of an East Timorese Governor, for a five-year term by the Assembly.

- Powers devolved to the East Timor Assembly to include legislation concerning international trade relations, investment, property, immigration and others.

- Withdrawal of remaining Indonesian troops and further reduction in Indonesian civil servants.

- Placement under the command of the elected governor of a territorial police force organized by the UN. The territory is to have no army.

Phase Two may be extended by mutual consent between Indonesia and the East Timorese population. A 2/3 vote by the Assembly would be required for a proposal for the extension of Phase Two to be put to a popular referendum.

If the referendum rejects extension of Phase Two, or at the end of an extension of Phase Two, Phase Three would commence.

Phase Three — Self determination

This phase covers:

- Preparation for a self-determination referendum, to be held within one year of the commencement of Phase Three, whereby the population may choose between independence, free association with, or, integration into Indonesia.

In the case of independence being chosen, the following would take place:

- Election of a Constituent Assembly, and adoption of a Constitution for East Timor.

- Election of a government of East Timor, and transfer of sovereign powers to this Government of National Unity.

- East Timor applies for United Nations membership.

- Declaration of East Timor as a Zone of Peace and of Neutrality, guaranteed by the Permanent Members of the UN Security Council and ASEAN.

- East Timor accedes to and ratifies all international human rights instruments.

- East Timor applies to join ASEAN and the South Pacific Forum.

Notes

Introduction

1. Amnesty International 1994: 5.
2. When speaking of the "West," I am referring to a political-economic grouping rather than a strictly geographical one. Specifically, I am referring to the member-countries of the OECD, the Organization of Economic Cooperation and Development, which include the countries of Western Europe, the United States, Canada, Australia, New Zealand, and Japan.
3. Wolf 1982: 129.
4. Taylor 1991: 1; Hanna 1966, Pt. 1: 10; and Jolliffe 1978: 23-24.
5. Jolliffe 1978: 22-25 and Taylor 1991: 2-3 and 8.
6. Dunn 1983: 17 and Weatherbee 1966: 685.
7. Taylor 1991: 12.
8. Boxer 1968: 189.
9. Taylor 1991: 10.
10. Wallace 1869: 307.
11. Jolliffe 1978: 34 and Taylor 1991: 10.
12. Telkamp 1979: 78; Clarence-Smith 1992: 178; and Lains e Silva 1956: 24-26.
13. Hill 1978: 10-11 and Taylor 1991: 11.
14. Jolliffe 1978: 36-39; Dunn 1983: 19-20; Boxer 1960: 355; and Taylor 1991: 11.
15. Clarence-Smith 1992: 18-19.
16. Dunn 1983: 54.
17. Weatherbee 1966: 684.
18. Taylor 1991: 16 and Dunn 1983: 7-8.
19. See Colegrove 1941 and Hall 1981, Chapter 50.
20. Dunn 1983: 25-26 and Turner 1992: 3.
21. Although the vast majority of the population were Australian sympathizers, the Australians also "routinely killed" East Timorese suspected of cooperating with the Japanese (Turner 1992: 5).
22. Had the Australians and the Allies left the territory alone, the Japanese might very well have ignored the territory or, at most, sent a token contingent of soldiers. See Dunn 1983: 23-26, Turner 1992: 4-5, and Taylor 1991: 14.
23. Taylor 1991: 14. Also see Francis 1960.

24. Taylor 1991: 21. The circumstances surrounding the revolt are quite complicated and not altogether clear. Also see Jolliffe 1978: 48-49 and Dunn 1983: 33-34.
25. Dunn 1983: 21.
26. Dunn 1983: 37.
27. Dunn 1983: 49-52 and Diaz de Rábago 1966: 166.
28. Dunn 1983: 53 and Taylor 1991: 27.
29. Telkamp 1979: 77 and Dunn 1983: 39.
30. Jolliffe 1978: 55-56.
31. Dunn 1983: 54.
32. Taylor 1991: 17 and Jolliffe 1978: 42-43.
33. Taylor 1991: 16 and Metzner 1978: 213.
34. Dunn 1983: 9-11.
35. Special Correspondent 1960: 585.
36. Taylor 1991: 26-27.
37. Taylor 1991: 26; Horta 1987: 29-31; and Dunn 1983: 61.
38. Dunn 1983: 63; Taylor 1991: 27; and Horta 1987: 35.
39. Taylor 1991: 23, 27-28 and Dunn 1983: 71.
40. Jolliffe 1978: 74; Dunn 1983: 68; and Taylor 1991: 32-33.
41. Hill 1978, Chapter 4; Dunn 1983: 69; Jolliffe 1978: 75-76; and Taylor 1991: 33-35.
42. Taylor 1991: 38-39 and Hill 1978: 143-144.
43. Dunn 1983: 116 and Taylor 1991: 31.
44. Taylor 1991: 41-51; Horta 1987: 54-56; and Jolliffe 1978: 115-119.
45. Budiardjo and Liem 1984: 55; Taylor 1991: 51; Dunn 1983: 180; and Jolliffe 1978, Chapter 4.
46. Dunn 1983: 171-174; Taylor 1991: 51-54; and Jolliffe 1978: 124-125.
47. Horta 1987: 55.
48. Dunn 1983: 210.
49. Taylor 1991: 56.
50. Horta 1987: 59.
51. Taylor 1991: 51; Jolliffe 1978: 146; and Van Atta et al. 1982: 2.
52. Van Atta et al. 1982.
53. Taylor 1991: 58-61; Budiardjo and Liem 1983: 20. Also see Turner 1992: 98-101.
54. *Los Angeles Times*, December 7, 1975.
55. Anderson 1979.
56. Southwood and Flanagan 1983: 22-23.
57. Marshall 1973: 7.
58. Hayes et al. 1986: 15-16.

59. From U.S. Congress, Committee of Naval Affairs and Merchant Marine and Fisheries Committee, "No. 67: Survey of Pacific Areas," Report to Chairman, May 29, 1946: 2. Quoted in Hayes et al. 1986: 20-21.
60. Kennan 1976: 524-5.
61. See "Why U.S. Risks War for Indo-China" 1954; Lodge 1965; and Southwood and Flanagan 1983: 19.
62. Scott 1975: 241.
63. See Chomsky 1993: 126-127.
64. See Budiardjo 1991 and Caldwell 1975.
65. Anderson and McVey 1978.
66. The circumstances surrounding the alleged coup are rather murky and certainly far more complex than presented by the Indonesian government. See Cribb and Brown 1995: 97-106, Kahin and Kahin 1995: 224-230, and Chomsky 1993: 121-125 on the alleged coup and its aftermath.
67. Chomsky 1993: 122-123.
68. See Chomsky 1993: 123-131 and Griswold 1973: 20.
69. Kahin and Kahin 1995: 224-230.
70. Quoted in Chomsky 1990: 15.
71. Kahin and Kahin 1995: 230.
72. Waby 1976.
73. Kohen and Quance 1980: 20-21; Harkin 1980: 46-47; Chomsky and Herman 1979: 144-145; Taylor 1991: 169; and Scheiner 1992: 51. Also see Hertsgaard 1990.
74. See Chomsky and Herman 1979.
75. See Jardine 1993a: 23.

Chapter 1

1. Remexio was one of four administrative sub-districts of Aileu. Portuguese Timor was made up of thirteen districts.
2. The increasing monetization of the East Timorese economy coincided with the rise of a new economic elite, composed largely of Chinese merchants. Chinese contact with the island of Timor began in the fifteenth century with the rise of the sandalwood trade. However, Chinese settlement on the island did not commence until the beginning of the twentieth century with the Portuguese and Dutch "pacification" campaigns in their respective halves of the island. Gradually, Chinese settlers ventured into the interior of the territory. Under the protection of nearby Portuguese military installations, Chinese merchants began to open shops (Taylor 1991: 16 and Metzner 1978: 213). While a number of Chinese were not involved in commercial activity, Chinese merchants dominated the commercial sector, owning and running 397 of the colony's 400 retail outlets by the late 1960s (Taylor 1991: 16). All but two of

the 25 largest enterprises in the colony were Chinese-owned (Dunn 1983: 47).

Many Chinese, mostly Hakka from Fukien Province (South China), eventually married into Timorese families. Most ethnic Chinese in East Timor were educated in Taiwanese schools and were Taiwanese citizens (Taylor 1991: 16 and Metzner 1978: 213). About half of East Timor's Chinese population were citizens of Taiwan where many of them fled in early 1975 (Hill 1976: 8). Also see Ramos de Oliveira 1971: 42.

3. Aileu is both the name of the district or *concelho* and of the district's principal town.
4. Taylor 1991: 17. Also see Jolliffe 1978: 42-43.
5. In traditional Timorese society, the title of *liurai* (local king) was inherited usually by the eldest son (Hill 1978: 2). According to Joachim Metzner, the term *liurai* means "beyond the earth" in the Tetum language (Metzner 1977: 3). According to Abilio Araujo, the term means "one who has unlimited land" (de Araujo 1975: 2).
6. For a description of traditional East Timorese political geography, see Hill 1978: 2 and Metzner 1977: 3.
7. Zacarias da Costa, the son, currently is the vice president of the UDT in exile and lives in Portugal.
8. *Policia Internacional e de Defesa do Estado*—International Police and in Defense of the State.
9. The local people elected the *suco* chiefs (Hill 1978: 2).
10. See Taylor 1991: 42 and Horta 1987: 37.
11. *Forças Armadas de Libertação Nacional de Timor Leste,* or Armed Forces for the National Liberation of East Timor.
12. See Jolliffe 1978: 217.
13. FRETILIN named Xavier do Amaral as president, Nicolau Lobato as prime minister, Rogerio Lobato as minister of defense, and José Ramos Horta as minister for foreign affairs and external information. For a detailed, eyewitness account of the ceremony see Jolliffe 1978, Chapter 8.
14. FRETILIN hoped that a relatively high level of recognition of its declaration of independence would protect East Timor from Indonesia. Despite promises of "certain recognition" within 10 days of the declaration from 25 countries that included China, Russia, Norway, Brazil, Sweden, East Germany, and Cuba, however, only Mozambique, Angola, Guinea-Bissau, and Cape Verde quickly granted official recognition of the newly independent country (Jolliffe 1978: 216-217).

Chapter 2

1. For detailed accounts of the first few days of the Indonesian invasion of Dili, see Taylor 1991, Turner 1992, and Jardine 1995c.

From an Indonesian military perspective, the invasion was hardly a masterpiece; see Budiardjo and Liem 1984: 24. ABRI also suffered heavy casualties at the hands of FALINTIL in the early stages of the war. See "Jakarta's Timor Dead . . . " 1976 and Taylor 1991: 70.

2. In the early stages of the war, FRETILIN had a number of advantages over the Indonesian military. FRETILIN had prepared for months for the invasion, having set up bases in the interior of the country to which FRETILIN groups retreated on or before December 7, 1975 (Taylor 1991: 70). ABRI had great difficulties in gaining control over large areas of the country. By August 1976, Indonesia controlled only the major towns, several regional centers and villages in the territory, and several "corridors" that connected several of the areas. Most of the rural areas, where the vast majority of the people lived, were still under the control of FRETILIN (Budiardjo and Liem 1984: 23). As of March 1977, the U.S. State Department estimated that two-thirds of the East Timorese population was still in FRETILIN-dominated areas (Chomsky and Herman 1979: 162).

FALINTIL had about 20,000 former soldiers, reservists, and trainees of the colonial army, as well as many fighters who had received military training from FALINTIL following the civil war. Thus, FRETILIN's military wing was quite formidable. FALINTIL also had large supplies of weapons left by the Portuguese and had detailed knowledge of East Timor's topography; thus it was able to retain effective control of East Timorese territory, with the exceptions of Dili, Baucau, Same, Aileu, and a few other administrative centers. FRETILIN radio continued to broadcast throughout the territory. Within the liberated areas, life continued as normal. Schools, agricultural cooperatives, and the like functioned under FRETILIN's administration; its control was so secure that it was able to hold a national conference in Soibada from May 20 to June 2, 1976 without disturbance (Budiardjo and Liem 1984: 57-59 and Taylor 1991: 70-71).

3. For a discussion of the severe decline in livestock in East Timor and its detrimental effects on East Timorese society, see Aditjondro 1994: 44-46.

4. For a brief discussion of the founding and activities of the OPMT, see Budiardjo and Liem 1984: 56-57. Rosa Bonaparte was the founding secretary of the mass organization, which was formally part of FRETILIN.

5. This refers to an Indonesian military operation that began in September 1978. See Chapter 3.

Chapter 3

1. In the face of a military stalemate, mounting international publicity of the brutality of their occupation, and growing criticism of the Indonesian occupation in the United States and Western Europe, Jakarta de-

cided it was to time to wipe out the resistance once and for all and thus put an end to any hopes for an independent East Timor (Dunn 1983: 311 and Taylor 1991: 82). Emboldened by the acquisition of advanced military technology, especially counter-insurgency aircraft, ABRI began an 18-month campaign that Catholic sources within East Timor have described as one of "encirclement" and "annihilation." Using tens of thousands of ground troops and aerial bombardment, ABRI forces penetrated inward from the border and the coasts. As part of the operation, Indonesia bombed forested areas, hoping to defoliate ground cover, and used chemical sprays to destroy crops and livestock (Taylor 1991: 85). The objective was to push the resistance into the center of the country where fighters could be killed or captured and to force the population living in the interior of the country to come to the coastal lowlands where they could be more easily controlled by the Indonesians (Budiardjo and Liem 1984: 27; also see Jardine 1995c).

2. For eyewitness accounts of the Indonesian military's use of napalm, see Turner 1992: 114 and 172.

3. The campaign resulted in the destruction of probably hundreds of villages and forced tens of thousands of people to flee the mountains. According to an Indonesian government publication, the number of villages declined from 1,717 prior to "integration" to 442 in 1991 (Department of Information 1991: 13).

4. KORAMIL is the Sub-District Military Command.

5. As early as April 1976, Radio Maubere reported the existence of "guarded camps" in the Indonesian-controlled areas of the territory (Kohen and Taylor 1979: 84-85). According to a July 1979 report by the Australian Council for Overseas Aid (ACFOA), there were 15 such centers in both urban and rural areas with a population of 318,921 "displaced persons" (Kohen and Taylor 1979: 87). According to ACFOA, ABRI ordered people to move from their own villages or districts into one of the 15 centers as part of its strategy against FRETILIN. The strategy, which resembles counter-insurgency techniques employed against guerrillas in places such as Rhodesia, Malaysia, and Viet-nam, has increased the Indonesian army's control over the local population and allowed it, in the words of an Indonesian parliamentarian, "to separate the people from the terrorists" (i.e., FRETILIN) (quoted in Kohen and Taylor 1979: 87).

6. Anthony Jenkins, a journalist visiting Remexio with a party of foreign diplomats around the time of the capture of Constâncio's family, described life in the town as follows:

> In Remexio, as in most other towns, the people are stunned, sullen and dispirited. Emaciated as a result of deprivation and hardship, they are struggling to make

sense of the nightmarish interlude in which as much as half the population was uprooted.

Recently, as a party of foreign diplomats called in on Remexio during a three-day inspection tour of East Timor, they found bewildered residents drawn up in two rows, jiggling Indonesian flags and mouthing the words [sic] *merdeka* (freedom) to the prompting of local cheerleaders. It was, as Indonesian officials themselves admitted, something less than an effusive welcome. . . .

The townspeople are undernourished and desperately in need of medical attention. Many have recently come down from the hills, where they lived on tapioca and leaves—and berries so poisonous they have to be cooked six times before they can be eaten. Tuberculosis is a major problem, and with so many people sleeping on the damp ground at night there is danger of widespread pneumonia. The children in Remexio are so undernourished that one ambassador said they reminded him of victims of an African famine.

Remexio is a singularly depressing place. It is not, however, by any means unique. Timorese officials say there are 14 similar "transit camps" in the province, many of them worse than Remexio. "This is nothing," said one official. "At Suai things are much worse and there are many more people. There is an urgent need for humanitarian aid" (Jenkins 1978).

Glen Shortliffe, Canada's ambassador to Indonesia, visited East Timor from September 6 to 8, 1978—probably as part of the delegation that Jenkins accompanied. His report to the Canadian government included the following description of conditions in Remexio:

The day before our arrival about 200 people had come down from the nearby mountains. They were in an appalling condition. Little children had the distended bellies of those in advanced state of starvation, their clothing was in rags; men, women and children were covered with running sores, in the grip of advanced respiratory illnesses, the hair of many had turned orange, and obviously some would not survive even with the assistance they were receiving . . . . I can confirm that the condition of these people was as bad as purported in more widely publicized refugee situations such as Bangladesh, Vietnam, etc. (Scharfe 1996: 141).

7. Since the beginning of Indonesia's aggression, Jakarta has been trying to paint the ongoing conflict in East Timor as a civil war. Thus, ABRI has long been trying to create a situation in which this is actually the case. Early on in the occupation, Jakarta established two East Timor-based ABRI battalions, 744 and 745, composed of a few APODETI volunteers but mostly of conscripted East Timorese. ABRI has also formed local "civil defense" militia, such as Hansip, with compulsory participation (Dunn 1983: 303-304. Also see Budiardjo and Liem 1984, Part II). See Turner 1992: 172-174 for the account of an East Timorese refugee who was forced to participate in Indonesia's war against his own people.

8. FRETILIN's central committee arrested Xavier do Amaral for "high treason" on September 14, 1977. The atrocities perpetrated by the Indonesian military and the resulting suffering drove Xavier to the conclusion early in the conflict that negotiations with the Indonesians were necessary to reduce the levels of fighting. Ultimately, he thought that the East Timorese had to reach a settlement with the Indonesians, at whatever cost, to end the hostilities and Indonesians atrocities. As a result, Xavier unilaterally entered into negotiations in his area of Turiscai, which resulted in local troop withdrawals and cease-fires—often to the detriment of neighboring areas.

   Increasingly, Xavier do Amaral clashed with members of the central committee, as his actions limited the ability of FRETILIN to realize national policies and strategies (Taylor 1991: 96).

9. Violence against women has been a systematic part of the Indonesian war in East Timor. Shortly after the initial assault on Dili in 1975, for example, the invading troops compelled young women, especially those related to FRETILIN activists and members of the FRETILIN-associated OPMT and UNETIM (National Union of Timorese Students), to join them in a "victory celebration." The soldiers arrested and imprisoned most of the women, many of whom were repeatedly tortured and raped (Dunn 1983: 285 and Taylor 1991: 69). Also see the story of Maria Gorete Joaquim in Turner 1992: 168-171.

10. *Pancasila*, which literally means "five foundations" or "five pillars," was first articulated by President Sukarno in 1945. The five principles of *Pancasila* are "belief in one almighty God; just and civilized humanitarianism; a united Indonesia; democracy guided by wisdom, through consultations and representation; and social justice for all the Indonesian people" (Asia Watch 1989: 41). Indonesia's state ideology emphasizes the subordination of ethnic and/or religious differences to national unity and stability.

11. While there are no precise estimates, there is no doubt that there have been thousands of Indonesian casualties in Jakarta's war to conquer East Timor. According to an East Timorese refugee who worked in the Indonesian administration in East Timor, more than 15,000 Indonesian

soldiers had lost their lives as of 1988 (*TAPOL Bulletin*, June 1988: 11). East Timorese resistance leader Xanana Gusmão estimates that between 25,000 and 30,000 Indonesian troops have died since the war's beginning (Aditjondro 1994: 37).

Chapter 4

1. SAPT, a plantation and trading company, stands for Sociedade Agricola Patria e Trabalho (Society, Agricultural Fatherland and Labor), founded in 1899. Along with SOTA—Sociedade Orientale do Transportes e Armagens, SAPT "covered the full spectrum of business activity in Timor: they possessed large plantations (mostly coffee) and engaged in import/export, wholesaling and retailing" (Dunn 1983: 47). SAPT began by establishing coffee plantations in the Ermera area (Taylor 1991: 11). According to James Dunn, the provincial government held 48 percent of the shares of the SAPT (Dunn 1983: 47). Another report states that 40 percent of the SAPT's shares were owned by the government, 53 percent by "Lisbon interests," and 7 percent by a bank (Hartley 1975: 62).

2. General Benny Murdani, along with Colonel Dading Kalbuadi, led Indonesia's invasion of East Timor, code-named Operasi Seroja or Operation Lotus.

3. The primary economic beneficiaries of East Timor's integration have been members of the Indonesian military who have established a number of monopolies within East Timor, initially and most notably P.T. Denok, a company set up by General Benny Murdani and a few associates in the immediate aftermath of the invasion (Wain 1982: 1). As an Indonesian military commander in East Timor stated in reference to P.T. Denok, it was "the only company that landed with the marines. They came together" (Wain 1982: 1). Soon after the invasion, Indonesian interests simply took over former Portuguese colonial business enterprises. East Timor's main coffee-growing area of Ermera was one of the first areas attacked in full-strength by ABRI (Budiardjo and Liem 1984: 104-106 and Taylor 1991: 125). Until 1994, East Timorese coffee producers had no choice but to sell their coffee to Denok. The transport or sale of coffee other than through the military monopoly became illegal. The profits generated through P.T. Denok's coffee monopoly, moreover, allowed the company to diversify. By 1982, only 30 percent of Denok's revenue came from coffee (Budiardjo and Liem 1984: 106 and Wain 1982: 3).

4. According to Hadi Soesastro (1989: 215), many Chinese left East Timor during the mid-1970s. Yet large numbers of ethnic Chinese in East Timor also died at the hands of the Indonesian military. ABRI specifically targeted ethnic Chinese during the invasion. According to John Taylor, "The Chinese population of Dili was singled out for selective killings.

Five hundred were killed on the first day of the attack" (Taylor 1991: 69). According to Andrew McMillan (1992: 67), out of the 2,000 people killed in Dili in the first two days of the Indonesian invasion, 700 were ethnic Chinese. In the towns of Maubara and Liquiça "the entire Chinese population was killed" (Taylor 1991: 70). In 1985, it was "reported that the Chinese population of 20,000 in 1974 had been reduced to 'a few thousand' by July 1985" (Taylor 1991: 164). Also see Turner 1992: 103-105. Regarding the situation of ethnic Chinese within Indonesian society, see Drake 1989.

5. See Dunn 1983: 285.

6. *Timur Timor* is Indonesian for East Timor.

7. In the aftermath of the encirclement and annihilation campaign and the massive blows to FALINTIL, the military resistance reorganized (especially in the east, which was less devastated than other parts of the country) under the leadership of Kay Rala Xanana (José Alexandre) Gusmão in 1979. A former construction worker during the Portuguese era, Xanana became an ASDT/FRETILIN militant in 1974 and was later elected as a member of the central committee. After the invasion, Xanana was a platoon commander for FALINTIL, subsequently becoming head of the Ponte Leste (eastern tip) sector during ABRI's 1977-78 campaign (Budiardjo and Liem 1984: 70).

Acting in a more localized fashion, which drew on traditional forms of socio-political organization, small and relatively independent FRETILIN units were soon engaging in clashes with the Indonesian troops, particularly in the border area, in the eastern sectors, and in regions such as Ermera, Venilale, Baucau, and especially Lospalos. In 1980, individual FALINTIL units attacked a number of Indonesian garrisons and even infrastructure and positions around Dili. Despite ABRI statements to the contrary, FRETILIN showed itself to be very much alive. By March 1981 there was enough communication among various FRETILIN units to hold a national conference at which Xanana was elected head of the newly formed Revolutionary Council of National Resistance (CRRN) and FALINTIL commander in chief (Taylor 1991: 115 and Budiardjo and Liem 1984: 67-69).

8. In response to FRETILIN's resurgence, ABRI launched Operation Security (Operasi Keamanan) in mid-1981, employing the "fence of legs" *(pagar betis)* in which ABRI forced about 80,000 East Timorese males (a conservative estimate) to walk in a line across the countryside in front of Indonesian troops to flush out FALINTIL guerrillas or force them to the center of the half-island where they could be massacred.

While many FRETILIN groups surrendered or were slaughtered during the operation, many evaded capture. The operation as a whole had very detrimental effects on the Timorese, as it greatly disrupted agricultural production, leading to severe food shortages in most regions of the country. Many of the males (ages 8 to 50) who were forced to participate in the campaign starved to death, given their meager food provisions from the Indonesian military (Taylor 1991: 117-120). For a personal account of the operation and its aftermath, see Turner 1991: 185-186.

9. For the account of a former prisoner on Atauro, see Turner 1992: 176-183.

10. Indonesia observes Hari Integrasi on July 17. Integration Day commemorates the day in 1976 when President Suharto signed the law formalizing East Timor's "integration" into the Republic of Indonesia and East Timor's status as Indonesia's "27th province." According to the Indonesian government, President Suharto signed the law in response to a petition requesting integration from the "Provisional Government of East Timor" and an "on-the-spot assessment" by an Indonesian government delegation that the East Timorese strongly desired integration (see Department of Foreign Affairs, no date). For information regarding Indonesia's staging of the events used to justify Suharto's signing into law East Timor's integration, see Taylor 1991: 73-74 and Dunn 1983: 298-301. For discussion of the legality of Indonesia's claim that the East Timorese have already exercised their right to self-determination, see Clark 1980 and 1992.

11. An "RT" is a *rukun tetangga*, which is an unsalaried position one or sometimes two notches below the *kepala desa*, or village head. Identity cards, land registration certificates, and school permits must first go through the RT for processing (and legal and illegal fees) prior to processing by the *kepala desa, camat, polisi,* or *bupati.* In rural Java, an RT usually coincides with one *kampong,* which resembles what we would call a hamlet or a village, while *desa,* which translates as village, is an administrative unit that actually comprises several little neighborhood clumps and their surrounding farms, each of which we would call a "village." RT stands for both the administrative unit and the person in charge. Thanks to Craig Thorburn of the Department of Geography, University of California, Los Angeles, for this explanation.

12. The Indonesian authorities present *gotong-royong* in a benign light. See, for example, Department of Foreign Affairs, no date: 52. For a critical description of the practice, see Budiardjo and Liem 1984: 108.

13. At the time of the Portuguese arrival there seems to have been two loose-knit "kingdoms" on the island. The Bello or Belu kingdom occupied the eastern part of the island while the Wehale or Servião kingdom occupied the west (Dunn 1983: 16). Some argue, however, that the two kingdoms were basically creations of the Portuguese, who, upon arriving in Timor, consolidated (based on geographical location and political alliances) what were actually numerous, separate, and loosely knit po-

East Timor's Unfinished Struggle

litical entities into kingdoms (Hill 1978: 5 and Taylor 1991: 2).

Chapter 5

1. By late 1982, FALINTIL was launching a number of attacks in many
parts of the country, especially the east and the south. In November,
FALINTIL even attacked Dili. Increasingly placed on the defensive, a
number of local Indonesian military leaders negotiated local cease-fire
agreements with FRETILIN, culminating in a country-wide cease-fire
agreement signed on March 23, 1983, by Xanana Gusmão for FRETILIN
and Colonel Purwanto for ABRI. Purwanto accepted a letter for Suharto
from Xanana outlining FRETILIN's proposals for peace. Hoping to keep
the talks secret, ABRI and the Indonesian government were greatly embarrassed when the news broke internationally. For its part, FRETILIN,
able to freely travel throughout the country, used the cease-fire to consolidate its underground network. This proved useful when General
Benny Murdani unilaterally broke the cease-fire, declaring, "This time
no fooling around. We are going to hit them without mercy" (*Sinar
Harapan*, August 17, 1983, quoted in Taylor 1991: 142). In August 1983,
ABRI launched Operasi Persatuan, or Operation Unity (see Budiardjo
and Liem 1984 and Taylor 1991).
2. A leading plantation owner, Mario Carrascalão was the UDT's first
president and served from 1981 to 1992 as Indonesia's governor of East
Timor. Currently, he is Indonesia's ambassador to Romania.
Jakarta provides a facade of effective East Timorese participation in local affairs. Ultimate power, however, remains firmly in the hands of the
Indonesian military, a fact even some of Indonesia's supposed East Timorese supporters admit. See, for example, Neales 1995.
3. Although Mario Carrascalão was essentially a figurehead governor for
the Indonesian military, he was able to limit somewhat the levels of Indonesian repression. For this reason, many East Timorese regard him in
a favorable light.
4. For a description of the Kraras Massacre, see Turner 1992: 174-176.
5. Like most of the FRETILIN leadership, Nicolau Lobato lost his life in
ABRI's "encirclement and annihilation" campaign. He was killed on
January 1, 1979, after a six-hour battle with Indonesian troops (Taylor
1991: 97).
6. Under Indonesia's occupation, Oecussi remains part of East Timor,
Jakarta's "27th province."
7. Today, P.T. Denok coffee trading and is handled by only one of 12 subsidiaries in East Timor under the control of the P.T. Batara Indra Group.
Subsidiaries within the group own Dili's only movie theater and the
city's three luxury hotels (including the Hotel Mahkota); control the territory's marble production; and engage in general trading, importing a

wide variety of consumer products. The group virtually controls the East Timorese economy, including the sandalwood trade and most civil engineering projects in the territory. While the companies are nominally owned by civilians, ABRI or interests close to the military are undoubtedly in ultimate control (Aditjondro 1994: 20-23).

Chapter 6

1. *Merah* means "red," and *putih* means "white." Red and white are the colors of the Indonesian flag.
2. The more than 500,000 Indonesians killed by Suharto is a reference to his bloody seizure of power from Sukarno in the period of late 1965 to early 1966. See the Introduction for a discussion of this matter.
3. From the time of the Indonesian invasion of December 7, 1975 until January 1989, Jakarta kept East Timor closed. Apart from official foreign delegations, some international aid workers, and a limited number of journalists, few people were able to enter the territory. On December 27, 1988, following a one-day visit in November to the territory by Indonesian president Suharto, the Indonesian authorities accorded East Timor open territory status. In addition to presenting an image to the outside world of normalcy in East Timor, Jakarta was keen on encouraging foreign and "domestic" (Indonesian) investment in its "27th province." On both accounts, Jakarta has largely failed in its objectives. (See, for example, "Few Investors Take Up Invite to East Timor," *Australian Financial Review* [reprinted from *Asian Wall Street Journal*], June 10, 1993.)
4. In a number of ways, the Church has helped to maintain East Timorese identity and has thus slowed the process of Indonesianization. When, for example, the Indonesian authorities tried to force the Church to replace Portuguese with Indonesian as the official language, East Timorese clergy successfully pressured the Vatican to allow Tetum to be used. Although the Vatican's position is rather ambiguous, the Vatican has resisted pressure to incorporate the East Timorese Church into the Catholic Church of Indonesia. To this day, the Catholic Church in East Timor is administered directly from Rome (Taylor 1991: 155-157 and Jardine 1993b: 17).
5. According to one report, about 40 percent of the population attended the Pope's mass (Vatikiotis, October 26, 1989: 32).
6. In a written report to Amnesty International, Donaciano described part of his torture:

> We were subject to beatings and immersed in tanks of excrement. Sometimes they would open the doors to soldiers returning from combat duty in the mountains and let them beat us up. They would come in at dawn in full combat gear, dust on their clothes, and start hitting and punching

us. They'd shout: "We're looking for the communists. So after all they are here in Dili, not in the mountains." They would cock their weapons and put them to our heads (International Commission of Jurists 1992: 23).

7. A "backgrounder" written by the United States Information Service of the U.S. Embassy in Jakarta clearly states the position of the U.S. Government on East Timor:

> The U.S. does not contest the integration of East Timor into Indonesia, but does not hold that an act of self-determination took place prior to integration. The U.S. actively pursues a policy to promote improvement in the situation in East Timor and underscores continuing U.S. interest in and concern about conditions there with the Indonesian government. This discussion takes place in the context of a broad-based and largely positive bilateral relationship.

The embassy sent the document, intended for public consumption, to the State Department in November 1994. A copy of the document is on file with Matthew Jardine.

8. A recent Radio Netherlands four-part series on East Timor broadcast to Indonesia in the Indonesian language included interviews with Indonesian soldiers who have refused to serve in East Timor. See *TAPOL Bulletin*, No. 133, February 1996.

9. For a detailed, eyewitness account of the Monjo demonstration, see McMillan 1992.

Chapter 7

1. Since the Indonesian invasion, the organization of the East Timorese resistance has changed significantly. In 1981, at its first party congress since its reorganization, FRETILIN declared itself to be a Marxist-Leninist party. This position was reversed at the next congress when FRETILIN decided to try to develop "a broad-based front" predicated on national unity. This led, in 1986, to a FRETILIN-UDT coalition called the National Convergence. As FALINTIL came to have more non-FRETILIN members, Xanana Gusmão left the party in 1989 (Gault-Williams 1990: 25).

2. TAPOL is the Indonesian Human Rights Campaign, based in the United Kingdom. The CDPM is the Comissão dos Direitos para o Povo Maubere, the Commission for the Rights of the Maubere People, based in Lisbon.

3. RENETIL stands for Resistencia Nacional dos Estudiantes de Timor Leste, the National Resistance of Students from East Timor. FECLETIL stands for Frente Clandestina dos Estudiantes de Timor Leste, the Clan-

destine Front of Students from East Timor. FECLETIL no longer exists.
4. See note 4 in Chapter 4.
5. For an account by Robert Domm of his visit with Xanana, see Turner 1992: 192-198. Also see Aarons and Domm 1992.

Chapter 8

1. In the aftermath of the Santa Cruz Massacre, the Indonesian government sentenced a few low-ranking soldiers to prison terms of not more than 18 months for disobeying orders. In contrast, East Timorese who participated in the Santa Cruz march and a demonstration in Jakarta to protest the massacre received sentences ranging from five years to life imprisonment. The sentences received by the handful of soldiers combined with the relieving of a few military commanders of their duties in East Timor were effective in helping to mollify Western governments. According to Constâncio, Martinho Alau received a sentence of 11 months in prison.
2. SGI is the Indonesian acronym for the Intelligence Task Force. For a report about the SGI's torture house in Colmera, Dili, see Cater 1995.

Chapter 10

1. Indonesia is placing a greater emphasis on "territorial" troops rather than combat troops in response to the evolving military situation. Jakarta claims to be greatly reducing the number of troops in East Timor, maintaining that the vast majority of the soldiers are engaged in development projects such as building houses, roads, and bridges. While those claims are highly exaggerated, such a change in strategy does not prevent ABRI from responding to military threats to its control of East Timor. If FALINTIL's threat were ever to increase, the military authorities could quickly dispatch rapid deployment troops (KOSTRAD), two combat-ready battalions of which are stationed in Java (TAPOL 1993; also see *TAPOL Bulletin*, December 1993).

   ABRI's territorial troops are trying to impose a new value system and a set of military structures to parallel indigenous civilian structures right down to the level of villages and neighborhoods. The aim is to isolate the resistance from the population and to further Indonesianize the society (see *TAPOL Bulletin*, February and April 1993).
2. Kopassus stands for Komando Pasukan Khusus, the Special Troops Commando. These elite troops have a reputation of being the most brutal in East Timor.
3. For an account of the events leading up to the Portuguese delegation's cancellation, see McMillan 1992, Chapter 9.
4. For RENETIL's report of ABRI's attack on the Motael Church, see "The Motael Shooting," *TAPOL Bulletin*, No. 108, December 1991.

5. Produced by Max Stahl for Yorkshire Television in the United Kingdom, *Cold Blood: The Massacre of East Timor* won Amnesty International's award for the best human rights video in 1992. Copies of the video can be obtained through the East Timor Action Network/U.S. (see Appendix for contact information).

6. According to the Australian Catholic Social Justice Council, there are about 40,000 orphans in contemporary East Timor, a result of Indonesia's war and occupation. Prior to the Indonesian invasion, orphans were virtually unknown in the territory.

   Thanks to Rev. John Chamberlin of East Timor Religious Outreach in the United States for this information.

Chapter 11

1. Indonesia argues that its troops acted in self-defense, provoked by the crowd gathered at the Santa Cruz Cemetery. An investigation of the massacre by a United Nations Special Rapporteur, however, found the following:

   > There are . . . reasons to believe that the actions of the security forces were not a spontaneous reaction to a riotous mob, but rather a planned military operation designed to deal with a public expression of political dissent in a way not in accordance with international human rights standards (Economic and Social Council of the United Nations 1994: 13).

2. For an interesting discussion of the alleged stabbing, see Stahl 1991. Reprinted in the *TAPOL Bulletin*, No. 108, December 1991.

3. See Goodman 1991 and Nairn 1991 and 1992.

4. See the *TAPOL Bulletin*, No. 108, December 1991, for a brief article about Kamal by James Gibbons, Kamal's stepbrother, and for excerpts from Kamal's diary of his time in East Timor.

5. In October 1975, Indonesian troops killed a team of journalists from Australia (two Australian, one British, and one New Zealander) who were in Balibó to document Indonesian military aggression (see Taylor 1991: 60-62 and Turner 1992: 95-101). Also, on the first day of the invasion, Indonesian troops executed the only foreign journalist left in East Timor, Roger East from Australia.

   More than 20 years later, the Australian government conducted an official inquiry into the deaths. The report seems to corroborate eyewitness accounts that invading Indonesian troops killed the journalists. The report also found that it was "more likely than not" that an Indonesian soldier summarily executed Roger East (see Williams 1996). Also see the *TAPOL Bulletin*, No. 136, August 1996.

6. The documentary *Cold Blood: The Massacre of East Timor* contains a brief interview with Domingos Segurado shortly before he was killed at the Santa Cruz Cemetery.

7. During Matthew Jardine's trip to East Timor in July-August 1992, he learned that there were 14 ABRI checkpoints on the road from Dili to Aileu (a distance of about 28 miles) after the November 1991 massacre; during his trip there was only one.

8. On a return visit to East Timor about two years after the Santa Cruz Massacre, Max Stahl learned of a second wave of killings. According to a lab technician at the Dili hospital and a survivor of the massacre interviewed by Stahl in late 1993, Indonesian soldiers killed survivors of the massacre at the hospital. The soldiers "crushed the skulls of the wounded with large rocks, ran over them with trucks, stabbed them, and administered—with doctors present—poisonous disinfecting chemicals as medicines to 'finish off' scores of wounded demonstrators in the wake of the massacre." Stahl thinks that anywhere from 50 to 200 wounded died in this manner (Stahl 1994).

9. For a summary of Fernando's defense plea to the Indonesian court, see *TAPOL Bulletin*, No. 11, June 1992. When the court sentenced him, Fernando stood up, gave a victory salute, and emphatically stated, "I want to say once again that I am not an Indonesian." Amnesty International has adopted Fernando as a prisoner of conscience.

10. For a detailed account of the *Lusitania Expresso* mission, see McMillan 1992, Chapters 11-14. Also see *TAPOL Bulletin*, April 1992.

Chapter 12

1. In September 1975, the ASDT changed its name to FRETILIN. In the aftermath of its September meeting, FRETILIN, energized by the return of a number of radical East Timorese university students from Lisbon, developed an explicit program emphasizing development and social justice in the areas of women's and workers' rights, health, education, and agriculture. FRETILIN also developed nationalist poems, songs, and dances exalting the indigenous roots of the East Timorese. FRETILIN's appropriation of the term *maubere* (*bibere* in its feminine form), a word used by the Portuguese to express contempt for the East Timorese masses and to convey to the Portuguese colonialists the idea of East Timorese inferiority, reversed the colonial meaning to one of cultural identity and pride. Thus FRETILIN named its ideology *mauberismo*, which proved to be the most successful political symbol of the FRETILIN campaign (Taylor 1991: 42 and Ramos Horta 1987: 37).

FRETILIN provided substance to the concept of *mauberismo* by working in a variety of concrete activities with the intent of laying the foundation for a new society and boosting the front's popularity and organizational structure in the process. These activities included organizing workers and students in the towns, conducting a literacy program in Tetum, establishing a number of agricultural production and distribution cooperatives, and doing extensive political organizing throughout the country (Hill 1978, Chapter 4; Dunn 1983: 69; Jolliffe 1978: 75-76; and Taylor 1991: 33-35).

Chapter 13

1. GPK stands for Gerombolan Pengacau Keamanan or Security Disrupter Gang. The Indonesian authorities use the term to describe guerrilla groups, like the East Timorese armed resistance, that challenge Jakarta's rule.
2. Shortly after the massacre, General Try Sutrisno, the commander of the Indonesian Armed Forces (ABRI), publicly stated the East Timorese who had gathered at the cemetery were "disrupters." "These delinquent people have to be shot and we will shoot them," he added. "ABRI is determined to wipe out anyone who disrupts stability" (*TAPOL Bulletin*, No. 108, December 1991: 9).

Chapter 14

1. See the *Far Eastern Economic Review*, April 22, 1993: 14. Also see Constâncio's letter to the editor in response to the report of his capture (*FEER*, May 13, 1993).
2. See the *United States Congressional Record* of May 24, 1993, pages S6358-S6361, for the text of Senator Pell's statement.
3. At the March 1993 meeting of the United Nations Human Rights Commission in Geneva, the United States, under grassroots and congressional pressure, reversed its historical opposition to resolutions criticizing Indonesia and cosponsored a resolution condemning Indonesian human rights violations in East Timor. A number of Western countries similarly changed their positions and followed suit, indicating the key role the U.S. could play in determining East Timor's future.
4. In a 1995 interview done with a miniature tape recorder smuggled into his Jakarta prison cell, Xanana Gusmão offered the following on the role people throughout the world can play in helping to bring about East Timor's freedom:

> Go out on the streets and protest in front of the nearest Indonesian Embassy. Put the lie to Indonesian claims that the problem of East Timor is a domestic one for Indonesia. During the African colonial wars, [Portuguese dictator] Marcelo Caetano was mobbed in the streets of London and forced to return to Portugal like a bandit fleeing from the

police. Actions such as these are worth more than a million letters written to Suharto or [UN Secretary General] Boutros-Ghali. This is what people should do. Show the regime that it will never be free of public displays of repudiation for as long as the question of East Timor remains unresolved (Pilger 1995: 823-824).

5. See Stahl 1994.
6. Businessman Manuel Carrascalão, a member of the local parliament and a longtime supporter of integration, is one of a growing number of local elites who are become increasingly uneasy about East Timor's shotgun marriage with Indonesia. "We don't have a democratic system here. . . . [I]t's rule by force, oppression, and suffering," Carrascalão now argues. "In 1975, I thought that integration would be best for the people. But they haven't given us integration, they have given us occupation" (Neales 1995).

Epilogue

1. Jardine 1995d.
2. Eban 1995: 43.
3. Jardine 1995d.
4. Moynihan 1978: 247.
5. For an in-depth analysis and account of the West's support for Indonesia and the occupation, see Taylor 1991 and Jardine 1995c.
6. See, for example, Sanger 1995 and United States Congress 1987.
7. APEC is the Pacific Rim's version of NAFTA. Begun in Canberra, Australia, in 1989, APEC has quickly grown to 18 members-states: the six members of the Association of Southeast Asian Nations, or ASEAN—Brunei, Indonesia, Malaysia, the Philippines, Singapore, and Thailand—as well as Australia, Canada, Chile, China, Hong Kong, Japan, Mexico, Papua New Guinea, New Zealand, South Korea, Taiwan, and the United States. In the first four years of its existence, APEC was simply an annual meeting among foreign ministers that focused on dialogue about customs procedures. While APEC was originally seen as an Australian project, the United States has come to play the dominant role.

In 1993, the Clinton administration decided to elevate the dialogue to an actual organization by hosting the first meeting of APEC leaders on Blake Island, near Seattle. In the short term, U.S. objective for APEC is to accelerate the integration of APEC member-states into the General Agreement on Tariffs and Trade (GATT). In the long term, the United States would like to see the APEC countries move beyond GATT in terms of lowering tariffs outside of the purview of GATT; this would include telecommunications and further agreements on intellectual property.

From the U.S. perspective, APEC represents an opportunity to regain its economic preeminence through the establishment of a U.S.-dominated free-trade region to counter the European trading bloc. In this sense, we should not view APEC in isolation, but rather as one component of an overall U.S. effort to open up the markets of the Asia-Pacific region (and the world in general) and to provide U.S.-based multinationals access to the human and natural resources of the area (Jardine 1995a).

8. Sanger 1995.
9. *TAPOL Bulletin*, February 1990: 18.
10. For a discussion of the relationship between Australian foreign policy toward Indonesia and East Timor and the Timor Gap, see Taylor 1991: 170 and 75, Walsh and Munster 1980: 197-200, and "Timor Sold for Oil" 1976. Regarding the legality of the *Timor Gap Treaty*, see Clark 1992 and Stepan 1990.
11. For a discussion of Portuguese foreign policy toward East Timor, see Taylor 1991: 171-174. Also see Walsh 1995: 150-151.
12. Saldanha 1994: 355.
13. Colchester 1986: 103; Taylor 1991: 124; and Aditjondro 1994: 62-63.
14. Otten 1986: 74-75.
15. Carey et al. 1995: 2.
16. See, for example, Crossette 1994.
17. Mubyarto et al. 1991: 51-52.
18. Taylor 1991: 160-161.
19. See Jones 1996.
20. Stahl 1994.
21. *TAPOL Bulletin*, No. 132, December 1995: 4.
22. See *TAPOL Bulletin*, No. 132, December 1995; No. 133, February 1996; and No. 134, April 1996.
23. Jardine 1992: 21.
24. See, for example, Cumming-Bruce 1996. Regarding growing labor unrest in Indonesia, see *TAPOL Bulletin*, No. 130, August 1995.
25. For an interesting discussion of the future prospects for change in Indonesia, see Cribb and Brown 1995, Chapter 10. Cribb and Brown do not include in their analysis organized labor, a social movement of growing importance in Indonesia, as the number of work stoppages by organized labor has increased significantly over the last few years.

Bibliography

Aarons, Mark and Robert Domm. *East Timor: A Western-Made Tragedy*. Sydney: The Left Book Club, 1992.

Aditjondro, George J. *In the Shadow of Mount Ramelau: The Impact of the Occupation of East Timor*. Leiden (The Netherlands): Indonesian Documentation Centre, 1994.

Amnesty International. *Power and Impunity: Human Rights under the New Order*. New York: Amnesty International, 1994.

Anderson, Benedict and Ruth McVey. "What Happened in Indonesia," letter to the editor in *The New York Review*, June 1, 1978: 40-42.

Anderson, Jack. "Another Slaughter," *San Francisco Chronicle*, November 9, 1979: 61.

Araujo, Abilio. *Timorese Elites* (eds. J. Jolliffe and B. Reece). Canberra, 1975.

Asia Watch. *Human Rights in Indonesia and East Timor*. New York: Human Rights Watch, 1989.

Awanohara, Susumu. "Falling into Step," *Far Eastern Economic Review*, August 6, 1982: 19-23.

Boxer, C.R. *Fidalgos in the Far East 1550-1770*. New York: Oxford University Press, 1968.

Boxer, C.R. "Portuguese Timor: A Rough Island Story: 1515-1960," *History Today*, Vol. 10, No. 5, May 1960: 349-355.

Budiardjo, Carmel and Liem Soei Liong. *The War Against East Timor*. London: Zed, 1984.

Budiardjo, Carmel. "Indonesia: Mass Extermination and the Consolidation of Authoritarian Power," in Alexander George (ed.), *Western State Terrorism*. Cambridge: Polity Press, 1991.

Caldwell, Malcolm (ed.). *Ten Years' Military Terror in Indonesia*. Nottingham: Bertrand Russell Peace Foundation for Spokesman Books, 1975.

Carey, Peter. "The Forging of a Nation: East Timor," in Peter Carey and G. Carter Bentley (eds.), *East Timor at the Crossroads: The Forging of a Nation*. Honolulu: University of Hawaii Press and Social Science Research Council, 1995: 1-18.

Cater, Nick. "Timorese Bears the Scars of Repression," *The West Australian*, September 30, 1995: 18-19.

Chomsky, Noam. "A Gleam of Light in Asia," *Z Magazine*, Vol. 3, No. 9, September 1990a: 15-23.

Chomsky, Noam. *Year 501: The Conquest Continues*. Boston: South End Press, 1993.

Chomsky, Noam and Edward S. Herman. *The Washington Connection and Third World Fascism—The Political Economy of Human Rights, Volume I*. Boston: South End Press, 1979: 176.

Clarence-Smith, G. "Planters and smallholders in Portuguese Timor in the nineteenth and twentieth centuries," *Indonesia Circle* (London, School of Oriental and African Studies), No. 57, March 1992: 15-30.

Clark, Roger S. "The 'Decolonization' of East Timor and the United Nations Norms on Self-Determination and Aggression," *Yale Journal of World Public Order*, Vol. 7, No. 1, Fall 1980: 2-44.

Clark, Roger S. "Timor Gap: The Legality of the 'Treaty on the Zone of Cooperation in an Area between the Indonesian Province of East Timor and Northern Australia,'" *Pace Yearbook of International Law*, Vol. 4, No. 69, 1992: 69-95.

Colchester, Marcus. "The Struggle for Land—Tribal Peoples in the Face of the Transmigration Programme," *The Ecologist*, Vol. 16, No. 2/3, 1986: 99-110.

Cribb, Robert and Colin Brown. *Modern Indonesia: A History Since 1945*. London and New York: Longman, 1995.

Cumming-Bruce, Nick. "Indonesia Cracks Down on Unrest," *Manchester Guardian Weekly*, August 4, 1996: 1.

Department of Foreign Affairs (DFA), Republic of Indonesia. *Decolonization in East Timor*, no date.

Department of Information, Republic of Indonesia. *East Timor—15 years of development*, 1991.

Diaz de Rábago, A. "Portuguese Timor," *New Catholic Encyclopedia*, Vol. 14. New York: McGraw-Hill Book Company, 1967: 165-166.

Drake, Christine. *National Integration in Indonesia—Patterns and Policies*. Honolulu: University of Hawaii Press, 1989.

Dunn, James. *Timor—A People Betrayed*. Milton, Queensland: The Jacaranda Press, 1983.

Eban, Abba. "The U.N. Idea Revisited," *Foreign Affairs*, Vol. 74, No. 5, September/October 1995: 39-55.

Economic and Social Council of the United Nations, *Report by the Special Rapporteur, Mr. Bacre Waly Ndiaye, on his Mission to Indonesia and East Timor from 3 to 13 July 1994*, E/CN.4/1995/61/Add. 1, November 1, 1994.

"Few Investors Take Up Invite to East Timor," *Australian Financial Review* (reprinted from *Asian Wall Street Journal*), June 10, 1993.

Francis, Glen. "Slavery in Timor," *The Observer* (Sydney, Australia), Vol. 3, No. 22, October 29, 1960: 12.

Gault-Williams, Malcolm. "Funu—Liberation War—Continues in East Timor," *Bulletin of Concerned Asian Scholars*, Vol. 22, No. 3, July-September 1990: 21-31.

Goodman, Amy. "Troops Fire on East Timorese—An Eyewitness Account," *Third World Resurgence*, No. 16, December 1991: 34.

Griswold, Lawrence. "Garuda and the Emerald Archipelago: Strategic Indonesia Forges New Ties with the West," *Sea Power* (Navy League of the United States), Vol. 16, No. 2, February 1973: 20-25.

Hadi Soesastro, M. "East Timor: Questions of Economic Viability," in Hal Hill (ed.), *Unity and Diversity: Regional Economic Development in Indonesia Since 1970*. Singapore: Oxford University Press, 1989.

Hanna, William A. "Reanimated Relic—Part I: Target Timor," American Universities Field Staff (AUFS) Reports Service, Southeast Asia Series, Vol. 14, No. 7, 1966.

Harkin, Tom. "Our Proxy War in East Timor—The U.S. Abets a Brutal Annexation," *The Progressive*, December 1980: 45-47.

Hartley, William. "Letter from Dili," *Far Eastern Economic Review*, Vol. 87, No. 10, March 7, 1975: 62.

Hayes, Peter, Lyuba Zarsky, and Walden Bello. *American Lake: Nuclear Peril in the Pacific*. Rigwood, Victoria (Australia): Penguin Books, 1986.

Hertsgaard, Mark. "The Secret Life of Henry Kissinger," *The Nation*, October 29, 1990.

Hill, Helen. *FRETILIN: The Origins, Ideologies and Strategies of a Nationalist Movement in East Timor*, M.A. Thesis, Monash University, Australia, 1978.

Hill, Helen. *The Timor Story*. Victoria (Australia): Timor Information Service, 1976.

Horta, José Ramos. *Funu—The Unfinished Saga of East Timor*. Trenton: The Red Sea Press, 1987.

International Commission of Jurists, Australian Section. "Timor Tragedy, Incident at Santa Cruz: 12 November, 1991," Sydney, July 1992.

"Jakarta's Timor Dead . . . , " *Washington Post*, January 9, 1976.

Jardine, Matthew. "APEC, the United States and East Timor," *Z Magazine*, January 1995a: 34-39.

Jardine, Matthew. "A Changed Church: Two Decades of Struggle in East Timor Has Made Friends and Enemies," *Sojourners*, November-December 1995b: 74-76.

Jardine, Matthew. *East Timor: Genocide in Paradise*. Tucson: Odonian Press, 1995c.

Jardine, Matthew. "East Timor: Media Ignored Genocide," *Extra!*, November/December 1993a.

Jardine, Matthew. "Forgotten Genocide—A Little Attention, at Last, for East Timor," *The Progressive*, Vol. 56, No. 12, December 1992: 19-21.

Jardine, Matthew. "Pacification, Resistance, and Territoriality: Prospects for a Space of Peace in East Timor," *GeoJournal*, Vol. 39, No. 4, August 1996: 397-404.

Jardine, Matthew. "The Secret Sacrifice of East Timor—Amid Invasion, Massacre, and Insurrection, the Church Takes a Stand," *Christianity & Crisis*, February 1, 1993b: 16-18.

Jardine, Matthew. "U.N. Pledge Forgotten in War-Torn East Timor," *London Free Press* (Ontario, Canada), December 2, 1995d.

Jenkins, Anthony. "Timor's Arithmetic of Despair," *Far Eastern Economic Review*, September 29, 1978.

Jolliffe, Jill. *East Timor—Nationalism and Colonialism*. St. Lucia, Queensland: University of Queensland Press, 1978.

Jones, Sidney. "Human Rights in Indonesia," Testimony Before the United States Senate Foreign Relations Committee, September 18, 1996.

Kahin, Audrey R. and McT. George Kahin. *Subversion as Foreign Policy: The Secret Eisenhower and Dulles Debacle in Indonesia*. New York: The New Press, 1995.

Kennan, George F. "Review of Current Trends, U.S. Foreign Policy," PPS/23, Top Secret. Included in *Foreign Relations of the United States, 1948*, Vol. I, Part 2. Washington, D.C.: Government Printing Office, 1976: 509-529.

Kohen, Arnold and John Taylor. *An Act of Genocide: Indonesia's Invasion of East Timor*. London: TAPOL, 1979.

Kohen, Arnold S. and Roberta A. Quance. "The Politics of Starvation," *Inquiry*, San Francisco: the Cato Institute, February 18, 1980: 18-22.

Lains e Silva, Helder. *Timor e a cultura do café*, Lisbon: Ministério do Ultramar, 1956.

Lodge, Henry Cabot. "We Can Win in Vietnam," *The New York Times Magazine*, January 17, 1965.

Malan, Andre. "Truth First Casualty of Swift, Brutal Invasion," *The West Australian*, March 12, 1994.

Marshall, Jonathan. "Southeast Asia and U.S.-Japan Relations: 1940-1941," *Pacific Research and World Empire Telegram*, Vol. 4, No. 3, March-April 1973: 1-23.

McMillan, Andrew. *Death in Dili*. Rydalmere (NSW, Australia): Hodder and Stoughton, 1992.

Metzner, Joachim K. *Man and Environment in Eastern Timor: A Geo-ecological Analysis of the Baucau-Viqueque Area as a Possible Basis for Regional Planning*. Canberra: The Australian National University, Development Studies Centre Monograph No. 8, 1977.

Moynihan, Daniel Patrick (with Suzanne Weaver). *A Dangerous Place*, Boston: Little, Brown, 1978.

Mubyarto, Loekaman Soetrisno *et al. East Timor: The Impact of Integration—Indonesian Socio-Anthropological Study.* Northcote (Australia): Indonesia Resources and Information Program (IRIP), 1991.

Nairn, Allan. "A Narrow Escape from East Timor," *USA Today,* November 21, 1991.

Nairn, Allan. "'I Witnessed and Survived the Massacre at the Santa Cruz Cemetery,'" Testimony before the United States Senate Committee on Foreign Relations on the Crisis in East Timor and U.S. Policy Towards Indonesia, February 27, 1992.

Neales, Sue. "East Timor: Two Decades of Death, Despair and Torture in Indonesia's Achilles' Heel," *Sydney Morning Herald,* October 21, 1995.

Otten, Mariel. "'Transmigrasi': From Poverty to Bare Subsistence," *The Ecologist,* Vol. 16, No. 2/3, 1986: 71-76.

Pilger, John. "Messages from a Jakarta Prison," *The Nation,* December 25, 1995: 820-824.

Provincial Government of East Timor (PGET). *East Timor—A Decade of Development.* Jakarta: Department of Information, Republic of Indonesia, 1986.

Ramos de Oliveira, Carlos M.G. "Dili: Panorama de uma Sociedade," *Boletim da Sociedade de Geografia de Lisboa,* Vol. 89, Nos. 1-3, January-March 1971: 33-49.

"Remnants of Empire, II: Portuguese Timor," *Far Eastern Economic Review,* Vol. 30, No. 11, December 15, 1960: 585.

Sanger, David E. "Real Politics: Why Suharto Is In and Castro Is Out," *The New York Times,* October 31, 1995.

Scharfe, Sharon. *Complicity: Human Rights and Canadian Foreign Policy: The Case of East Timor.* Montreal: Black Rose Books, 1996.

Scheiner, Charles. "No U.S. Military Aid to Indonesia in Fiscal Year 1993!" *Bulletin of Concerned Asian Scholars,* Vol. 24, No. 3, July-September 1992: 51.

Southwood, Julie and Patrick Flanagan. *Indonesia—Law, Propaganda and Terror.* London: Zed, 1983.

Stahl, Max. "Dili, the Bloody Aftermath," *Sydney Morning Herald,* February 12, 1994.

Stahl, Max. "Guerillas in the Mist: The War of Resistance in East Timor," *Sydney Morning Herald,* February 15, 1994a.

Stahl, Max. "Massacre Among the Graves," *Independent on Sunday* (London), November 17, 1991.

Stepan, Sasha. *Credibility Gap—Australia and the Timor Gap Treaty,* Fitzroy (Australia): Australian Council for Overseas Aid, 1990.

Taylor, John G. *Indonesia's Forgotten War—The Hidden History of East Timor.* London: Zed, 1991.

Telkamp, Gerard J. "The Economic Structure of an Outpost in the Outer Islands in the Indonesian Archipelago: Portuguese Timor 1850-1975," in P. Creutzberg (ed.), *Between Peoples and Statistics—Essays on Modern Indonesian History.* The Hague: Martinus Nijhoff, 1979.

"Timor Sold for Oil," *Tribune* (Australia), October 27, 1976.

Turner, Michele. *Telling: East Timor, Personal Testimonies 1942-1992.* New South Wales (Australia): New South Wales University Press, 1992.

Van Atta, Dale and Brian Toohey. "The Timor Papers" (Parts 1 and 2), *The National Times* (Australia), May 30-June 5, 1982 and June 6 to June 12, 1982, reprints from TAPOL.

Vatikiotis, Michael. "Unresolved Tensions—Papal Visit Renews International Focus on East Timor," *Far Eastern Economic Review,* October 26, 1989: 32-33.

Wain, Barry. "Military Seen Behind Firm Controlling Timor's Coffee," *Asian Wall Street Journal,* June 16, 1982.

Walsh, J.R. and George Munster. *Documents on Australian Defence and Foreign Policy, 1968-1975.* Hong Kong: J.R. Walsh and G.J. Munster, 1980.

Walsh, Pat. "Towards a Just Peace," in Peter Carey and G. Carter Bentley (eds.), *East Timor at the Crossroads: The Forging of a Nation.* Honolulu: University of Hawaii Press and Social Science Research Council, 1995: 148-158.

Weatherbee, Donald E. "Portuguese Timor: An Indonesian Dilemma," *Asian Survey,* Vol. 6, No. 12, December 1966: 683-695.

Williams, Louise. "Indonesia Warns on Relations," *Sydney Morning Herald,* June 29, 1996.

Wolf, Eric R. *Europe and the People Without History.* Berkeley and Los Angeles: University of California Press, 1982.

Appendix

East Timor Support and Solidarity Groups

East Timorese in the Diaspora

National Council of Maubere Resistance
(CNRM)
GPO Box 2155
Darwin, NT 0801 AUSTRALIA
61-69-855-678 fax: 61-89-855-622
etio@ozemail.com.au

CANADA

East Timor Alert Network/National
PO BOX 562, Station P
Toronto ON M5S 2T1
416-531-5850 fax: 416-588-5556
etantor@web.net

UNITED KINGDOM

TAPOL
111 Northwood Road
Thornton Heath, Surrey CR7 8HW
44-181-771-2904 fax: 44-81-653-0322
tapol@gn.apc.org

UNITED STATES

East Timor Action Network (ETAN/US)
Int'l Federation for East Timor UN
Representative
Charles Scheiner
PO Box 1182
White Plains, NY 10602
914-428-7299 fax: 914-428-7383
etan-us@igc.apc.org

For a complete list of East Timor supporters around the world, or of ETAN chapters in the United States, contact:

Charles Scheiner
Int'l Federation for East Timor
PO Box 1182
White Plains, NY 10602
fax: 914-428-7383
etan-us@igc.apc.org

For information on East Timor, write to:
timor-info@igc.apc.org

Index

About the Authors

CONSTÂNCIO PINTO is an international leader in the struggle to achieve self-determination for East Timor who fled the country after Indonesian troops killed more than 200 demonstrators at a pro-independence protest he helped organize. Pinto was the leader of the Timorese underground movement of the National Council of Maubere Resistance (CNRM), the leading coalition of Timorese independence organizations. An undergraduate in development studies at Brown University, he is married and has two children. Pinto is currently CNRM representative to the United Nations and the United States.

MATTHEW JARDINE is a researcher and activist based in Los Angeles who has written and lectured extensively on the politics and history of East Timor. Jardine is the author of *East Timor: Genocide in Paradise* (Tucson: Odonian Press, 1995), and his articles on East Timor have appeared in a number of publications, including *The Los Angeles Times*, *Bulletin of Concerned Asian Scholars*, *O Publico* (Lisbon), *The Progressive*, and *Z Magazine*.

ALLAN NAIRN has covered U.S. foreign policy and operations since 1980. His articles have appeared in *The New Yorker*, *The Nation*, *The New York Times*, and many other publications. His coverage of the 1991 Santa Cruz Massacre in East Timor won several awards, including the RFK Journalism Award. He was formally banned from Indonesia in 1991 as a "threat to national security."

About the Cover Photographer

STEVE COX is a British photojournalist whose photographs of the Santa Cruz Massacre in East Timor were published around the world. His photographs of East Timor are featured in *Generations of Resistance: East Timor* (London: Cassell, 1995).